# The Imperial
# Imagination

Lewis D. Wurgaft

# The Imperial Imagination

*Magic and Myth
in Kipling's India*

*Wesleyan University Press*

*Middletown, Connecticut*

All inquiries and permissions requests should be addressed to the Publisher, Wesleyan University Press, 110 Mt. Vernon Street, Middletown, Connecticut 06457

Distributed by Harper & Row Publishers, Keystone Industrial Park, Scranton, Pennsylvania 18512

Parts of Chapters 2 and 3 previously appeared in somewhat different form as "Another Look at Prospero and Caliban: Magic and Magical Thinking in British India," in *The Psychohistory Review* 6 (Summer 1977), 2–26; and "History as Mythology: 'The Punjab Style' in British India," in *The Psychohistory Review* 6 (Spring 1978), 33–44.

First Edition

Lines from "The Sea and the Mirror," from *Collected Poems*, by W. H. Auden, edited by Edward Mendelson, reprinted by permission of Random House, Inc.

Manufactured in the United States of America

LIBRARY OF CONGRESS CATALOGING IN PUBLICATION DATA

Wurgaft, Lewis D.
    The imperial imagination.

    Includes index.
    1. India—History—British occupation, 1765–1947.    2. British—India—
Attitudes.    3. British—India—Psychology.    4. Kipling, Rudyard, 1865–
1936—Criticism and interpretation.    5. India in literature.    I. Title.
DS475.W87    1983        954.03        82-23678
ISBN  0-8195-5082-5

## TO CORKY

*Ship me somewheres east of Suez where the best is like the worst,*
*Where there aren't no Ten Commandments an' a man can raise a*
*   thirst;*
*For the temple-bells are callin', an' it's there that I would be—*
                                              —Rudyard Kipling

# CONTENTS

vii

*But Caliban remains my impervious disgrace.*
*We did it, Ariel, between us; you found on me a wish*
*For absolute devotion; result—his wreck*
*That sprawls in the weeds and will not be repaired. . . .*
Prospero to Ariel
*The Sea and the Mirror:*
*A Commentary on Shakespeare's* The Tempest
—W. H. Auden

# ILLUSTRATIONS

ix

# PREFACE

*I*n 1891, a few years after Rudyard Kipling's emergence on the British literary scene, the critic Edmund Gosse described how his work "produces on the reader a peculiar thrill, a voluptuous and agitating sentiment of intellectual uneasiness. . . . It excites, disturbs, and attracts me; I cannot throw off its disquieting influence."[1] Gosse's ambivalent but ineluctable attraction to Kipling mirrored the response of an entire generation, not only to Kipling but also to India and to the imperial endeavor itself. The writings of the men who served in India, and of those who tried to memorialize that service, suggest—in their extremes of attraction and aversion— an extraordinary imaginative investment in that experience.

Despite the continuing legacy of imperialism, its capacity to stimulate "a peculiar thrill" has declined in the contemporary world. The political mystique imperialism once possessed has largely been undermined in the awakening of the colonized nations. Moreover, the exoticism of India and other imperial outposts has been worn away by greater familiarity and by the infiltration, to one degree or another, of Western values and Western institutions.

This study sets out to recapture and to examine the imaginative element in the British involvement in India. It poses and then explores a fundamental tension between two contrasting British attitudes toward India: the attraction to India as a land unknown, mysterious, and seductive; and the self-mastering and self-sacrificing repression and denial involved in the commitment to govern. This tension gave birth to a rich literature of political memoirs, histories, biographies, and fictional accounts that touched on the imperial experience. Such literature looked with curiosity—and anxiety—at what Rudyard Kipling called "the dark places of the earth"[2] that epitomized the native presence in British India, at the same time that it sought a means of mastering the temptations and dangers perceived there.

This literature also presented a dimension of human experience felt to be missing or diminished at home—the daily encounter with death that fosters self-mastery and personal insight. Kipling captures this in his story "Without Benefit of Clergy" in the contrast between the pompous M.P. "wandering about India in a top-hat and frock-coat" and the laconic district administrator who knows the country and its vulnerability to natural disaster. While the M.P. "talked largely of the benefits of British rule, and suggested as the one thing needful the establishment of a duly qualified electoral system," the administrator saw the tell-tale signs of impending famine and disease. The M.P.'s "long-suffering hosts smiled and made him welcome, and when he paused to admire, with pretty picked words, the blossom of the blood-red dhak tree, that had flowered untimely for a sign of the sickness that was coming, they smiled more than ever. . . . Two months later, as the deputy had foretold, Nature began to audit her accounts with a red pencil."[3] As Kipling writes:

It struck a pilgrim gathering of half a million at a sacred shrine. Many died at the feet of their god, the others broke and ran over the face of the land, carrying the pestilence with them. It smote a walled city and killed two hundred a day. The people crowded the trains, hanging on to the footboards and squatting on the roofs of the carriages; and the cholera followed them, for at each station they dragged out the dead and the dying on the platforms reeking of lime wash and carbolic acid. They died by the roadside, and the horses of Englishmen shied at the corpses in the grass.[4]

When the frightened M.P. views a death by cholera, he wants "to take his enlightened self out of India." In contrast to the apparent superficiality of life in Britain, the familiarity with the elemental—be it death, sensuality, or the cruelty of native tribes—gave India a larger-than-life quality that drew on the imaginative resources of the practitioners and observers of late-nineteenth-century imperialism. Reflecting on this phenomenon, the critic Alan Sandison has commented on "the astonishing capacity" of the imperial endeavor "for fulfilling fantasies."[5]

Along with the use of historical and literary sources, the study employs some perspectives drawn from psychoanalytic theory. At one level this approach would seem a natural one, given the emotional investment and rigid defensiveness so manifest in the British reaction to India. Yet it is controversial for two reasons: first, because it employs an approach that has been subject to spirited attack by historians; and second, because it undertakes to go beyond the individual psyche and explore the response of an entire culture to the imperial experience.

The criticisms of psychoanalytically informed historical work have often focused on psychoanalytic theory rather than the scholarship derived from it.[6] Critics have challenged the scientific validity of psychoanalysis, and questioned the appropriateness of such an approach to the structure of historical reasoning.[7] In part, these criticisms belong to a broader debate on the nature of historical explanation that has implications for a number of specialized approaches to historical writing. In giving so much attention to the scientific status of psychohistory, these critics tend to neglect the fact that the broader influence of psychoanalysis has rested on its continuing capacity to strike compelling metaphors that clarify the ideals or conflicts of a particular era. A more stimulating criticism—especially for the theorists and practitioners of psychohistory—maintains that psychoanalytic theory is inherently reductionist in its claims that universal, biologically rooted psychological characteristics exist, and that psychohistory is likewise reductionist in seeking to strip away moral or political conventions to reveal human pathology.

Such criticisms almost invariably emphasize Freud's classic drive theory, in which behavior is understood in terms of the resolution of unconscious and unchanging infantile wishes. According to this essentially ahistorical and acultural perspective, environmental factors in human development are regarded as subordinate (devalued in comparison) to the unfolding of a biologically based psychological determinism. In this theory, personality structure is assumed to be fixed by the resolution (or irresolution) of Oedipal conflict; psychoanalytic treatment was, and to a considerable extent still is, geared to the uncovering of unconscious fantasy, with little attention to the current life of the patient.

Much has happened in psychoanalysis within the past half century to qualify this picture. The further elaboration of concepts that Freud himself set forth initially in later major works like *The Ego and the Id* provided a structure for better understanding the interrelationship of psychic and social phenomena. Perhaps the best-known representative of this tendency is Erik Erikson, whose work in developing a psychosocial perspective contributed both to the clinical theory and also to its cultural applications. By suggesting a timetable for emotional growth that complements and extends psychosexual development, and by integrating it into a series of cultural and moral imperatives more responsive to social influence, Erikson dramatized the status of psychoanalysis as a cultural artifact as well as a clinical theory.[8]

Another influential theoretical paradigm has been offered by the object relations theorists. Object relations theory has provided a general framework for a psychodynamic interpretation of very early intrapsychic experience, of borderline personality organization, and most recently of pathological narcissism and the development of the self.[9] Object relations theory sets out to describe the development of increasingly complex ego and self systems through the incorporation of "objects" encountered in the immediate parenting environment of the infant and young child—not ordinary objects, but rather the intrapsychic representations of persons (initially, primarily the mother) that reflect, among other things, the child's level of development and the nature of its contact with the environment.[10] These introjected or taken-in "objects" are subject to massive distortion in response to the repeated experience of frustration or deprivation, or to extreme idealization in keeping with the needs of the child to protect its fragile psychic systems. It is possible to describe appropriate psychological development as a function of the child's ability to achieve a realistic view of its intrapsychic objects, free of excessive distortion. The character and quality of these objects, according to this theory, is ultimately decisive for our capacity to tolerate intimacy, for the nature of our self-regard and our ideals, and for our capacity to employ appropriate and productive psychological defenses.

The notion of the intrapsychic object is highly suggestive for social or historical applications of psychoanalytic theory. Culture and society represent the developing individual's ultimate object world. The process of introjection or of identification extends to less concrete "objects"—values, ideals, ideologies—drawn from the wider culture; and provides a conceptual tool for grasping the continuing pressures on personality structures in later life. Object relations theory facilitates the cultural application of psychoanalysis by providing a vocabulary—especially a vocabulary for the power relationships so critical to psychological development—to describe the intrapsychic world in interpersonal terms. In effect, this allows a "translation" into psychosocial categories of the phenomena that Freud's drive theory deals with psychosexually. It also provides a framework for understanding how shared social values, as well as cognitive and affective orientations, as "objects" can penetrate to unconscious levels of personality across an entire group and influence collective behavior.[11] Just as the individual remains vulnerable to psychic regression under the threat of object loss, so groups can react collectively to threats to culturally sanctioned objects. For instance, the capacity to mobilize mass support for extreme or simplistic solutions to situations of social or political chaos—e.g., Naziism—illustrates this process of mass regression.

Criticisms of reductionism within psychohistory carry more weight.[12] Too often scholars have employed a psychohistorical or psychobiographical approach in an effort to unmask the "real" individual—presented in terms of instinctual conflict or character pathology—who hides beneath a public façade. The reduction of a historical figure to psychic conflicts often serves only to undercut the significance of the person's historical role.[13] The identity of a public figure should be seen not so much as a function of his personal dynamics as of the image that made the person a compelling individual to contemporaries. A leader's appeal may relate more to the psychic needs of the times than to the leader's own personality.

From the point of view of object relations or self psychology, such an individual could function for a group as a shared "object" around which a set of more or less formalized ideals—religious, political, or social—could cohere. The leader, or rather the leader's public image, provides the idealizing content necessary to stimulate achievement or to define values at a social level.[14] Whether an individual or some other entity is the source of social coherence of this kind, psychohistorical studies should be judged by the contribution they make to understanding the affective bases on which groups cohere and generate values. The dissection of personality as an end in itself should, in my view, be left to the clinical practitioner.

Two popular concerns of cultural historians—ideology and mythology—provide natural sources for the psychohistorical study of value formation. Both relate to beliefs or systems of belief with significant emotional underpinnings; for both, a significant distortion of reality in pursuit of some political or cultural objective is implied. To the sociologist Gerald Platt the language of ideology is an especially powerful force in a situation of social change or disintegration, because through it "the experiences of chaos and emotional arousal are harnessed and the sense of loss resolved."[15] Especially within this context the language of ideology helps to ascertain "the meaning of emotional arousal, suggesting the reestablishment of a coherent world and one's place in it."[16]

Mythology, as many commentators have pointed out, can also be measured by its capacity to place the individual within a communal framework—one which employs the past as a medium for conferring meaning. It provides a bridge between the domains of fantasy and reality, neutralizing the tension between the regressive pull of omnipotent wishes and the adaptation to more realistic aims. Although it has often seemed necessary to magnify history to heroic or mythic proportions, the primitive impulses behind this process have also been tailored to the historical needs of given cultures. In terms of this adaptive function of mythology, the psychoanalyst Jacob Arlow writes:

The myth is a particular kind of communal experience. It is a special form of shared fantasy, and it serves to bring the individual into relationship with members of his cultural group on the basis of certain common needs. Accordingly, the myth can be studied from the point of view of its function in psychic integration—how it plays a role in warding off feelings of guilt and anxiety, how it constitutes a form of adaptation to reality and to the group in which the individual lives, and how it influences the crystallization of the individual identity and the formation of the superego.[17]

Through the emotional power vested in myth, a social group is better able to defend itself against external threat. Myth also shapes the history and identity of a group as part of a broader culture. In regenerating and reshaping a community's idealizing fantasies, mythology helps to liberate the individual ego and the culture itself for the conquest or control of external reality. Thus the "inner" or "absolute" reality of the myth provides an emotional medium for the articulation of the community's political or social beliefs.[18] The social and cultural homogeneity of a group and its response to the pressure to forge a self-conscious group identity can be assessed by the extent to which fantasy material becomes institutionalized and idealized.

In these respects the Anglo-Indian community in the latter part of the nineteenth century—especially the few thousand civil and military officers who made up the community's social elite—constituted a tightly knit group. There was considerable homogeneity among them both in social background and cultural outlook.[19] As a group they were exposed to grave pressures that found expression in increasingly rigid social behavior, and in the cultivation of political and racial stereotypes. This process was reinforced by a relationship to native Indians centered on issues of authority and control that have inherent emotional significance.

My study attempts to point out some of the underlying psychological concerns of the British community in its relationships with Indians and with India, and to describe how these concerns found expression in a heroic mythology generated by British achievements there. Recent historians have noted an increasingly conservative ideological stance among British officers serving in India in the late nineteenth century, compared with their counterparts a half century earlier. In the face of pressures from native Indians for political recognition, these men became increasingly dependent on authoritarian institutions and notions of racial and moral superiority to defend and rationalize their political hegemony. They turned for inspiration to the exploits of a group of British soldiers and administrators who had conquered an important province of northern India, the Punjab, at mid-century, and who then were instrumental in crushing a large-scale rebellion against British rule—the Indian Mutiny—that broke out in 1857. In focusing on a frontier region, and on the activities of men like John and Henry Lawrence—brothers, collaborators, and ultimately antagonists in the administration of the Punjab—they tried to turn away from the complexities of contemporary India to a simpler reality that reflected their ideal of paternal rule. And in portraying the steely determination with which the Lawrences and their protégés helped to subdue mutinous natives, they drew a parallel to their perceived position as embattled rulers. Faced with the prospective loss of India as an "object," the British responded with an increasing reliance on political and instinctual control—on the qualities of character that were said to distinguish Victorian Britain—and with a mythology of British heroism in which instinctual and social control were major constituents.

The ability of the imperial experience to assume mythic stature has been reinforced by a mechanism that psychologists call projection: the displacement of one's own deep-seated wishes and fears onto some external object. In his personal observation of another colonial situation, the French in Madagascar, the psychiatrist Octave Mannoni has described this projective process in terms of the mutual illusions of Prospero and Caliban—those stalwart representatives of magical omnipotence and slavish dependency. In observing the patterns of Malagasy life and culture, Mannoni detected a wish for dependency perfectly congruent with a desire for domination on the part of the French drawn to that African island. Psychologically, white domination in Madagascar was as much a case of collusion as of conquest.

It cannot be force alone . . . which vanquished Madagascar; force would not have conquered and kept the island had not the Malagasy people, long before our arrival, been ready for our coming. Moreover, the Europeans themselves only made a show of believing in military force; they knew instinctively, and barely consciously, where their strength lay—in a certain "weakness" of personality on the part of the Malagasies. They were not to know that their position of dominance was due to the fact that in the network of dependencies they occupied roughly the same position as the dead ancestors. . . . But they were aware that the psychological situation favored them and knew that force alone would be powerless once that situation changed.[20]

I do not wish to challenge this interpretation directly, but rather to place it in a broader perspective. Mannoni, after all, was himself a member of the colonial establishment in Madagascar. This point, and the fact that his book is largely directed to a Western audience, helps to account for his decision to focus on the "dependency complex" of the Malagasies, rather than on the conflicts of the colonialists themselves, who, he informs us, have "worked through" the problem of dependency.[21] The effect of this approach is one-sided enough to have provoked spirited responses. Yet Mannoni's treatment of the French in Madagascar grows out of a perception central to any psychology of colonialism—the notion that the external circumstances of colonial life have always been thickly shadowed by the projected images of internal conflict. Like Prospero, Mannoni suggests, the French inhabited their island in search of a simpler reality—one more responsive to the internal imperialism of infantile desire.[22] Mannoni does disappointingly little to elaborate the urge for omnipotence that fuels Prospero's magic. The psychological dynamics behind the French—and the colonialist—urge to dominate, and its concrete relation to native culture, remain largely unexamined.

Rudyard Kipling and his contemporaries in British India present the other side of the imperial equation. My intention is to examine the psychology of the Anglo-Indian community in terms of its encounter with native society, rather than vice versa. I will consider the British in India as latter-day Prosperos, and explore the penetration of magic and magical thinking into the routine of imperial rule. The extensive literature of British India defines and delineates these magical beliefs, and demonstrates how they were molded into the myths that sustained the Anglo-Indian community against its native critics. The increasingly rigid posture the British assumed was supported by fantasies that compounded their isolation from Indian life, and obstructed a realistic approach to native political aspirations. Precisely because the elements of projection and wish fulfillment were so apparent in this period of British rule, it constitutes a prime subject for a historical inquiry into the psychology of colonialism.

It would be useful, in a study of "Kipling's India," to offer a word of caution concerning the relationship between the psychologically oriented exploration of Kipling's works and that of British India itself. Despite the intimate connection I suggest between Kipling's portrayal of India and India's meaning to the British community, neither Kipling nor his literary creations can be identified with India, nor for that matter British India with Kipling, in a simple correlation. Any individual life has too many idiosyncratic elements to be reduced to the culture or cultures in which it develops. Nevertheless, although individuals vary with genetic make-up or constitutional endowment, personality itself can be viewed as a complex symbolic code incorporated to a significant degree in the socialization process.[23] By extension, it is possible to speak cautiously of groups of individuals with similar cultural experience who share similar psychological characteristics—inhibitions, aggressive and erotic strivings, etc. Society and personality can by this theory be conceived as "somewhat interdependent action systems," related but not reducible to one another.[24] In this relationship, mythology and the mythmaker bridge the gap between the dynamic elements in society and in the individual psyche. As a mythmaker for a culture under protracted stress, Rudyard Kipling helped to articulate such a symbolic code. The idea of "Kipling's India" is at once a construct, and a compelling reality in the history of British imperialism.

# ACKNOWLEDGMENTS

*M*uch of the research for this book was carried out with the help of a grant from the Old Dominion Foundation. I wish to thank the staff of the India Office Library in London, both its Manuscript and Newspaper Divisions, for its assistance in my work in the library's collection of memoirs, documents, and newspapers. The Houghton Library, at Harvard University, kindly allowed me access to its collection of letters and manuscripts by and about Rudyard Kipling.

I wish to thank a number of people who generously provided me with advice and support while this book was being put together. I am especially grateful to Bruce Mazlish, who initiated my interest in psychoanalytically oriented historical work and who, as a colleague and friend, has been a constant source of encouragement and critical stimulation. He read an earlier version of two of the book's present chapters and made many valuable suggestions. Francis Hutchins, Martin Jay, David Lelyveld, Standish Meacham, and Thomas Metcalf also read sections of earlier drafts and pointed out many errors of fact, emphasis, and interpretation. Michael Gilmore read early drafts of each chapter with unflagging patience and interest. His suggestions have contributed immeasurably to the final shape of the book, and I am indebted to him for his advice and friendship throughout its preparation. My wife, Merry White, read versions of the manuscript at every stage in its composition and managed to combine insightful criticism with encouragement and support. Equally important, over the past several years she has stimulated me to extend my intellectual horizons far enough to consider many of the issues I take up here.

My editors, Jeannette Hopkins and Clifford Browder, have been instrumental in helping me to produce a more readable and intelligible book. Penelope Douglas and Kenje Ogata typed the manuscript with good humor, patience, and skill. Henry Isaacs provided me with invaluable help in assembling the illustrations.

# The Imperial
# Imagination

___

# India in the British Imagination

*A Stone's throw out on either hand*
*From that well-ordered road we tread,*
*And all the world is wild and strange. . . .*
*For we have reached the oldest land*
*Wherein the Powers of Darkness range.*
*—Rudyard Kipling*

*R*eflecting on his experience as a colonial administrator in Cey-
lon during the still palmy days of the British Raj early in this
century, Leonard Woolf makes this observation:

The white people were . . . in many ways astonishingly like characters in a
Kipling story. I could never make up my mind whether Kipling had
moulded his characters accurately in the image of Anglo-Indian society or
whether we were moulding our characters accurately in the image of a Kipling story. In the stories and in the conversations on the Jaffna tennis court
(and off it) there was the same incongruous mixture of public school
toughness, sentimentality, and melancholy.[1]

Rudyard Kipling's India has an almost uncanny quality of verisi-
militude. If he did not actually create Anglo-Indian society,[2] he left
its more reflective members feeling stuck in time, as if acting out
roles prescribed for them in a tragicomic play. Certainly Kipling's
identification with India arises initially out of the most accessible
aspects of his work, his virtuosity in capturing the shallowness of
Anglo-Indian social life, and his empathy for the soldiers and bureaucrats who governed there. Characters such as Bobby Wicks,
who is "only a Subaltern," and Orde, the grizzled Deputy Commissioner, possess unstinting energy and a devotion to duty that have

become hallmarks of an unmistakable style of imperial rule, one alternately honored and caricatured in our own "post-imperial" era.

For Woolf, however, Kipling's power to evoke his experience of India relied ultimately on something more subjective than mere photographic reproduction. "When in the tropics the glaring, flaring day ends with the suddenness to which the northerner never becomes insensitive," Woolf recalls, "it is impossible not to feel the beauty, the emptiness, the profundity, the sadness in the warm, gently stirring insect humming air. Our talk after the game, as we sipped our whisky and sodas, consisted almost entirely of platitudes, chaff, or gossip, and yet it was permeated by an incongruous melancholy, which, if we had known the word, we might even have called 'Weltschmerz.'"[3] Beneath the hard and taciturn surface of British rule there was a greater depth, a pathos responsive in part to a universal restiveness in man, in part to the vast landscape of India that heightened the sense of isolation and melancholy, and—not least—the grandiosity that afflicted its alien rulers. The emotional chemistry of Woolf's reaction to the exotic character of India tallied with the experience of other British who served there, and with the fantasies of those who stayed at home. The mysterious and the unknown in Indian life remained as central to the British experience in India as the tactile and familiar.

## The "Permanent" Raj

Kipling was born in Bombay on December 30, 1865, and spent the first five years of his childhood there, a time he always recalled with special vividness and warmth. He perceived the happiness of these first years in sharp contrast to the period that followed, when he and his younger sister Trix were taken to England and placed in the care of a stranger, the tyrannical Aunty Rosa of the autobiographical story "Baa, Baa Black Sheep." Many years later Kipling recalled being "regularly beaten" and humiliated by the "Woman" and her teen-age son, all in the name of Evangelical devotion. The gloom and chill of England and the terrors of Aunty Rosa's household were, in Trix's words, "experienced like an avalanche that had swept away everything happy and familiar."[4] Kipling's torment eased and literary education began when he was sent at age twelve to the

United Service College in southwest England. He returned to India at age sixteen and in the next seven years developed his talents as a journalist and a creative writer.

The shaping of Kipling's identity as a writer coincided with a period of deepening crisis in British rule in India, first openly acknowledged in the 1880s when Kipling was serving his journalistic apprenticeship. The distinctive character that the British community in India acquired by the end of the century crystallized out of this protracted crisis. Francis Hutchins has described a decisive change in the relationship between British India and native India:

> In the latter half of the century thinking about India bore a distinctly different face. . . . Once the target of reformers, India had now become the hope of reactionaries . . . excited by the desire to rule rather than reform, concerned with British might, not Indian hopes. . . . the ideology of permanence clearly exerted a strong pressure on British life and thought. A permanent *raj* seemed a practical possibility and to be confirmed by racial and political and religious theories as both sound and high principled. In retrospect, the extent of the British dedication to this illusion of permanence seems to have been both regrettable and dangerous. The Empire, seemingly so stable, was in reality growing ever more fragile. . . . The certainty of a permanent Empire in these years, however, seemed to increase in proportion to its fragility, and to serve for many people as a defense and retreat from reason long after the course of events had proved its impossibility.[5]

Rudyard Kipling became a prominent spokesman for this "ideology of permanence." He never experienced the "different face" of British policy—the reformist impulse—espoused in his time only by the despised native middle class. Yet just a half century earlier, British representatives in India had been animated by the zeal for reform that had inspired both philosophical radicals and evangelicals in England.[6] Although these men decried political "backwardness" and religious superstition as vehemently as the conservatives who succeeded them later in the nineteenth century, they felt confident that in the coming generations India would advance along the same civilized path the Western nations had followed before it. Writing in 1835, the Whig liberal Thomas B. Macaulay stressed the value of education in creating a new middle class and eventually establishing a capacity for self-government in the fragmented and demoralized India of his time. Others, imbued with the utilitarian principles of Bentham and Mill, emphasized constitutional and legal reform as an instrument of progress. In each instance their thought had its foundations in an Enlightenment sense of universal human destiny, and by and large such a conviction set the tone for British rule in the 1830s and 1840s.

More recent historical writing, such as Erik Stokes's *The English Utilitarians in India*, has, however, qualified this benevolent picture. Stokes has shown the extent to which the authoritarian strain in British rule made manifest in the late nineteenth century was implicit in the assumptions of earlier evangelical and utilitarian reformers.[7] But Stokes recognizes the radically different spirit of reform that divides the 1870s from the 1830s. The policies of a reforming Governor General like William Bentinck in the 1830s were envisaged as a co-operative effort between the British and a nascent Indian middle class. In the later period, however, such reform was carried out at sword's-point to what Lord George Curzon, British Viceroy at the turn of the century, described as "a benighted people" that "had to be compelled toward the light."[8]

## The Mutiny and After

The Indian Mutiny is the event conventionally used to divide the enlightened era of British rule from the more authoritarian one that succeeded it. In May 1857 the Bengal Army revolted against its British officers over what they perceived as a threat to their religious practices. Behind the revolt was a general suspicion—stimulated by Christian missionary activity, by the prohibition of some traditional religious practices, and by the introduction of Western education—that the British intended to promote a massive conversion of Indians to Christianity. Within the Bengal Army this fear was stimulated by the introduction of the new Enfield rifle that required cartridges greased with fat. The native soldiers (known as sepoys) became convinced that the grease contained beef or pork fat they were prohibited, by religious scruple, from touching. The government quickly withdrew the objectionable fat and allowed the sepoys to grease their own cartridges, but many refused to believe that their caste status or religious integrity was not in danger.[9]

After eighty-five sepoys stationed at Meerut, outside of Delhi, were imprisoned for refusing the cartridges, a regiment of native cavalry mutinied. Two battalions of infantry joined in the uprising. The British community in Meerut was taken by surprise. Officers were cut down and houses set on fire before the Mutineers marched to Delhi, where a similar scene took place. The Mutineers, along with new recruits from the Delhi cantonments, seized a major cache of arms stored outside the city walls and then triumphantly entered the city proper. They declared the titular Mughal emperor, Bahadur Shah, an old and powerless man who lived in Delhi, their leader. Europeans who failed to escape Delhi were shot or cut to pieces.

While the unprepared British tried to organize a response in the weeks that followed, the Mutiny spread to much of north and central India. With British forces concentrated on the northwest frontier, native troops mutinied at such major centers as Agra, Lucknow, and Bareilly; and many of the native princes suppressed by the British were able, for a time, to reassert their authority. The most notorious instance of insurrection occurred at Kanpur on the Ganges. Four regiments of sepoys, under the leadership of Nana Sahib, one of the most prominent mutineering princes, surrounded the British garrison of soldiers, women, and children. On June 26, after a three-week siege, the British surrendered with a promise of safe conduct to Allahabad. But when they boarded the barge provided for their passage, the boats were set on fire and attacked from the shore. Women and children who survived were taken prisoner, but when news came of a British advance up the river, the Nana Sahib ordered them killed. The grisly mass murder, enshrined as the Kanpur Massacre, came to be symbolic of native ferocity in the Mutiny and of the British need to extract revenge. When a British force under General Henry Havelock entered the city two days later, they punished the sepoys deemed responsible by forcing them to lick the bloodstains of the murdered Britons before being hanged.

The first major British action was to send a force under Colonel James Neill up the Ganges to secure important stations at Benares and Allahabad. Colonel Neill tried to stamp out all signs of resistance by a reign of terror throughout the surrounding countryside. Under Neill's orders British troops destroyed villages and killed natives indiscriminately on the streets of Allahabad.

By September 1857 the British force outside Delhi was reconstituted with reinforcements from the Punjab, and in an action that proved the turning point the Mutineers were driven from the city in five days of fierce fighting. The British turned their attention to relieving their besieged garrison at Lucknow. Their first two assaults, in July and September, were strongly resisted by the Mutineers; only with the arrival of fresh troops from outside India was Lucknow finally recaptured, in March 1858, by a British force under Sir Colin Campbell. Large-scale fighting continued throughout 1858, but from this point on ultimate British success seemed assured. Under Campbell the British regained control of the Ganges-Jumna area, the strategic center of the revolt, and ultimately conquered the province of Oudh, the only area where the Mutiny had spread to a significant section of the civilian population.

The Mutiny became a seminal event in the history of British India. Acts of unbridled violence on both sides left a legacy of bitterness. For the British, in the post-Mutiny period, the cruelty and impulsiveness of the Mutineers justified the moral and racial condemnation of native Indians. The sepoys' betrayal symbolized the suspicion with which Indian natives and their political aspirations came to be viewed, and legitimized the highhandedness of the Anglo-Indian community in dealing with them. The Mutiny was not solely responsible for these changes, but it did accelerate them. For instance, the pre-Mutiny army was largely recruited on the basis of individual qualities without regard to caste; the post-Mutiny Bengal army was rebuilt with greater attention to regional, caste, and religious differences. Rather than attempting to convert their recruits or at least trying to loosen their caste loyalties, British officers sought to maintain the orthodoxy of their troops by hiring Hindu, Muslim, and Sikh priests and by enacting regulations to enforce orthodox behavior.[10] The British were now satisfied to exploit traditional social and regional distinctions, rather than to reform them.

With few exceptions, the British leadership of Kipling's India perceived its role in opposition to political reform. The forty-odd years from the suppression of the Mutiny to the viceroyalty of Lord Curzon at the turn of the century witnessed the growth of an articulate and politically self-conscious native middle class, the founding of the Indian National Congress, and the widespread demand for a broader political and administrative role for native Indians. Although committed in theory to these objectives, the British government in India did its utmost to ignore these persistent claims, and to obstruct the access of Indians to responsible political and administrative positions. More than ever the Viceroys of the period—since the Mutiny, the direct representatives of the Queen Empress—acknowledged that the British position in India rested ultimately on force. These men continued to be advocates of progress, yet they interpreted that term quite differently from their more liberal predecessors. They placed the value of administrative fiat high above the potential benefit of political reform, and became zealous advocates of practical improvements in areas such as sanitation and transportation, even as they grew increasingly suspicious of the "subversive" effects of Western education on their native subjects.

The viceroyalty of Lord Curzon from 1898 to 1905 represents the culmination of this trend in British rule. Curzon redoubled the effort to defuse political aspirations with administrative reforms. Efficiency of administration was to him "a synonym for the contentment of the governed."[11] From the time of the Mutiny forward, this preoccupation with administrative reform had shaped the ethos of the prestigious Indian Civil Service, which was responsible for the day-to-day administration of the Indian Empire. Working in the vast stretches of rural India, these civilian officers acquired a reputation for paternal devotion to their native charges and for a scrupulous sense of duty and honesty. Philip Mason has termed them the Guardians—"soldiers" who served the state in the spirit of the defenders of Plato's authoritarian republic.[12] And as the men charged with the practical—often unacknowledged—work of empire, they became the stolid heroes of many of Kipling's Indian stories. "No one wants my post," says Gallio, the assistant collector of "The Judgment of Dungara." "He had long been in the district and the Buria Kol loved him and brought him offerings. . . . In return he gave them quinine . . . and controlled their simple policies."[13]

The social and cultural concerns of the Anglo-Indian community narrowed accordingly. For a variety of reasons Anglo-Indian society became much more insular in the latter part of the nineteenth century, and the gap between it and the native community widened perceptibly. This trend reflected such concrete developments as improved communications between Britain and India, and a shift in the career patterns of the British who went out to India. Throughout the nineteenth century, as direct British administration expanded throughout much of the subcontinent, the civil servant replaced the fortune seeker, the fabled Nabob,[14] as the typical Briton in India, or at least as the figure who set the standards for Anglo-Indian society. As a public official whose reputation was identified with that of the government he served, the "civilian"[15] could mingle less freely in native society than the commercial adventurer. Rather than a quick fortune in mercantile activity, he sought his rewards in India over the longer span of a career in service. Fifty years earlier the Nabobs had often taken native Indian mistresses, but these middle-class bureaucrats—aided by improved communications with Britain—brought families out to India, and with them the full train of Victorian values. The sexual taboos and moral self-consciousness of Victorian society were successfully transplanted to Indian soil, and perhaps exaggerated by the physical and moral climate experienced there. Compared to their counterparts in Britain, the "underworld" of India appears to have been more rigidly segregated from Anglo-Indian society.[16]

The increasing insularity of Anglo-Indian society was reflected in the attitude of Englishmen in India toward their native subjects. Reformers in the first half of the nineteenth century had interpreted the immorality and idolatry of their native charges largely in terms of "relative backwardness." After mid-century, these "deficiencies" tended to be interpreted in racial categories. It was forcefully asserted that racial differences effectively divided the two communities into permanently separate camps. To some degree this perspective was the product of changed conditions in India, and to some degree it reflected the popularity of such views in European thought.

The growing attention to race in nineteenth-century Europe was a consequence of greater contact with darker-skinned Oriental and Negro groups, and of the self-confidence engendered by a technologically superior, expansive industrial system. Although writers described differences among peoples in racial terms, for the most part they focused on what twentieth-century biologists would regard as social or cultural, not genetic, characteristics.[17] Nonetheless, the articulation of "scientific" approaches to the problem of race at mid-century, encouraged by the emergence of anthropology as an organized field of inquiry, reinforced the ascription of differences in cultural and economic development to race. Ethnologists attempted to draw broad inferences from the precise measurement of physical characteristics like cranial capacity. Some maintained that these "findings" supported the notion that the different races represented separate, distinct acts of creation.[18] The acceptance of Darwin's evolutionary theories gradually undermined the ideas of multiple creation and the fixity of racial types, but popularized notions of Darwinism, emphasizing the struggle for survival, appeared to some to support conclusions of the multiple creation theory with regard to race. A hierarchy of races was developed by white social scientists, said to reflect levels of physical and intellectual advancement and adaptability. The white races stood at the top of this hierarchy, the Negro at the bottom.

Within this spectrum of color, Indians were placed in an intermediate position and compared to one another relative to the fairness of their skin. In some instances the caste system itself divided men by color as well as by occupation and social status—the lower the caste, the darker the color, and the British found justification in this for their own racial views. The British also emphasized Hindu religious texts that described the Dravidians of south India as black, apelike, woolly-haired, and thick-lipped.[19] Said a writer for the *Contemporary Review* in 1866: "To this black race, passionate, magnetic, of wild imaginings, we must trace every lurid and demonic element in the beliefs of India. This is their contribution to the common sum: a contribution fitting in the kin of the African Voodoo, the Australian cannibal, the Papuan head-hunter."[20]

The impact of such racial thinking, combined with events in India, was dramatic. Until mid-century, racial slurs had apparently been unusual among the British in India, especially within the morally self-conscious ranks of the military and the Civil Service. The Mutiny changed all that, igniting racial antagonisms that had begun to surface before the outbreak of the conflict, and encouraging what George Trevelyan, who visited India in the early 1860s and produced a widely read account of his travels, called "the 'damned nigger' style."[21] In another context he commented on the tendency to describe *all* Indians as "niggers" as a result of ill feelings arising from the Mutiny: "That hateful word nigger which is now constantly on the tongues of all Anglo-Indians, except civilians and missionaries, made its first appearance in decent society during the years which immediately preceded the Mutiny."[22]

Trevelyan and other observers described incidents of indiscriminate violence against Indians in the immediate post-Mutiny period that they attributed to racial antagonism. In the decades after the Mutiny such open and arrogant racism was identified largely with the nonofficial British population in India who had much direct contact with natives, who enjoyed less prestige than the civil and military hierarchies, and whose views often clashed with the imperial government. These British outside the official ranks were sometimes labeled the "d—d nigger party."[23] By the 1880s there was a growing feeling of racial antagonism even within the Civil Service. According to Henry Cotton, a civilian of the period, "the official body has now succumbed as completely as the non-official to anti-native prejudice."[24]

Although the public official in post-Mutiny India generally avoided direct racial slurs, he conceived the gap between Britain and India in absolute moral and racial terms, rather than as an aspect of intellectual or cultural progress. The British came to regard themselves as the incarnation of austerity, courage, and self-control; natives were caricatured to an increasing extent as their emotional opposites, and as captives of a constitutional weakness for emotional excess and moral depravity. Such moral shortcomings were said to reflect the inroads of centuries of breeding and climate, and were not amenable to simple legislative or educational remedies.[25] As an antidote to the degradations of native life, the cult of character—the British public school code of morality borrowed and fortified—was invoked time and again. Only such spirit, commented Lord Herbert Kitchener, military commander in India just after the turn of the century, could save his men from the dangers of the native prostitute. "No soldier who is unable to exercise due restraint in these matters," Kitchener explained, "can expect to be entrusted with command over his comrades. . . . Every man can, by self-control, restrain the indulgence of these imprudent and reckless impulses that so often lead men astray."[26] Through such exhortation India became an arena in which to test and reinforce the Victorian character. The meeting point between British and native culture had vanished. Bound by its own values and assailed by native demands for reform, the Anglo-Indian community became increasingly defensive, and increasingly isolated from the realities of Indian social and political life.

### The "Real India": The Rugged Frontier

Such a development in the life of the Anglo-Indian community takes on a concrete unity—or at least a common geographical expression—in the history of British India from the 1840s forward through the prominence of the northwest frontier and the province in which it was located, the Punjab. The Punjab was an area of northern India added to the British Raj in 1848 after a series of wars with its Sikh rulers. Under British control it became both a flourishing agricultural area and, as a frontier province, a focal point of military and diplomatic concern because of the wild and vulnerable border it shared with Afghanistan.

Most of Kipling's adult residence in India was spent in the Punjab as a newspaper reporter for the *Civil and Military Gazette*, published in the province's capital, Lahore. His work as a reporter brought him out to the vast agricultural stretches of the Punjab, within territorial enclaves still ruled by native princes, and among the military and civilian castes he so admired. In this setting he imbibed the lore of the frontier, whose rugged landscape and rude tribesmen figured so prominently in his Indian stories.

Beyond Kipling's personal experience of the frontier, the general role of the British who governed there was expressive of a major reorientation in imperial policy in the post-Mutiny period. Earlier in the century, under the standard of liberal reform, the focus of British policy had been India's major urban centers, where reformers had sought to educate the kernel of a new native middle class. The goal of self-government was acknowledged as a distant but nonetheless explicit part of this Westernizing policy. In the post-Mutiny period, however, British attention shifted from the cities to the frontier regions in the north, and to the peasant populations

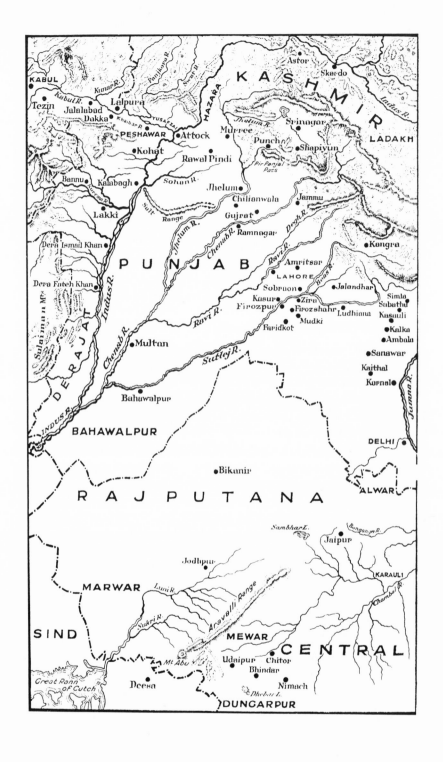

that inhabited them. Such a shift reflected political priorities, the product of decades of territorial expansion and the growing possibility of conflict with Russia. Yet it can also be attributed to a marked change in attitude toward the middle classes whom the British had previously nurtured, and who by the 1870s were becoming forceful and impatient critics of the dominant British role in politics and administration, particularly in populous Bengal, where British influence was perhaps greatest, and where British educational policies had produced the most outspoken and articulate native critics.

In the face of such pressures the British literally turned their backs on Bengal and the urban centers and focused attention on the frontier areas, where they could cultivate a rugged and paternalistic style of imperial stewardship, untrammeled by the stagnant atmosphere of the Indian cities.[27] Here also they could assert their absolute authority over warlike tribes and what they regarded as a simple but manly peasantry.

The British perception of the Indian in the post-Mutiny period as basically passive politically could in large measure be attributed to this shift in focus. Indians who failed to conform to such a stereotype were conveniently ignored, or condemned as dissidents. S. S. Thorburn, a civilian who served in the Punjab in this period, summed up this sentiment when he asserted that "the 'people of India' are the dumb toiling millions of peasants inhabiting the villages, hamlets, and scattered homesteads of the land." He compared the India of toiling peasants with "the town-bred exotics who are annually forced through in our educational hot-houses, and glibly mouth the phrase." Although posing as representatives of that people, they "have less claim to the title than the puny representatives of our manufacturing towns have of being representatives of John Bull."[28] Increasingly, from the Mutiny onward, it became part of the conventional wisdom of British India to contrast a stereotype of the effeminate resident of Bengal unfavorably with a stereotype of the vigorous and sturdy peasant of the Punjab.[29] Many of the conflicts rooted in the British identity as imperial rulers were implicit in that dichotomy.

One measure of the imaginative appeal of the frontier region was the remarkable extent to which Anglo-Indian fiction and historical works focused on the settlements of the northwest frontier and on the exploits of the civil and military men stationed there. Perhaps ninety percent of the stories and novels produced in this period took the northwest area as their locus, and most of this writing was steeped in the conventional values and concerns of the Anglo-Indian community.[30] This was especially the case by the 1890s, when the administrative zeal that had initially marked the British attraction to the frontier had been eroded by native political dissent and by a sense of bureaucratic inertia even within the Punjab itself. One response to these threats was to raise the achievements of the men stationed on the frontier to an unmistakably mythic level, a level at which they could function as a communal rejoinder to native demands for greater administrative and political power. Kipling's Indian stories of the late 1880s and early 1890s were immersed in the heroism of the frontier, but his genuine fascination with native life and ironic attitude toward at least some aspects of British administration served to leaven its mythologizing function. By contrast, the Anglo-Indian fiction of the 1890s and early 1900s, as best represented by the novels of Flora Annie Steel and Maud Diver—wives of British officers in India—constitutes an unalloyed celebration of British heroism on the frontier.[31]

This celebration of the frontier was only one aspect of the imperial ideology that evolved in late nineteenth-century Britain and British India. The other side of this strident expression of British strength was an equally self-conscious insistence on the alien and mysterious character of native India. This response was not only related to the social and political distance between the two communities, but also to an almost obsessive awareness of the gulf that divided what was quintessentially Western from what was quintessentially Oriental. In contrast to the confidence expressed early in the century that education would make Indians conform to Western patterns of thought and behavior, the conventional wisdom of the late nineteenth century stressed the unassailable distance between the European and the Indian mind. Repeatedly, in the novels and commentaries of this period, India was said to be essentially unknowable, and what was unknown was assumed to be corrupted by a chronic sexual and moral degeneracy. Even Malcolm Darling, a

relatively liberal civil servant in the Punjab at the turn of the century, found Eastern eyes to be unfathomable, and asserted that it
was impossible to bridge the gap between East and West.[32] From
the British perspective there remained an illogic and indifference at
the core of native life that could not be harnessed to the demands of
a rationalized society or expunged through education.

Focusing on one product of Western training, Maud Diver, in
her novel *The Great Amulet*, derided the effort to demystify the native mind. The plot of the book revolves, in part, around a Sikh
prince, Govind Singh, who had "been zealously inculcated with
Western knowledge" and had submitted to the process "with the
deceptive pliancy of the Oriental." He merely tolerated cricket,
polo, and the pressure to reform corrupt administrative practices,
while "in the unplumbed heart of him he waited for the day when
he would be rid of these well-meaning interlopers." Moreover,
Diver informs us, "in the heart of Govind Singh you have a fair epitome of the great heart of India herself: aloof, long-suffering, illogi-
cal to a degree inconceivable by Western minds." India was "not
an inch nearer . . . to the inner significance of English life and character" than she had been fifty years before.[33] India remained an
"area of darkness" to the British, who, behind barriers of moral and
racial superiority, were unable or unwilling to comprehend the life
around them.

The reception of Kipling's work by the British reading public reflected this notion of India as an abode of mystery and intrigue. Although reviewers of Kipling's early stories admired his often satiric
portrait of Anglo-Indian society and were stirred by his soldiers and
isolated civilians, their most unstinted praise was reserved for his
presentation of India itself, for the "muffled passions and mysterious instincts" he uncovered there.[34] The literary critic Edmund
Gosse expressed the wish to "be told more of what happened, out
of the moonlight, in the blackness of Amir Nath's Gully . . . to
know who it is who dances the Halli Hukk, and how, and why, and
where. . . . I want to know all the things that Mr. Kipling does not
like to tell—to see the devils of the East 'rioting as the stallions riot
in the spring.' It is the strength of this new story-teller that he re-
awakens in us the primitive emotions of curiosity, mystery, and ro-

mance in action. He is the master of a new kind of terrible and enchanting peepshow, and we crowd around him begging for 'just one more look.'"[35]

It was this aspect of India—its capacity to stir up strange and often troublesome emotions—that was instrumental in attracting Kipling's readers. An identical emotional response to India prompted the Anglo-Indians themselves so insistently to deny that they could understand the inner workings of the native mind. This mysterious or magical conception of native India was placed directly in opposition to the mythical achievements of the British in the Punjab. The heroic stature of the one image was designed to contain and to control the dangerously seductive qualities of the other. But more than the British would acknowledge, and more than their physical and emotional isolation would suggest, these images were dependent upon one another in the structure of the imperial imagination.

*Chapter One*

# Post-Mutiny India and the Development of the Punjab Style

*"Why is my District death-rate low?"*
*Said Binks of Hezabad.*
*"Wells, drains, and sewage-outfalls are*
*My own peculiar fad."*
—*Rudyard Kipling*

*I*n the midst of her tale of corrosive relations between Indian natives and Englishmen, *The Waters of Destruction*, the novelist Alice Perrin, also the wife of a British official in India, speaks out for her exasperated British protagonist.

There are many who, speaking from years of experience and study, would say . . . that the West can never truly interpret the East, because by origin and inheritance the two have nothing in common; because the thought, belief, speech, manner of feeding, living, marrying, and dying are all totally and fundamentally different. And though there are some who, possibly from susceptible temperament, or a far-off strain of Oriental descent, may succeed in throwing a plank across the chasm, it is the Westerner who has to venture over to the other side, for there is never a meeting half way.[1]

In Perrin's novel, published in 1909, even the English dog Sally treats the natives who care for her with an instinctive "insolence . . . a contemptuous hitch of her hind-quarters."[2] In her confident and condescending assertion of the chasm between East and West, she speaks for the Anglo-Indian community in a tone far removed from that of Rudyard Kipling. Kipling's stories of native life are charged with wonder and inchoate passion; Perrin's rings with arrogance and disdain.

The young Kipling did identify with such views as Perrin's, as

17

much from emotional confusion as from self-righteous conviction. By contrast, Perrin and her fellow Anglo-Indians were the willing captives of their own cultural isolation. In noting that only some exotically "susceptible temperament" could bridge the gap between the Westerner and the Oriental, she describes the plight of the British in India by the turn of the century, and asserts the blatantly racial ideology with which they rationalized that isolation.

In expressing the need to meet native India more than half way, Perrin reveals some of the rage and disappointment that underlay the confident doctrine of imperial supremacy. The British in India were also impelled by the wish to be loved and appreciated by their native subjects. A tragedy of British rule in India was that these two goals—of mastery, and of the desire for affection and gratitude—seemed so often irreconcilable. The iron hand of imperial stewardship—symbolized by its panoply of administrative codes and regulations—precluded the warm response of either partner to the imperial relationship, or became confused with that response in the British imagination. In the final analysis the institutions that supported the "illusion of permanence" reflected the emotional confusion and frustration of their exponents. The institutional and ideological fabric of British rule in the post-Mutiny period was informed by a persuasive emotional dynamic.

### Authoritarian Rule in Post-Mutiny India

At dawn on September 14, 1857, a force under John Nicholson, an intrepid young officer known for heroic service in the Punjab, stormed the walled city of Delhi, held by mutineering native troops. The attacking columns encountered devastating enemy fire but established a foothold within the city's walls during the first day's fighting. For the next several days the British inched their way through Delhi's tangled streets and bazaars, obstructed by resisting Mutineers and by their own penchant for the liquor left for them by the enemy. When the city capitulated, it signaled the effective collapse of the Indian Mutiny. Although bitter fighting continued for another year in other parts of India, the conquest of the old imperial city came to symbolize, at least for the historians who chronicled

British military achievements in India in the subsequent half century, both the definitive defeat of the rebellious native princes, and the re-establishment of British rule on a more resolute footing. In the years that followed the Mutiny this tendency was confirmed, in general terms, by the increasingly authoritarian tone of British administration in India, as well as in specific acts such as the substitution of direct governmental control for that of the East India Company, and the declaration of Queen Victoria as Empress of India in 1877. The militant righteousness of the late nineteenth-century British Raj was rooted in its conquest in the Indian Mutiny.

Yet the Mutiny and its outcome were not alone responsible for the movement toward more authoritarian rule in India. The Sepoy Revolt did bring British government in Hindustan to a standstill and unleashed a seismic shock throughout the Anglo-Indian community—reverberations that did not wholly subside over the next half century. Furthermore, the policies that evolved out of this imposed pause in British administration, in contrast to the liberal policies pursued in the pre-Mutiny era, demonstrated a renewed—indeed, an exaggerated—respect for the weight of tradition in Indian social and political life, as well as a more inflexible estimation of native character as immutably alien.

These two threads of British policy represented continuity as well as change in Britain's imperial posture. The events of the Mutiny cannot be drawn in a straight line across the history of nineteenth-century India to separate a predominantly liberal from a predominantly conservative era of British rule. The reformist impulse of the 1830s and 1840s was too overlaid with paternalistic and authoritarian assumptions to warrant such a simple division. Even during the high tide of liberal influence in the 1830s, certain areas of British administration like Bombay and Madras were much more resistant to the reform of traditional Indian institutions. Sir John Malcolm, who served as Governor of Bombay, pointed out the importance of regional differences in the condition and character of the people, and warned of any precipitous effort to impose changes on them. Lord Edward Ellenborough, Governor-General from 1842 to 1844, was the most influential conservative in India in the years immediately prior to the Mutiny. He rejected the liberal notion that education could function as a vehicle of moral improvement, and denounced as dangerous the liberal British attempts at religious conversion and social reform, emphasizing instead the development of public works and the promotion of useful technical skills.[3] At the level of the district officer, the work of R. M. Bird and James Thomason in the land settlement of the North-West Provinces in the 1830s and 1840s also ran counter in some respects to the predominant liberal creed. Fearful of the social effects of a sudden dissolution of joint proprietorship, they tried to protect the peasantry from a rigorous enforcement of individual proprietary title and revenue responsibility.[4]

The violence of 1857 was preceded by deterioration of relations between British officers and native soldiers in the Bengal army, a source of grave concern to many observers by mid-century. The British officer, so it was said, had been wholeheartedly involved with his native troops early in the century. But by 1850 greater access to Britain through improved communications and more liberal furloughs had promoted estrangement from the sepoy, and a greater awareness of the conflict between British and native values.[5] The Mutiny became an event around which British stereotypes of native treachery, impulsiveness, and brutality could crystallize. It provided an ultimate rationalization for authoritarian rule. The Mutiny sanctioned these attitudes and accelerated their adoption as conventional beliefs, but it did not create them.

Developments in India were responsive to two societies, and two sets of historical conditions. The ultimate responsibility for British rule in India in the nineteenth century lay in London, not Calcutta; the policies pursued by Governors-General and Viceroys both before and after the Mutiny reflected not only events and conditions in India, but also attitudes in Britain. The Viceroy, as an emissary of Her Majesty's government and a political appointee, often had to mediate between the desires of the home government and an entrenched and provincial Civil Service in India. If anything, improved communications and greater interest in imperial policy later in the century strengthened the hand of Prime Ministers and Secretaries of State against that of the Viceroy and his government in India. And from the ideological point of view it appears that the impulse for change in this period came often from England. The authoritarian strain in Indian policy after the Mutiny must be regarded, at least partially, as a reflection of the attitudes of middle-class conservatives in England who feared the further extension of the franchise in their own country. The policies of the 1870s and 1880s were strongly influenced also by the authoritarian liberalism of men like John Strachey, a prominent civil servant, and James Fitzjames Stephen, the political philosopher who served as Legal Member of the Viceroy's Council from 1869 to 1872. As spokesmen for strong government in India, they stressed the necessity of administrative order above the potential benefits of political freedom. In fact, as in the case of the Punjab, Indian conditions as well as the intellectual baggage of British rulers were instrumental in determining policy. But it is not a simple matter to disentangle these two threads of influence.

The two separate and sometimes contradictory impulses that informed British rule in post-Mutiny India seemed to call for more authoritarian or conservative political practices. The first of these, the restoration of an "Oriental" approach to Indian policy, was said to be justified by the Mutiny; it received intellectual sustenance from the racial theories popular in the latter half of the nineteenth century. The second, the appeal to an administrative over a political program of Indian reform, remained utilitarian in its broad outline, but reflected both the impact of Indian conditions and the altered character of English liberalism by the 1860s.

The principal political lesson the British derived from the Mutiny was that native India was incorrigibly conservative. The British construed the rebellion of the sepoy army—and the support the revolt received in some areas of Hindustan—as a reaction to the pressure of Britain's reformist policies on a culture permeated with superstitious beliefs and debilitated by decadent practices. It was not the alien character of British rule, they concluded, but the inroads imperial government had made in the traditional structure of society and culture, that had alarmed their native subjects and led to the uprising of 1857. They focused on the imagined danger to caste and religion that had animated many of the sepoys, and the apparent peasant support for the traditional landholding class in the country-

side—a class at times dispossessed by the leavening land tenure policies of the British in the pre-Mutiny period. In the years that followed the Mutiny the British came to have an exaggerated image of
Indian conservatism, labeled by Thomas Metcalf a species of "imperial folklore."[6]

The British, responding to this image of Indian conservatism in
the years between 1859 and 1870, sought to restore the Indian aristocracy to its paramount position in native society. As initiated by
Lord Canning in the immediate aftermath of the Mutiny, such a
policy assumed that only a loyal landholding class could anchor Indian society in its sustaining traditions and forestall the anarchy and
revolt engendered by a "liberal" approach to imperial administration. The cornerstone of such an effort was a land tenure policy that
favored the aristocracy and large landholders. It led to renewed
British support for the Indian states still ruled by native princes, and
an effort to ensure that any political, social, or educational reforms
enhanced the position of the native aristocracy.[7]

This approach validated the deeper awareness of the Oriental
character of Indian society. At its best it fostered a new respect for
Hindu religion and culture among inquisitive and broad-minded
Englishmen, but at its worst its reliance on racial ideas and politics
tended to reinforce the most stereotypical images of native life.

In political terms the notion of the "changeless East" stressed the
indifference or hostility of the average Indians to practical progress,
their childlike devotion to a paternalistic ruler, and their insatiable
appetite for the trappings of Oriental monarchy. In inviting the prospective Indian tourist "to enter into the political ideas of the people of India," Theodore Morison,[8] who was principal of a Mohammedan college in Aligarh, described how "when the glare of day
has softened to a golden haze . . . the Rajah's elephant, in long
housings of velvet and cloth of gold, comes shuffling down the
steep declivity." Morison enthusiastically wrote that "the women
and children rush to the doors of their houses, and all the people
gaze upon their prince with an expression of almost ecstatic delight;
as the elephant passes, each man puts one hand to the ground and
shouts 'Majaraj Ram Ram!'" Morison concludes: "The most indo-
lent tourist cannot fail to notice the joy upon all the people's faces;

and when the cavalcade winds home and he realises the intensity of delight which the mere sight of their prince has caused the subjects, he will begin to understand the suitability of monarchy to certain phases of social evolution."[9]

Many similar observers of late nineteenth-century British rule hoped to impart some of this Oriental circumstance into the drab cadres of British administration. One favorite instrument was the Durbar, a traditional ceremonial gathering of native princes at which they affirmed their loyalty to British rule in elaborate and lavish ritual. This device was employed by Viceroys from John Lawrence in the 1860s to George Curzon, whose Delhi Durbar of 1903 to celebrate the coronation of King Edward was the crowning expression of such Oriental pomp in the history of the British Raj.[10]

Conservative Viceroys like Lord Edward Lytton expressed this Orientalist view in emphasizing the native attraction to strength and authority. Lytton arrived in India in 1876, bringing with him a deep distaste for liberalism and a romantic conception of Britain's imperial dignity in India. On the occasion of the crowning of Queen Victoria as Empress of India, he proposed the formal establishment of an Indian peerage that would recognize the British crown as its head, and the formation of an imperial privy council composed exclusively of the most eminent native princes. Lytton's plan represented an effort to wed a paternalistic notion of British authority with a regard for flamboyant and aristocratic government. Behind this notion was the simple recognition that British rule rested ultimately on force and the forcefulness of its leaders, not on the willing co-operation of the broad range of native subjects, especially those with a Western education. As the cautious and clear-sighted Foreign Secretary Robert Salisbury suggested to his Prime Minister, Benjamin Disraeli, at the time: "Whether the aristocracy themselves are very powerful may be doubted, and any popularity we may achieve with them is not much to lean upon in a moment of trial. But it is good as far as it goes; their good will and co-operation, if we can obtain it, will at all events serve to hide to the eyes of our own people and perhaps, of the growing literary class in India the nakedness of the sword on which we really rely."[11] Lytton's anachronistic scheme was, however, rejected by the India

Council in London, which was unwilling to delegate any authority over the internal affairs of the Indian government to a native group, even an aristocratic one.[12]

The other authoritarian impulse—more consistently reflected in British policy—also drew on the Orientalist stereotype of the Indian, but it did so in the effort to find a satisfactory alternative to the anarchy and slothfulness of Oriental despotism. In insisting on the primacy of the law and of administrative procedure, it was influenced not only by conservative paternalism, but also by the utilitarian tradition established in British India early in the nineteenth century. Such administrative "rationalism" embodied its own distinction between the order associated with British rule and the anarchy endemic to native India. Yet it also constituted a reaction against democratic trends in Britain. Having learned to admire autocratic government through his service in British India, James Fitzjames Stephen published *Liberty, Equality, Fraternity*, a work that established him as a leading spokesman for the Hobbesian view that people need strong government, and that security rather than freedom is its principal objective. Having turned "an Indian lantern on European problems,"[13] Stephen turned it back again to argue that the heathenism and barbarism he perceived in India required and rationalized Britain's authoritarian rule.[14] In an article entitled "Foundations of the Government of India" published in 1883, Stephen expressed his ideal of government in these terms: "Now the essential parts of European civilization are peace, order, the supremacy of law, the prevention of crime, the redress of wrong, the enforcements of contracts, the development and concentration of the military force of the state, the construction of public works, the collection and expenditure of revenue required for these objects in such a way as to promote to the utmost the public interest, interfering as little as possible with the comfort, or wealth of the inhabitants, and improvement of the people."[15]

The first post-Mutiny Viceroy to associate himself wholeheartedly with this administrative ideal of force and justice was Lord Richard Mayo, who served in the early 1870s. Mayo regarded himself as working tirelessly for the welfare of the Indian people. Unlike earlier reformers, he avoided becoming embroiled with native culture and social structure, or with the political objectives of native

Indians, being determined that "we use all our power for the good of the blacks." He understood that power in narrow terms, and devoted his tenure to material improvements and to the establishment of efficient and rigorous administration.[16]

With Indian progress defined in terms of order, British rule became increasingly identified with the work of the Civil Service, and especially an elite group of a few thousand "covenanted civilians" at its head. This elite group, almost exclusively British, monopolized the responsible governmental posts in Calcutta and the districts. Administrative tasks at the district level such as the revision of assessments on the land, road building, and the extension of cultivation, preoccupied the British in these years, almost to the exclusion of broader political concerns such as the introduction of some measure of self-government. And the Civil Service effectively thwarted reforms which they disliked, either by vociferous dissent or noncooperation.[17] When Lytton arrived in India, he found the Civil Service too narrow in outlook for his visionary schemes. His regard for its administrative ethos increased with his experience as Viceroy. By 1877, he was professing "an immense faith in the energy, ability and ruling instinct of the man on the spot."[18]

The administrative orientation of British policy expressed not only a concern with practical improvement in the post-Mutiny period, but also a determination to maintain the political status quo. As long as it was energetically managed, and as long as Indian public opinion was relatively quiet and relatively unorganized, this approach served a concrete if limited purpose. The British government in India was not always distinguished by forceful leadership, however, and in the face of an articulate and impatient class of educated Indians, found it increasingly difficult to strike an effective balance between the excesses of romantic paternalism and the inertial tendencies of bureaucratic rule. Just before his tragic assassination by a Pathan convict during a visit to the Andaman Islands,[19] Mayo declared that he had subdued "many demons, but obstruction and delay are the many-headed monsters which bear on the present occasion."[20] After an ineffectual attempt at liberal reform by Lord George Ripon in the 1880s, and further erosion of power under the unimaginative leadership of Lord Henry Lansdowne and Lord Victor Elgin in the following decade, real authority passed from the executive to the administrative departments, where decision-making was delayed by bureaucratic procedures and paper work. Soon after Lord Curzon arrived in India in 1899, he complained of the sapping of the vitality of Indian government by the weight of reports and minutes it produced.[21]

Within the Civil Service at the level of local administration, the proliferation of bureaucratic procedures seemed to hamper the work of the "man on the spot." Although there was a recognition of the need for systematic administrative and judicial procedures, British civilians experienced a corresponding frustration at their constraint and a growing nostalgia for a more direct and more improvisational administrative style thought to have prevailed at mid-century.[22] The "outward and visible signs" of British authority—to use Kipling's phrase—as embodied in the district officer, remained the ideal of the Civil Service. But by the 1890s, thoughtful officers felt isolated from the people they hoped to serve by the very regulations designed to promote their welfare.

### Beginnings of Indian Dissent

Both bureaucrat and Orientalist—and often both views were espoused at various times by the same person—were isolated by their convictions from an important aspect of Indian life in the last third of the nineteenth century. Neither could respond sympathetically or realistically to the pressure for a more responsible role in government for the Western-educated Indian middle class. Implicit in the post-Mutiny policy of fostering an Indian aristocracy of wealth or influence was the neglect of, or opposition to, the commercial and professional middle class, especially that of Bengal, where native public opinion was best organized and most outspoken. The Bengali Babu became a stock figure universally condemned in Anglo-Indian society. In 1888 an editorial in Lahore's *Civil and Military Gazette*—where Kipling had worked as a reporter—declared that "nowhere in any corner of his character has the Bengali a spark of the spirit which has guided Englishmen in taking and ruling India; and upon occasions of legislative difficulty, it is impossible that he could offer, of his own motion, any reasonable advice toward the maintenance of that rule. He is a shrewd judge of all matters regarding his own comfort."[23]

As this statement suggests, the critique of the Bengali's political capacities was easily generalized into a sweeping disparagement of his character. The contrast between British strength and Bengali weakness, both physical and moral, became one of the most predictable themes in Anglo-Indian literature and political discourse. To illustrate this point, in his autobiography Sir O'Moore Creagh, who served as Commander-in-Chief of the Indian army, told an "amusing story" he had heard about a Bengali stationmaster of a small railway station ten miles into the jungle. After a wandering tiger had entered the station's compound, Creagh writes, the Bengali hurriedly sent the following telegram to his British superior: "'Tiger in charge, I on roof, please arrange.' The British officer at once went to the place, shot the tiger, and the station-master descended and resumed control."[24]

When the cowardice and deceitfulness regarded as inherent in Bengali character were compounded by Western education, it resulted, in the British view, in personal malice and political sedition. Native lawyers and journalists often adopted a mannered and flamboyant style in expressing their political aspirations and in criticizing British administration; still, there was little reason to question their basic loyalty in the decades following the Mutiny. Their outspokenness was inconsistent with imperial dignity, as Lord Lytton understood it. In 1878 he engineered the Vernacular Press Act to muzzle the "agitation" among the native language newspapers, a clear denial of the civil rights officially supported by the British. Although the act was largely directed against the Bengali press, the opposition to the Western-educated, politically aware native permeated Anglo-Indian opinion in every other section of India as well. By the turn of the century such "alien" and "rootless" figures were spotted even in the frontier regions of India, undermining the otherwise reliable peasantry. Writing on the Punjab city of Rawal Pindi, Creagh finds "many seditionists and agitators . . . some of them native lawyers. Such people are only found in the towns of India, for the agricultural classes are quite loyal and can only be stirred up to riot and disorder when some fire-brand from the town has worked upon their fears for themselves and their religion."[25] Such seditionists, Creagh writes, used local crises like an epidemic or plague to extract government favors for themselves at the same time as they stirred up "disturbances and outrages" in the villages.

In spite of this insistent distinction between the loyal Indian and the seditious Indian, the actual political pressures from the educated native middle class were relatively modest. The only political concessions made by the British in the second half of the nineteenth century were initiated in the 1880s, allowing some municipal self-government and granting limited native participation on provincial legislative councils. After 1885 the center of Indian political consciousness was the National Congress, organized largely by middle-class lawyers to create a national movement out of diverse and often conflicting regional interests and organizations.[26] For its first two decades the Congress was, if anything, a moderating influence on Indian public opinion. Even in petitioning the Indian government to move toward representative political institutions, it repeatedly affirmed its basic loyalty to British rule.

Almost from the first, the National Congress met with hostility or disdain from the British community. The official policy of the Indian government toward the Congress was neutrality, but individual Viceroys made no secret of their hostility toward natives in the movement. Behind its official protestations of loyalty, men like George Hamilton, Secretary of State for India in London, remained convinced of the Congress's seditious intent.[27] In Anglo-Indian public opinion, it was identified with all those traits conventionally ascribed to the educated Indian. When Curzon arrived in India at the end of the nineteenth century, he hoped and half expected that Congress would simply collapse of its own rhetorical weight.[28]

More serious than political agitation against British rule was the pressure from educated Indians for responsible positions within the judicial and administrative systems. Since the time of the Mutiny and before, the British government had been unambiguously committed to equal access to government service for all races in India. According to the Queen's Proclamation of 1858: "No native of the said territories, nor any natural born subjects of His Majesty resident therein, shall, by reason only of his religion, place of birth, descent, colour, or any of them, be disabled from holding any place, office, employment under the said Company." [29] Yet in the second half of the nineteenth century, with a few token exceptions, such access was effectively blocked by procedural barriers, and by the increasing determination of the British to reserve the most influential government posts for themselves. In minor bureaucratic posts and clerkships native Indians were needed and predominated, but genuine power was vested in the thousand-odd positions in the Covenanted Civil Service. Indians were free to compete for these positions, but against formidable obstacles. The examinations were held only in England. An Indian could sit for them only at great expense and, in the case of devout Hindus, at peril to their caste status. [30] When the Indian middle class lobbied for simultaneous examinations in England and India, they were turned down on the grounds that only preparation in Britain could provide the training in leadership required for successful administrative work.

At the hands of an authoritarian liberal such as John Strachey, this moral argument took on racial overtones. "Not the least important part of the competitive examination for the young Englishman was passed for him by his forefathers . . ." he wrote in 1888, "who have transmitted to him not only their physical courage, but the powers of independent judgment, the decision of character, the habits of thought, and generally those qualities that are necessary for the government of men, and the discharge of the various duties of civilised life, and which have given us our empire. The stock-in-trade with which Englishmen start in life is not that of Bengalis." [31] Whatever his intellectual attainments, Strachey added, the "feeble and effeminate" Bengali was both racially and morally unfit to rule. [32]

In the face of native demands—and sporadic pressures fron London—to place more Indian candidates in the Covenanted Civil Service, the basic strategy of the Calcutta government was to create alternate services that conferred prestige but not genuine power. In 1879 Lord Lytton's government set up a Statutory Service for native Indians; it included many of the more remunerative positions in the uncovenanted branch of the Civil Service, and moreover was not to be recruited in competition like the Covenanted Service, but on the basis of social position. By this means Lytton hoped to involve the natural ruling class, the native aristocracy, in government, and to exclude the hated Babu—the western-educated, middle-class Indian.[33] The obvious inferiority of the Statutory Service made it unpopular with native Indians, and in 1886 a commission under Charles Aitchison, then Lieutenant-Governor of the Punjab, was set up to recommend an alternative. The pressures to maintain the British monopoly of crucial administrative posts and to protect the position of the native aristocracy were too great to allow a significant break with existing policy. Aitchison's commission recommended the creation of a Provincial Service for native Indians with a number of posts formerly reserved for the Covenanted Service. The pre-eminent position of the Covenanted Service as a separate *corps d'élite* was reaffirmed. With no simultaneous examinations in England and India, by the end of the nineteenth century only a handful of natives had succeeded in entering the Covenanted Civil Service.[34]

Native Indians had more success in obtaining influential posts in the judiciary. There the political implications of their status seemed less great because, until 1883, these Indian judges had no jurisdiction over British subjects. However, a proposal to expand their authority, put forward in that year, rekindled fears that had been inflamed initially during the Mutiny, and galvanized the Anglo-Indian community against any program of liberal reform. The struggle over the so-called Ilbert Bill was the most controversial episode in the turbulent viceroyalty of Lord Ripon, who was sent to India by the liberal Gladstone government in 1880 to reverse the conservative policies of his predecessors. Although Ripon had little support from career officers serving in India, his goal was to re-establish in British rule the spirit of co-operative enterprise that prevailed earlier in the century. He revoked Lytton's Vernacular Press Act and put forward proposals for municipal self-government and for the election of native representatives to the legislative councils.

In February 1883, through his legal officer C. P. Ilbert, Ripon introduced an act to allow Indian judges to try European offenders in the rural areas, where until that time Europeans had been privileged to be tried by judicial officers of their own race. In the following months the bill aroused a storm of protest within the Anglo-Indian community. Virtually all the members of the Bengal Civil Service opposed the measure. Among the nonofficial Anglo-Indian community the agitation was immediate, especially among the planters of Bengal, Bihar, and Assam, who felt most vulnerable to native judges, and who had a reputation for racism. In Calcutta an Anglo-Indian Defense Association was organized—with the help of two major rallies in February and August 1883—to collect funds and to mobilize opinion against the bill in other parts of the country. Throughout the agitation the association served watch over the actions of the Indian government, scrutinizing its resolutions and warning of any dangers to the interests of Anglo-Indian settlers.[35]

The Anglo-Indian press, especially in Bengal, generally supported such vigilance; its commentary reflected the depths of racial feeling, the fear of native rebellion, and the resistance to further native encroachments into responsible government positions. This was particularly true in Calcutta where in May the *Englishman* first alluded to a supposed readiness among British settlers to establish a separatist Anglo-Indian republic. Subsequent issues put forward a number of immigration schemes to increase the supply of "white manhood" for such an enterprise.[36] Contributors to the *Englishman* and other newspapers derided the capacity of Bengalis to preside over Europeans in a judicial capacity. No amount of Western education, they wrote, could overcome the Bengali penchant for "subtility [*sic*] and corruption" and their "peculiar aptitude for crime," reflecting both "constitution and habit."[37] The evil influences of Hindu ignorance and superstition, transmitted from one generation to another, were sharply distinguished from British qualities of character: "courage, uprightness, truthfulness, independence."[38] Nothing, contended a memorial to the government from the Bengal Chamber of Commerce, could eradicate differences of character that arose from differences of race.[39]

In the pages of the *Civil and Military Gazette* the natives of India were identified with the "Bengal Tiger," which "has been observed wagging its tail at the dainty smell" of judicial privilege, a whiff of which would "inflame the eye and erect the bristles of every tiger within its range."[40] Even a relatively liberal civilian like Albert Lyall, writing in the same newspaper, opposed the bill on grounds of cultural superiority: "the average conscientiousness and firmness of character of the educated English gentleman is at present much higher than the educated native gentleman. . . . This difference may very well be due to no inherent superiority of race, it may be simply the result of free political life, a purer form of religion, high education and high civilization."[41]

The controversy over the bill, which provided Kipling with his journalistic baptism of fire in India, provided fuel for an all-out attack on Ripon's administration. The Viceroy was warned by his executive council that efforts to enforce the bill would ignite "white revolt, civil war and chaos."[42] When he retreated under pressure and revised the controversial clauses in the bill, any impetus for the reform movement was dissipated. There was a self-conscious retreat to caution and to the conciliation of English interests in India under the next Viceroy, Lord Dufferin. By the 1890s even the vigor of administrative rule and practical progress was sapped by the defense of the political and administrative status quo. The viceroys of the 1890s, Elgin and Lansdowne, functioned largely as bureaucrats controlled from London. In the face of the increase in communal rivalry and political agitation in western India, they were satisfied to maintain the British monopoly of administrative and political power. The Indian government Lord Curzon inherited at the turn of the century lacked both political vision and administrative vitality, reflecting both the inertia and the arrogance of entrenched authority.

## The Punjab Style

During much of the second half of the nineteenth century British accomplishments in the Punjab served as an antidote to their difficulties elsewhere in India. British administration in this frontier province, from the 1840s on, came closest to linking the legalist and paternalist strands of imperial policy into a forceful and highly principled whole. The shift from a reformist to a conservative posture in India that evolved with the century and reflected the geographical reorientation in British policy toward the Punjab was determined, in part, by the politics of imperial expansion. The incorporation of the Punjab into the area of direct British rule in 1849 brought a vast and wild territory into the British Raj. It was a challenge to domesticate and to administer such a region.

Special attention was focused on the strategic role of the Punjab province also because of the gradual expansion of the Russian Empire into Central Asia as the nineteenth century advanced. Russia and Britain struggled for paramount influence with the Amirs of Afghanistan, whose territories bordered the Punjab and provided access to a traditional invasion route to India. The question of the proper stance toward the Amirs and toward the warlike tribes that populated the northwest frontier gradually became linked to the broadest questions of international diplomacy. At mid-century the Lawrence brothers, Henry and John, who administered the Punjab in its first years under British rule, had generally been satisfied with a *de facto* armistice with the Pathan tribes, a policy which became known somewhat deceptively as "masterful inactivity." In exchange for a guarantee of their independence and territorial integrity, the tribes were admonished not to descend from their mountain strongholds into populated and cultivated areas such as the Indus valley. The result was a rough-hewn pragmatic peace, subject to sudden explosions of violence and rapid but limited British incursions into the hills.

Lord Lytton took a more pugnacious attitude toward Afghanistan and toward the alleged designs of the Russians. After a British emissary was murdered in Kabul in 1878, the British defeated the regular Afghan army. In the 1890s, under the "forward policy" pursued by Lansdowne and Elgin, the British tried to establish a so-called "scientific frontier," consisting of a series of advanced military positions extending to the Hindu Kush range of the Himalayas. From there they felt they could better resist a Russian invasion. The principal consequence of this more aggressive frontier policy was a rash of fighting with Pathan tribes, who resented the British presence in their mountain territories.[43] As in Kipling's *Kim* and the Anglo-Indian fiction of the 1890s generally, the northwest frontier became identified with the intrigue and adventure of the imperial struggle. "I go North again upon the Great Game. What else?" declares a Pathan who has befriended Kim and engaged in espionage on the British side.[44] The human cost of the struggle was considered by Kipling in "Arithmetic on the Frontier":

> A scrimmage in a Border station—
> A canter down some dark defile—
> Two thousand pounds of education
> Drops to a ten-rupee *jezail*—[45]

Beyond its strategic significance, the Punjab had an appeal to the British both physical and emotional. The "Land of Five Rivers," named for the streams that coursed through it, swept down from the snowy reaches of the Himalayas across a vast and often arid plain. Beauty contrasted with stark desolation was a seduction and a challenge to its British rulers. The province's climate was divided between a temperate season conducive to "European" exertion, and a summer heat that tested the mettle of the most devoted district officer. In his book on the frontier tribes Olaf Caroe, who lived on the northwest frontier in the later years of the British Raj, wrote of "a strange fascination in living among the Pathans." Caroe attributed it to "the tremendous scenic canvas against which the Pathan plays out his life, a canvas brought into vivid relief by sharp, cruel changes of climate. Sometimes the assault on the spirits is that of stark ugliness and discomfort . . . more often it is an impression of beauty indescribable in its clarity and contrast with the barren emptiness that went before. The weft and warp of this tapestry is woven into the souls and bodies of the men who move before it."[46] To Caroe such a landscape constituted "the magic of the frontier."

Such "magic" did lend a special flavor to British rule in the Punjab. The open expanses of the Punjab and the northwest frontier provided an outlet for civil and military officers, disillusioned with the Indian middle classes, who felt hemmed in by the bureaucratic fetters imposed upon them in the more developed regions of Bengal and elsewhere in India. Unburdened by elaborate administrative regulations—at least in the first decades of British rule there—they could work as all-powerful and paternalistic despots, dispensing their own scrupulous justice to native subjects. They found the Sikhs and Punjabi peasants over whom they ruled malleable politically and, unlike the intractable and contentious Bengalis, responsive to administrative direction.[47] The British passion for physical improvements—roads, sanitation, and irrigation—was relatively well received by the Punjabis, and agriculture flourished in the province under the Pax Britannica imposed after 1850. The border tribes themselves, except in a few dramatic instances,[48] were never subdued by the British, who were content initially to curb their most outrageous acts of felony and revenge. The very ferocity and independence of these Pathan warriors seemed to exercise a spell over the British that attracted the most zealous of them to the hardships and the dangers of frontier service.

The heroic era in the Punjab was the 1840s and 1850s, the years of its conquest and initial administrative settlement, and the period before the inevitable introduction of the procedural codes that already applied in other areas of British India. The province was ruled by two of the most renowned British officers who served in nineteenth-century India, Henry and John Lawrence, and by a legion of picked lieutenants who shared the Lawrences' reputation for courage, ardor, and devotion to duty. The earmarks of the "Punjab Style" were heroic action, the exercise of unlimited power, and evangelical zeal. Far from the red tape of the more settled areas, leaders like Henry Lawrence cultivated an ideology of action and independence as the primary instruments of imperial control. "We do not want antique generals, and brigadiers with antiquated notions, in such quarters; but energetic, active-minded men, with considerable discretionary power, civil and military," Lawrence declared. "It is all nonsense, sticking to rules and formalities, and reporting on foolscap paper, when you ought to be on the heels of a body of marauders, far within their own fastness, or riding into the villages and glens consoling, coaxing, or bullying as it may be, the wild inhabitants."[49]

Such "bullying" was accomplished with a strength and purity that captured the imagination of the biographers and historians who extolled their labors. Their zealousness was inextricably connected to a sense of dawning personal power, described eloquently by Robert Cust, a civilian who served in the Punjab in the Lawrences' time.

Much had there been in the natural features of the country, the blending of hill and plain, the union of mountain and river, but it was the development of my own faculties, the first sweet taste of unbounded power for good over others, the joy of working out one's own design, the contagious pleasure of influencing hundreds, the new dignity of independence, the novelty of Rule and swift obedience, this and the worship of nature in the solemnity of its grandeur and the simplicity of its children, were the fascinations which had enchanted me.[50]

This sense of authority was inseparable from the environment in which it flourished, and from the affection for a vigorous style of life, for the rugged countryside, and for its peasant population. It seemed to spark a spiritual chord in the officers who served there, and to excite their zeal and ambition.

Such spiritual susceptibility was enhanced by the evangelical background of many Punjab pioneers, inspired by the "magic" of messianic conviction. Evangelical feeling in India was at high tide in this period. Henry Lawrence and his wife Honoria were active and earnest Christians who believed that the hand of God was manifest in all their actions.[51] Lawrence's closest associate during much of his work in the Punjab, Herbert Edwardes, was perhaps the most zealous evangelical in the frontier region. His memoirs bristle with the rhetoric and moral absolutism of the Old Testament prophets, and with an exacting sense of duty in the evangelical tradition. He declared that God "must be supposed to wish us to remain unhomed, pilgrims ever while on earth, seeking to be placed only where we can do the most for Him."[52] Edwardes's "determination to make many barbarous wills give way to one that was civilized" was inseparable from a conviction that India had been given to the British to evangelize and to improve.[53]

Like so many of his colleagues on the frontier, Edwardes was convinced that the Pathans among whom he had been sent, with their traditional robes and patriarchal bearing, were the lost tribes of Israel. This Biblical fantasy was something of an *idée fixe* among the British along the entire length of the frontier, and excited individual Guardians to proclaim the tribes of Pathans or Baluchs with whom they worked as the reincarnation of Israel.[54] The patriarchal tone the Punjab pioneers employed as rulers seems directly drawn from the rhetoric of the Old Testament.[55] Robert Cust cajoled the principal landholders of his district: "If your lands are heavily assessed, tell me so and I will relieve you: if you have any grievance, let me know it, and I will try to remove it: if you have any plans, let me know them, and I will give you my advice: *if you will excite rebellion, as I live I will severely punish you*. I have ruled this district three years by the sole agency of the pen, and, if necessary, *I will rule it by the sword*. God forbid, that matters should come to that."[56] Although not every Punjab officer shared Edwardes's and Cust's evangelical enthusiasm, almost all adhered to its secular equivalent, a scrupulous sense of justice and an unswerving devotion to duty.

The ability of these men was measured by their character, and the definitive expression of character consisted in the readiness to take on a staggering burden of work. John Lawrence, as Chief Commissioner of the Punjab, was less concerned with the intellect of his officers than with their willingness to throw themselves into that work, and their skill in carrying it out quickly and resourcefully. Consistent with the messianic flavor of the Punjab experience, the commitment to work was itself idealized and spiritualized. Reflecting on his experience as one of Lawrence's subordinates, Alexander Taylor cited "a glow of work and duty round us all in the Punjab in those days, such as I have never felt before or since. I well remember the reaction of feeling when I went on furlough to England, the want of pressure of any kind, the self-seeking, the want of high aims which seemed to dull and dwarf you."[57] The physical and emotional strain which so concerned Kipling in his Indian stories was accepted by the "Punjabis" as an occupational hazard. They often worked themselves to or over the brink of physical breakdown, especially in the premonsoon heat which descended on the Punjab in spring and early summer. The term *Punjab head* became a proverbial expression throughout India for the breakdown from overwork that often forced these men to recruit their health in the hill resorts.[58]

The accomplishments of this first generation of "Punjabis"—as embroidered by the custodians of Anglo-Indian culture—became legendary in India and Britain by the end of the nineteenth century. For their successors this rough-and-ready form of rule had to yield gradually to the implacable demands of administrative regulation, yet their idealism and activism were still alive among the district officers in the Punjab in the 1870s and 1880s, and were exported beyond the boundaries of the province itself. In the post-Mutiny period many of the Lawrences' protégés, such as Richard Temple and George Campbell, became prominent in other parts of India. They brought with them, as an antidote to the more bureaucratic methods they encountered in Bengal and Bombay, the tireless devotion to duty and the style of simple and direct administration that had succeeded in the Punjab.[59] They helped to establish and maintain the reputation of the Punjab as a model of imperial administration.

Kipling promoted the Punjab style in his own work, most notably in a story of the 1890s entitled "William the Conqueror." In it a group of resourceful civilians from the Punjab, drafted to serve in southern India, is instrumental in combatting a famine which has beleaguered an extensive area of that region. Only the "Punjabis" possess the confidence and vigor equal to such an emergency. "When in doubt," a civil servant explains, "hire a Punjabi."[60]

Even at the turn of the century, when such enthusiasm was less universal, in the letters of a young civilian like Malcolm Darling one still finds some of these same qualities. Assigned to a remote outpost in the Punjab, Darling expressed his delight "to have got away from the artificialities and conventions of civilization" and to eat "a plain dinner" in informal dress. "Though the work is interminable . . . ," Darling confided, "it is full of responsibility and it is your own."[61] Like his predecessors, Darling was deeply impressed with the dignity of the Punjab peasant, and also with his own power as a magistrate to impress them "as if for a moment the fear of God had suddenly descended upon them."[62]

Darling's exuberant experience was more than balanced by the concerned responses of other officers who served in the Punjab from the 1860s on. Although the province flourished under British rule, it did so at the expense of traditional social institutions, and often at the cost of the morale of the men who worked there. The "absolute despotism" of district officers gave way gradually to more bureaucratic methods in which, for one thing, administrator and magistrate divided the work formerly vested in one office. The multiplication of paper work under the so-called "regulation" codes hemmed in the restive district official, leaving him less time to survey his district on horseback, and fewer opportunities to deal directly with his subjects. One of the first casualties was the *esprit de corps* of the original Punjab officers, who had regarded themselves as a brotherhood of committed soldiers and administrators uniting in a civilizing mission. Writing in the late 1870s, one of the original band, A. W. H. Coxe, complained that "one can hardly venture to say that that feeling exists now, at any rate to the same extent as formerly. All the old associations are broken up, and no attempt has been made to renew them."[63]

From the 1870s on many of the Punjab officers were involved in a struggle to preserve a way of life for themselves and the Punjab peasantry—an order threatened by the progressive measures the British had introduced into the province. In the Punjab, as in all of agricultural India, the foundation of social structure was in the land tenure system. Under John Lawrence in the 1850s the British had pushed through a land tenure settlement that had favored the Punjab peasantry over their defeated Sikh masters. Because, in part, of the loyalty of the Punjab during the Mutiny, the province had been able to resist the aristocratic trend in land tenure. This system was introduced into other parts of India as well—into Oudh especially—to promote a loyal and influential native landholding upper class. The district officers in the Punjab, by contrast, continued to regard the peasantry as the foundation of the province's social system. For them the survival of the peasantry preserved the simplicity and dignity of the "real India," and helped to perpetuate the paternalistic environment in which the Punjab Style could thrive.

The legal and paternalistic principles of the British ruling elite were in conflict over land tenure, and their devotion to the Punjab peasantry was complicated, if not contradicted, by their competing allegiance to the principles of political economy. Land had possessed only marginal value under the exacting and sometimes ruthless administration of the Sikhs, but it rose steadily in price under British sovereignty. Through promotion of physical improvement—especially roads and irrigation—and through their introduction of a legal system based on contract and orderly judicial procedure, the British created a relatively prosperous agricultural economy and a free market in land.[64] The consequences of this new prosperity for the peasantry were not always favorable. Many, bound by traditional values and unaccustomed to operating in a free market, became hopelessly indebted to local moneylenders. Rural indebtedness and, ultimately, foreclosures on debts multiplied as the moneylending class realized the profit to be made in land. The potential for economic conflict was exacerbated by religious hostility between the largely Muslim Punjab peasantry and the moneylending class, or *bunniahs*, generally Hindu.

The problem of land transfer, or alienation, began to trouble individual district officers in the Punjab after the 1860s. Although they remained true to their economic principles, they began to fear the social impact of land transfer on the structure of the village community, as well as the political consequences for Britain's fragile hold on India. By the late 1880s most of the revenue officers in the Punjab—the men who were closest to the problem of landed indebtedness—favored some sort of limitation on the transfer of land, especially to the nonagricultural classes.[65] Their concern was directed primarily at the moneylenders, whose exactions, they believed, would deprive the rural areas of a physically robust and politically loyal peasantry.

Perhaps the most outspoken, if not the most repected, advocate of a policy of rural protection was S. S. Thorburn, a district officer and sometime novelist who served in the Punjab in this period. Thorburn first noted the problem of rural indebtedness in the 1870s after his experience as a district officer in Bannu,[66] and his advocacy of protective legislation was sustained over the next twenty years. Writing in *Musselmans and Moneylenders*, published in 1886, he decried the infiltration of native lawyers into the frontier district of Dera-Ghazi-Khan: "the district will be invaded by hungry pleaders . . . and then the demoralization of the Biluches and the disintegration of the clan organization will go on rapidly."[67] He recognized that the success of the moneylender was a consequence of thrift and business energy, but he deplored the *bunniah* and the social process he set in motion. "As a body," Thorburn wrote, "the *Bunniah* are men of miserable physique and no manliness of character." Before the British annexation of the Punjab, Thorburn said, he had been "a poor, cringing creature . . . the humble accountant and servant of the dominant class—the agricultural community."[68] The introduction of a money economy into the area had reversed this class relationship to an alarming degree. The only remedy, in Thorburn's view, was to make it illegal for any person deriving profit from moneylending to acquire an interest in agricultural land. By 1895, when Thorburn was asked by the Punjab's Lieutenant-Governor Dennis Fitzpatrick to prepare a report on the consequences of alienation in his administrative division, there was a general awareness at the upper echelons of government of the seriousness of the threat to rural stability.[69] The material progress which the British had introduced into the Punjab was undermining the foundations of peasant loyalty so carefully cultivated during the previous half century.

# MUTINY

Attack on British troops at Kanpur
*From E. Gilliat,* Heroes of the Indian
Mutiny, *Seeley, Service & Co., 1922. Courtesy of Frederick Warne, Ltd.*

Nana Sahib, who instigated the
Kanpur massacre
*From* Narrative of the Indian Revolt, *1858*

Havelock's troops attacking mutineers at Kanpur
*From C. Ball,* The History of the Indian Mutiny, *1859*

Mutinous Sepoys dividing the spoils
*From W. Forbes-Mitchell,* The Relief of Lucknow, *1962. Courtesy of The Folio Society, Ltd.*

Procession for the Goddess Kali
*From* Narrative of the Indian Revolt, *1858*

Colonel Edwardes's troops at Peshawur, 1857
*From* Memorials of the Life and Letters of Major-general Sir Herbert B. Edwardes, *1886*

Siege train advancing to Delhi
*From George MacMunn,* The Indian Mutiny in Perspective, *G. Bell & Sons, 1931. Courtesy of Bell & Hyman*

British troops storming Delhi
*From George MacMunn,* The Indian Mutiny in Perspective, *G. Bell & Sons, 1931. Courtesy of Bell & Hyman*

General Nicholson found wounded in Delhi
*From E. Gilliat,* Heroes of the Indian Mutiny, *Seeley, Service & Co., 1922.*
*Courtesy of Frederick Warne, Ltd.*

The hanging of two mutineers
*Copyright by Aperture, Inc., as published in* The Last Empire: Photography in British
India, 1855–1911, *Aperture, Millerton, 1976*

The Sikh horse regiment, Lucknow, March, 1858
*Copyright by Aperture, Inc., as published in* The Last Empire: Photography in British India, 1855–1911,
*Aperture, Millerton, 1976*

Wounded officers recuperating at Simla
*From G. Atkinson,* The Campaign in India, *1859, Harvard College Library*

Lord Canning at Grand Durbar at Kanpura investing loyal Rajahs after Mutiny,
engraving by Bourne
*Marshall Claxton's picture, courtesy of the BBC Hulton Picture Library*

The Punjab Alienation of Land Act, introduced in 1901 under the viceroyalty of Lord Curzon, was designed to achieve Thorburn's purpose. But if it did succor the peasantry it could not, in the eyes of Punjabi civilians, reverse the social and political trends that agricultural prosperity had set in motion. The spread of education and the growth of cities in the Punjab had bequeathed to the province its own class of Western-educated, "seditious" natives who seemed ubiquitous in the eyes of Anglo-Indians. Thanks to the nearly equal division of the population among Moslems, Hindus, and Sikhs, the Punjab also became a hotbed of the communal conflict that plagued India in the 1890s. Worst of all, a province whose reputation had been built on political loyalty was shaken by political dissent shortly after the turn of the century. Seditious articles in the native press led to rioting in Lahore and other major cities. Not surprisingly, as Malcolm Darling then noted, "it caused deep indignation" among the British community.[70] In the face of political danger and social disintegration, Thorburn's appeal to return to the paternalism of the Lawrences struck a responsive chord among the British, in the Punjab and elsewhere in India.

## "East" and "West" in Opposition

The growing isolation of British officials—behind barriers of administrative codes, paper work, and political distrust—was complemented by the general isolation of the Anglo-Indian community within native society by the end of the nineteenth century. This process of social isolation was responsive to the political disenchantment with native India, yet it possessed a logic of its own that further reinforced the racial stereotypes dominating Anglo-Indian thinking. The extension and bureaucratization of British administration by mid-century, as well as the increasing accessibility of India to Britain, brought with it what might be termed the domestication of Anglo-Indian social life: its organization around the ideal of career service in India; the growth of family life within the Anglo-Indian community; and the introduction into India of the panoply of Victorian social and cultural institutions. These institutions came to constitute, in their own right, another formidable barrier between the British and their native subjects.

The most obvious evidence of this process of domestication was the arrival in large numbers of the *memsahib*, the wife of the British professional or businessman. Many contemporary British observers blamed the increasing parochialism of Anglo-Indian society on her arrival. One consequence was the increasingly elaborate character of Anglo-Indian social life. Thanks to improved communications, especially after the opening of the Suez Canal, it became relatively easy to import clothing and all the paraphernalia of "civilized" living from England. Maud Diver's *The Englishwoman in India*, published just after the turn of the century, catalogued the rather complex social demands on the *memsahib* as wife, hostess, and head of household. "India is the land of dinners, as England is the land of five o'clock teas," wrote Diver. "From the Colonels' and Commissioners' wives, who conscientiously 'dine the station' every cold weather, to the wives of subalterns and junior civilians,—whose cheery, informal little parties of six or eight are by no means to be despised by lovers of good company and simple fare,—all Anglo-India is in a chronic state of giving and receiving this—the most delightful, or the most excruciating form of hospitality."[71] Giving the "ubiquitous dinner party" required an instinct for the niceties of hierarchy in a very status-minded society, and the capacity to command a retinue of servants with the correct proportions of sternness and leniency. Within this framework, and safely behind the walls of the station or compound, the Englishwomen in India attended "to the chief business of their lives—a round of social functions and amusements."[72]

This focus on the role of the *memsahib* must be viewed as a rationalization for the bigotry and status consciousness that had permeated the Anglo-Indian community at large. The gentility of the *memsahib* could now be employed as a justification for the narrow moralism and racism that became more conventional in India. Her idealized "purity" became symbolic of the aristocratic pretense that marked the British in India after mid-century. Unlike the middle-class British radicals who came out to India before the Mutiny, those who went out later on were more conservative in their political and social bearing and valued their "instant aristocracy" in the Indian context. The average Englishman in late-nineteenth-century India could count on living at a station above that from which he came in Britain.[73] Especially within the dominant civil and military hierarchies, the paternalism and authoritarianism of official life were mirrored in the status consciousness of social life. The civil servant John Beames, remarking on the eccentricities of an Anglo-Indian hotelkeeper, suggested that his manner was "typical of the tone assumed by the middle and lower classes of Europeans in India, everyone of whom considered himself a 'Sahib' or gentleman."[74]

The hill station contributed further to the process of separation from native society. These outposts in the hills, established in the 1830s, reached the height of their political and social vitality in the post-Mutiny period, when large numbers of British women and children came to India. With their cool and healthy summer climates, these settlements provided a retreat from the ferocious heat and killing epidemics of the Indian plains. Simla, in the foothills of the Himalayas, became famous as the summer capital of the Raj from March to October, and the haven for Kipling's philandering Anglo-Indians in *Plain Tales from the Hills*. It was only one of many such stations scattered throughout India. Writing of Ootacamund in 1877, the Viceroy Lord Lytton commented, "I affirm it to be a paradise, and declare without hesitation that in every particular it far surpasses all that its most enthusiastic admirers and devoted lovers have said to us about it." The climate and the Victorian comforts he found there reminded Lytton of home. "The afternoon was rainy and the road muddy, but such beautiful *English* rain, such delicious *English* mud."[75] Through access to these oases of health and comfort, the British became more isolated from their native subjects, and geographically elevated above them.

Although the British maintained some contact with the Indian upper classes—the native princes and large landholders—there were few social links with the educated Indian middle class. Malcolm Darling recalled that he spent a full year in Lahore before his first conversation with an educated Indian who was not a government official.[76] G. R. Elsmie, a prominent civil servant in the Punjab and a friend of the Kiplings, noted in his memoirs that a garden party he attended in Lahore in 1882 was his first "mixed" social gathering of natives and Anglo-Indians in twenty-four years in India.[77]

It is hardly surprising that the British attitude toward their native subjects was rooted in a few unquestioned stereotypes. These characterizations took on a rigidity and an obsessional quality that reflected not only the social distance in which they developed, but also the fantasies of sexuality and power shared within the Anglo-Indian community at large, and then projected onto native life. The unreality of these stereotypes is evidenced by a striking tension in the British understanding of India and her native population. When it served their purpose, as it often did, the British were acutely aware of the wide diversity—regional, ethnic, religious, and social—of the population they ruled in India. They regarded the communal rioting of the 1890s, and the regional hostilities exemplified in texts like Kipling's "The Head of the District," as ample proof that only British administration could maintain order throughout the entire subcontinent. Their disdain for the Congress in the 1880s and 1890s was predicated on the same conviction. When Alice Perrin, in her novel *The Anglo-Indians*, suggested that the English word "country" came only haltingly to the lips of the Western-educated Indian because the concept was foreign to him, she caricatured a notion conventionally believed among her fellow Anglo-Indians.[78] Time and again one finds repeated in the British community the notion that native India is too fragmented into warring factions—vertically by caste and horizontally by religion, race, and region—ever to achieve political cohesion of its own making.

Under the impress of Victorian values the Anglo-Indian community distinguished itself from native India on the high ground of uprightness and character, but not intellectual advancement or creativity. The blunt Englishman's distrust of pure intellect never found more fertile soil than in India. His was a sturdy and unyielding character, above all. John Lawrence's dispatches to his subordinates in the Punjab at mid-century had fixed zeal and character above inherent ability as the distinctive attribute of the successful British officer. Fifty years later, when Malcolm Darling was breaking into the Civil Service in the Punjab, his senior officer was still insisting "that for our work in India character was more important than intellect."[79]

Many British commentators were, indeed, content to concede that Indian natives were frequently superior in intellect.[80] The cleverness and precociousness of the native Indian often made him suspicious in British eyes. Such precociousness was regarded as a hothouse creation, a growth without firm roots in strong character and moral sensitivity. In Flora Annie Steel's novel *Voices in the Night*, it is the straightforward and sympathetic Englishman, Jack Raymond, not the Western-educated Indian Chris Davenant, who is able to assess Davenant's ill-fated marriage to an Englishwoman. When he confronted the Indian over this issue, "a curious mixture of pity and repugnance came to the Englishman as he looked at the face opposite him—the gentle face so full of intelligence, so devoid of character."[81]

Henry Lawrence, perhaps the most energetic champion of traditional Indian society, insisted that even the most eminent Indian leader suffered from some major flaw of character.[82] In 1886 Kipling's newspaper, the *Civil and Military Gazette*, declared that the deficiencies in British rule in those years be attributed to shortcomings in native character rather than any failure of the British themselves.[83] The grounds of this alleged weakness varied, but the litany of complaints against native character included indifference to order and cleanliness, sexual depravity, and passivity—defects attributed to inextricable racial differences. Not even five years of education in England and "incessant instructions" from his English wife had taught Chris Davenant the value of an orderly life.[84] By contrast, the Englishman was portrayed as an instinctive organizer and leader. In Maud Diver's historical novel of British involvement in Afghanistan, *The Hero of Herat*, only an Englishman disguised as a native is able to lead a caravan out of disarray.

Before long all were at a standstill. Women fell to whimpering, men to swearing . . . Pottinger saw that unless he asserted himself the fluent interchange . . . might go on till dawn. The plight of the women and children afflicted his chivalrous soul; and conquering his reluctance to attract attention, he silenced the combatants with the scathing comment that as none of them seemed to be able to find a way, he, a stranger, would do what he could; let those follow who chose. Quiet words, quietly spoken; but the note of decision had its effect. The wettest and weariest took heart of grace, little dreaming that the stranger of the deep-toned voice and reputed holiness was but a Feringhi subaltern exercising his racial instinct for leadership and resource.[85]

Such differences of endowment, from the Anglo-Indian perspective, made understanding or empathy between the races all but impossible. In an instance in which those racial barriers do break down and genuine love develops between an Indian prince and an Englishwoman, as in I. A. R. Wylie's novel *The Native Born*, it turns out that, unknown to anyone, the "native" prince possessed an English parent.[86] No manner of education or achievement could obliterate the truth that all shades of Indians, in the final analysis, could be lumped together under the demeaning term "native." When Diver, that indefatigable defender of British authority, noted in *The Englishwoman in India* that servants "thieve almost as instinctively as the monkey and the squirrel,"[87] she revealed the depth and character of the division between ruler and ruled. Despite the bewildering mosaic of Indian life, from the British perspective Prospero and Caliban still confronted each other just beneath its surface.

The cult of character served to settle—once and for all—the British relationship to a politically subordinate population. This cult was built upon a sense of national superiority, a confidence bred by commercial and political expansion. Yet only the claim of moral and racial superiority—as mysterious and as deeply rooted in its own way as the notion of native depravity—could support the exclusive mandate to order Indian political life. In its very simplicity, and in its obsessive concern with the stark contrast between strength and weakness, this claim depended as much on the projection of conflicting emotional states onto native society as it did on the realistic depiction of a *paysage moralisé*.

In fact, this projective process achieved its fuller elaboration only through the insistent identification of dominant and subordinate types within native society itself. In contrast to the universal image of man implicitly endorsed in the liberal period of British rule in India, the British in the post-Mutiny era sought out regional and racial stereotypes with a typography of aggressive and passive characteristics. In their recruitment of the post-Mutiny Indian army, and in their general assessment of Indian social life, the British made a sweeping distinction between the virile and effeminate "races" of India. This distinction was well suited to the behavioral modalities of the Punjab Style, and was most conventionally rendered in terms of the division between the sturdy peasants and wild tribesmen of the north and the allegedly effeminate residents of Bengal. This is a central theme in Kipling's Indian journalism, but in this respect he merely reflected a habit of mind all but universal among Englishmen in India.

There were, in fact, significant physical differences between these two populations. The Punjabis and Pathans were fair-skinned, tall, and sturdy, while the Bengalis tended to be darker and more slightly built. The peasants of the Punjab and the tribesmen of the hills were reknowned as soldiers; the Bengalis shunned military service for business and education. There were religious differences as well. The tribesmen of the hills were Moslems—often fanatical Moslems—of one variety or another, and most of the peasant proprietors in the Punjab were Sikhs or Moslems. With the exception of one area Bengal was, by comparison, largely Hindu in population and culture, with a deeply entrenched Brahminical tradition. Finally, Bengal was the first area under British rule in India, and the most settled. The Punjab was still regarded primarily as a frontier province in the 1880s.

These real differences, however, were magnified in the Anglo-Indian press. In fact, the denunciation of the middle-class Bengali as a rootless hybrid was most glaringly revealed only in contrast with the virility of the northern tribes. The *Civil and Military Gazette* in 1887 threatened to expose politically ambitious Bengalis to the revenge of the northern tribes: "he is the last person whom we would expect to go," the *Gazette* warned, "however fat and contented he might be, to fight the Russians. He is the spoiled child of the Indian family, whose voice in season and out of season is heard clamouring for private advantages; but who, if the eye of authority were removed, would promptly be beaten by his stronger brothers."[88]

Contempt for the Bengali and admiration for the Punjab peasant and tribesman reflected, in part, the Anglo-Indian choice between Hindu and Moslem creeds. The British regarded Hinduism as a "grotesque invention," but they could relate their own religious beliefs to Islam—a monotheistic and prophetic religion that in these respects was like Christianity. This was especially the case for those evangelicals who wished to wage a *jihad* or religious crusade of their own in India. Much to the displeasure of the British it had been high-caste Hindus, not Moslems, who had filled the schools established for native Indians and who had clamored for the oppor-

tunities education seemed to open to them. On both counts British
sympathy was with the Moslems, who remained true to their creed
and to their social traditions.

In the last analysis, however, the strength of the British identification with the northern tribesmen had little to do with religion. Nor
did it center on the morals or customs of the Pathans. The British
denunciation of Pathan treachery, filth, and licentiousness rings almost as harshly as their grievances against the Bengali. But even in
denouncing the Pathan—in administrative dispatches, letters, and
memoirs—elements of admiration almost invariably surface. A
characteristic Punjab government report of 1865 describes the Pathans as "thievish and predatory to the last degree. . . . They are
perpetually at war with each other. There is hardly a man whose
hands are unstained. . . . In their eyes the one great commandment
is blood for blood, and fire and sword for the infidels. They are superstitious and priest-ridden." On the other hand, the report comments, "they possess courage and gallantry themselves, and admire
such qualities in others. Such briefly is their character, replete with
the unaccountable inconsistencies, with that mixture of opposite
vices and virtues, belonging to savages." [89]

One measure of this undoubted, if severely qualified admiration,
was the myth of the "noble savage," which had wide currency in the
post-Mutiny period, especially within the British army on the
northwest frontier.[90] If the Bengali was the spoiled child of British
India—spoiled, as Kipling suggested, on the sweets of Western
education—the Pathan was by contrast the natural child—natural,
from the British perspective, insofar as he was an unregenerate child.
In his barbarity and utter disregard for instinctual limitations, he
embodied the rebellious spirit of the young man and, unlike the
Bengali, his rebellion had no threatening political consequences for
the British. Rather, it seemed more to them the expression of a
fierce and admirable independence of spirit. Herbert Edwardes expressed the conviction at mid-century that it was a pleasure to
struggle with the Pathans after spending many years fighting the
slavish natives of the plains.[91] After his experience on the frontier
Olaf Caroe noted that the Englishman and the Pathan could look
each other in the eye. The tradition of British heroism on the frontier, he felt, was imbibed in part from the example of the Pathan

himself.[92] Visiting India in the 1880s, George Stevens described the sense of identification between Englishman and Pathan in spite of, or because of, the Pathan's barbaric ways.

It is true that here, on the thin line between elaborate civiliation and primeval barbarism, where you may begin your morning by trying a duet with a lady on a grand piano and finish it with a *tulwar* through your belly—here there is more sympathy between white man and native than anywhere else in India. British soldiers pull tugs-of-war against Kohati school boys, whose fathers may easily have shot their room-mates. British gentlemen sit down to table with Mussalmans—each considering the other irretrievably ripe for damnation, but each knowing the other to be a man. The Briton was made to do with the barbarian, being—the more you think of it the clearer you see it—half barbarian himself.[93]

Not surprisingly, these fantasized images were tied to sexual characterization as well. It was generally assumed that the Indian male was sexually licentious, but he was not portrayed to any marked extent as a phallic figure or as a threatening sexual rival. Rather, his sensuality was viewed as one facet of a general pattern of moral shortcomings, and as a reflection of the presence of a diffuse but debilitating sexuality that permeated Indian society. To the Anglo-Indian imagination, as to Kipling's, India itself was thoroughly and threateningly libidinized, and the dislike of native India was rooted in a fundamental fear of its seductive and mysterious qualities. This "dark" side of Indian life was both alluring and frightening. The very configuration of native cities, with crowded and twisted alleyways that defied a secure sense of time and place, and seemed to swallow up anyone who encroached on their borders, conspired to deepen this impression.[94] This response to the seductive quality of Indian life was also apparent in the ambivalent British attitude to the Hindu worship of this period, overlaid as aspects of it were with overt sexual symbolism which Western commentators found both intriguing and repugnant.[95] It was not the phallic god Shiva who most commanded British attention, however, but rather the mercurial mother goddess Kali—associated with debauchery, violence, and death—who seemed to inspire paralyzing fear among her devotees and to threaten them with spiritual possession or annihilation.[96] Both the image of instinctual regression and its destructive potentiality seemed to fascinate the British.

Such apparent involvement with fantasies of destructive female sexuality illuminates one aspect of the appeal of the frontier to the British. The male-dominated life of frontier fighting, where women were altogether absent, and where Englishman and Pathan confronted each other in open warfare, allowed the most unconflicted expression of male aggressiveness. By contrast, the "stink" of the plains which Kipling described was constituted, at least partially, of the contaminating "odor" of female sexuality. Of course the British experience on the frontier had a sexual side of its own, in this instance predominantly homosexual. The British expressed repugnance at the homosexual practices, such as pederasty, that they believed common among the Pathans in the mountains and among the Sikh aristocracy. Writing of his experience as a British army officer in the Punjab in the *Underworld of India*, George MacMunn stated, "Unfortunately homosexuality in one form or another is very rife. In Afghanistan, especially among the nobles, it has been a byword for generations as it has in Persia. . . . In Afghanistan and in the frontier the shameless proverb runs 'A woman for business and a boy for pleasure.' . . . The senseless murders which occur at times in Indian regiments and villages are often due to such unpleasant origins as sodomistical [*sic*] jealousy."[97] Yet observers like MacMunn found it fascinating that the practice of pederasty—allegedly the sign of degeneracy or mental instability in the West—could exist among "the most resolute characters," natives who were "the last word in daring and reckless courage."[98] Whatever its sexual connotations, the attraction of a pure and strong masculine life style, rationalized and reinforced by the ascetic male society of the Victorian public school, promised a saving refuge from the highly charged female sensuality associated with native India's plains and cities.

It was precisely their inherited and acquired exposure to a bracing, self-strengthening environment at home that made leaders of the British, while their native counterparts were "emasculated" by Hindu marriage customs and the supposed degeneracy of princely life in the native courts. Mr. Dina Nath, the grandiloquent but vapid student of Kipling's "Enlightenments of Pagett, M.P."—"a sort of English schoolboy, but married three years, and the father of two weaklings"—typified a problem pointed out repeatedly by

Anglo-Indian critics of Hindu social life. The precocity and creativity of the young Indian, they felt, was eroded by the physical and moral ravages of too early sexual intimacy. The ultimate product of this imbroglio was the physical and moral weakling who had lost the taste or capacity for vigorous leadership. Still worse were the evil consequences of the princely courts, where sexual depravity and the overcharged environment of the prince's harem were depicted as deadly to the human spirit. O'Moore Creagh, for instance, insisted that the young prince's life in the female-dominated seraglio inevitably reduced him to impotence and degeneracy. As a ruler such a man could never control himself or his subjects.[99] It is from just such a fate that Nicholas Tarvin tries to deliver the young prince in Kipling's *Naulahka*. Lurid descriptions of the Indian harem and its enervating influence on Indian children were a staple of Anglo-Indian memoirs and fiction.[100]

The British image of the Indian woman, and their notion of sexuality among natives as a draining and destructive experience, is drawn from these fantasized portraits of the *zenana*, "where," as in Diver's *Englishwoman in India*, "India's women lie in their pain and anguish, nursed by superstition, and doctored by incantations and charms."[101] More than any other Indian institution, the locked doors with its *zenana* symbolized the barrier between Anglo-Indian society and the unsettling mysteries of native life. In this respect it is hardly surprising that the British responded to the seclusion of Indian women in the *zenana* with an unstable mixture of sexual interest and excitement, mitigated by humanitarian concern. And these two attitudes were often curiously intertwined. Even Diver, whose book was largely an appeal to Western women to come to the aid of their Indian counterparts, wrote of the Englishwoman that "the mysterious, compelling fascination of the East must, sooner or later, creep into her heart and dominate her imagination."[102] Anglo-Indian literature generally was marked by a conventional contrast between the idealized, chaste Englishwoman and her sensual counterpart.[103] In Steel's *Hosts of the Lord* a Western-educated woman of native blood embodies the respectability and purity of the Victorian woman as long as she remains in her English dress. But when she dons the local costume and jewelry sent to her by an unknown native, the sensual dimension of her personality emerges dramatically.[104]

The sexual aspects of the Hindu creed often led to an equation of sexuality and religion as the formative elements—the female elements—in Indian culture. In "On the Second Story," Steel's story of the futile efforts of a young Hindu to become fully enlightened, the youth's studious attempts are shadowed by unceasing reminders of his cultural heritage.

... he would go on with his elementary treatise on logarithms until the tinkle of the anklets merged into the giggle which generally followed when, in the comparative seclusion of the ante-shrine, the veils could be lifted for a peep at the handsome young man. But Ramamund, albeit a lineal descendant of the original Brahmin priests of the temple, had read Herbert Spencer and John Stuart Mill; so he would go on his way careless alike of the unseen woman and the unseen shrine—of the mysteries of sex and religion as presented in his natural environment. There are dozens of young men in India nowadays in this position; who stand figuratively, as he did actually, giving the go-by to one half of life alternately, and letting the cressets and the chaplets and the unseen women pass unchallenged into the alcove, where the speckled light of the lattice bejewelled their gay garments, and a blue cloud of incense floated sideways among the dim archives.[105]

Anglo-Indian writers tended to enlarge upon the despotic power wielded behind the walls of the *zenana*. Diver described the secluded woman as "a shrill-tongued virago; a tyrant unassailable in her own domain. . . . Cheap sensation-mongers . . . will find . . . a true and terrible picture of the scope and unscrupulousness of feminine tyranny behind the veil."[106] More than any other element in native culture, the Indian woman embodied what was unknown and inscrutable in Indian life. And for the Englishman in India, himself trained and educated in a male culture, this mystery was charged with the emotional appeal of power, and the threat of a destructive sexuality.

On a practical level, the British were seriously concerned in this period with bringing the Indian woman out of the darkness and into the light. The one area of social reform the British universally acknowledged as necessary was the liberation of the Indian woman from *purdah*, or seclusion. Diver's *Englishwoman in India* was dedicated to revealing the plight of the Indian woman, as was Kipling's *Naulahka*, in which an energetic young American girl ministers to the physical and spiritual torments that are experienced "behind the veil." [107] And the heroine of "The Enlightenments of Pagett, M.P." is a young American doctor whose work in setting up a women's hospital gives her special insight into the genuine problems of India.

Well, what's the matter with this country is not in the least political, but an all-round entanglement of physical, social, and moral evils and corruptions, all more or less due to the unnatural treatment of women. You can't gather figs from thistles, and so long as the system of infant marriages, the prohibition of the remarriage of widows, the lifelong imprisonment of wives and mothers in a worse than penal confinement, and the withholding from them of any kind of education or treatment as rational beings continues, the country can't advance a step. Half of it is morally dead, and worse than dead, and that's just the half from which we have right to look for the best impulses. It's right here where the trouble is, and not in any political considerations whatsoever. [108]

Part of the impulse behind this need for reform was genuinely humanitarian. Part of it, as the quote suggests, helped to rationalize the British conviction that the political ambitions of native critics were irrelevant to India's legitimate needs. Social rather than political reform was necessary for genuine progress and only Britain could guide India to that end. Yet there was a third element in this uncharacteristic commitment to reform, the psychic need to bring Indian sexuality out of the shadows of pure fantasy into a more reassuring emotional sphere, where it could be controlled and tailored to the requirements of the imperial imagination. As the civil servant Walter Lawrence put it, "India could never grow and prosper unless the women were healthy and free to look on the daylight and see the world around them." [109] He might have added that the British would never feel comfortable in India until they could see its women. At an emotional level, this was the ultimate "liberation" of India which the British desired, as well as a measure of the efficacy of their own "magic" in contending with the seductive qualities of Indian life.

## Chapter Two

# Magic and Magical Thinking in British India

*The God and the Godlings*
*On dust-laden shelves*
*Repose for a sign.*
*We are all Gods ourselves!*
—*Rudyard Kipling*

With the advantage of hindsight the civil servant Walter Lawrence, a veteran of the Punjab and then private secretary to Lord Curzon, observed about his experience in India:

Our life in India, our very work more or less, rests on illusion. I had the illusion, wherever I was, that I was infallible and invulnerable in my dealing with Indians. How else could I have dealt with angry mobs, with cholera-stricken masses, and with processions of religious fanatics? It was not conceit, Heaven knows: it was not the prestige of the British Raj, but it was the illusion which is in the very air of India. They expressed something of the idea when they called us the "Heaven born," and the idea is really make believe—mutual make believe. They, the millions, made us believe we had a divine mission. We made them believe they were right. Unconsciously perhaps, I may have had at the back of my mind that there was a British Battalion and a Battery of Artillery at the Cantonment near Ajmere; but I never thought of this, and I do not think that many of the primitive and simple Mers had ever heard of or seen English soldiers. But they saw the head of the Queen-Empress on the rupee, and worshipped it. They had a vague conception of the Raj, which they looked on as a power, omnipotent, all-pervading, benevolent for the most part but capricious, a deity of many shapes and many moods.[1]

To a much greater extent than the British ruling elite realized, their power in India rested on the perpetuation of such illusions as Lawrence described. This power was itself inspired by a form of magic dynamically related to the superstitious or magical beliefs that these rulers attributed to their native subjects. And it produced a deeper bond between Briton and Indian than either party to this political relationship suspected. The examination of British power—or rather the illusion of power—can help to clarify the nature of the imperial "magic" on which it was partially based.

## *"Magic" and Control*

During the past century magic has been a major concern of two human sciences, cultural anthropology and psychoanalysis, studies of the primitive in social life and in mental life. Anthropologists have catalogued efforts of primitive cultures to control their environment through magical practices; psychoanalysis has defined magic as "omnipotence of thought."[2] Freud perceived the connection that exists between that most "civilized" of all neurotics, the obsessive, and the ritual acts of cultures steeped in magic and superstition.[3] The role of magical thinking in the experience of the infant and young child has become widely recognized in psychoanalytic theory and other developmental psychologies. "We grow up through magic and in magic," writes the Hungarian psychoanalyst and anthropologist Geza Roheim, "and we can never outgrow the illusion of magic. Our first responses to the frustration of reality is magic; and without this belief in ourselves, in our own specific ability or magic, we cannot hold our own against the environment and against the superego."[4] Roheim and certain other analysts describe psychic development as the gradual abandonment of magical beliefs through which the primal tie to the mother, and the omnipotent feeling it engenders, are exchanged for a more realistic relationship to self and environment.[5] The pathological potential of this growing up can be described as the perseverance of magical assumptions. Magic is seen as rooted in the primitive past—of either the race or the individual—but accessible to the supposedly demystified present.

Though hardly primitive, the Indian culture which the British observed and commented on during the nineteenth century was steeped in magic and superstition. Hinduism, especially the popular Hinduism of the Indian masses, was regarded by the British as an elaborate idolatry of cultic practices and superstitious beliefs, incoherent at best and all too frequently debased and licentious.[6] The rationalist John Strachey dismissed Hinduism as a grotesque invention.[7] Even the British Orientalists of the period, who were dedicated to reinvigorating venerable Hindu traditions such as the Books of the Vedas, bemoaned the contemporary state of Hindu beliefs. The British denigrated the tantric cults, with its advocacy of erotic experience as a means of cultivating mystical awareness. Special distaste was reserved for the mercurial goddess Kali, who seemed to demand personal debasement and blood sacrifice.[8] Although Indian Islam was more congenial in theory to the Anglo-Indian, it was viewed as degraded in practice, as infiltrated by Hindu caste conceptions and vulnerable to the manipulation of religious charlatans.

In Anglo-Indian literature the preoccupation with native magic and superstition crystallized at the most intense points of contact between the two communities: in dealings with Indian servants,[9] and in accounts of district officers, whose administrative and judicial tasks brought them into direct touch with Indian life. Flora Annie Steel's "Little Henry and His Bearer" is a poignant story of a native servant's sacrifices to the goddess Kali in a futile effort to preserve the health of a young Sahib in his charge.[10] In Kipling's "At the End of the Passage," a British physician derides a servant's belief that his dead master "has descended into the Dark Places, and there has been caught because he was not able to escape with sufficient speed. 'Chuma, you're a mud-head,'" responds the doctor, although his own confidence in medical science has been shaken by the circumstances of the death.[11] The letters of a typical district officer, H. M. Kisch, who served in Bengal from 1873 to 1904,[12] are replete with accounts of native superstition: music boxes regarded as gods; tales of demonic posssession and exorcism; animal sacrifices to appease the gods who control the rainfall.[13] Almost any district officer's letters or memoirs of the period contain similar reports. George Trevelyan wrote that the natives "attribute to magic our uniform success in everything we take in hand." The blunt, plain-spoken, beer-drinking district official with whom Trevelyan was familiar was "regarded by our Eastern subjects as a species of quaint and somewhat objectionable demons, with a rare aptitude for fighting and administration."[14]

Native superstition seemed often to encroach on the efforts at practical reform in the 1870s and 1880s: projects such as road construction, famine relief, and the improvement of sanitary facilities to control the spread of disease. In A. E. W. Mason's *The Broken Road* and Maud Diver's *Candles in the Wind*, British engineers have to overcome not only natural obstacles but also native superstition to extend their network of roads in northern India.[15] Indian religious pilgrims, often unwitting agents for the dissemination of infectious disease, were singled out by the British as a menace to public health. The Anglo-Indian concern for sanitation became a governing metaphor to characterize the gap between East and West.[16]

Such self-conscious opposition between their own progressive rule and native superstition coexisted with curiosity. Ann Wilson, the wife of a civil servant in the Punjab, described superstition as "a branch of universal pathology which can be studied in no place better than in India. . . . The old gnarled tree still flourishes in India; it still shoots out grotesque buds and branches, and there anyone can witness still their strange abortive birth."[17] In his memoirs Walter Lawrence rejected the suggestion that an incident was merely a "hallucination." "I have seen so much in India of what we would call the supernatural," he commented, "that I have an open mind, and I think that if we lived with the Hindus, apart from the influence of our own people, we should soon find in that land of enchantment there is indeed more than is dreamt of in our philosophy."[18] In Alice Perrin's novel *The Waters of Destruction*, a British civilian in an isolated outpost is "drawn to the shallow, murmuring water as though to a living thing that could see and hear him. Standing on the brink . . . he thought as he watched the warm, lazy stream, that perhaps the natives might not be so far wrong when they worshipped and propitiated her as an incarnation of Kali, the goddess of destruction, for there seemed a subtle note of power hidden in the gentle, soothing song."[19] Perrin's civilian is stirred by a tension symbolic of the seductive appeal that so many British associated with India.[20]

The revival of "Orientalism" in the 1870s was accompanied by a wide-ranging Anglo-Indian concern with the occult and the supernatural. Anglo-Indian fiction displayed an explicit concern with supernatural phenomena, tales of inexplicable curses, demonic possession, and ghostly visitations.[21] Many books on exotic cults and superstitions appeared, and the visit of Madame Helena Blavatsky of the Theosophical Society was a dazzling, if brief, success. Madame Blavatsky was an itinerant Russian mystic who had studied in Tibet and traveled to many of the major cities of Europe, the Far East, and America in behalf of her occult, pantheistic religious philosophy. She helped to found the Theosophical Society in New York City in 1875. After the publication of her major work, *Isis Unveiled*, in 1877, she and her collaborator, Henry Steel Alcott, moved to India and established a theosophist temple near Madras in 1879. The society converted a number of prominent Anglo-Indians to a belief in occult phenomena and spiritualism. Theosophy was popular also in Britain at this time, but in England the magical elements in theosophy were balanced by a more conventional philosophical idealism. Among Anglo-Indians it was largely a cult of the supernatural, the reverse side of their aversion to superstition.[22]

The British fascination with magic—and the identification of India with illusion supported by it—existed in contrapuntal relationship to the supposedly demystified doctrine of administrative order, the pillar of imperial policy. The precondition for British domination in India was, Walter Lawrence said, "mutual make believe." He felt himself "infallible and invulnerable," and the natives addressed him as "Heaven born," representative of a power "omnipotent, all-pervading . . . a deity of many shapes and many moods." For both master and subject this was a magical relationship. Both purchased a sense of omnipotent satisfaction at the expense of a retreat from reality. Their goals were mutually dependent, yet the ways in which these goals were pursued seemed to diverge dramatically. For the British, power was the elixir. It was the appeal of untrammeled power that drew the most earnest and zealous of them to the frontier regions of northwest India and the Punjab in the last half of the nineteenth century. S. S. Thorburn, who served initially in the Punjab in the 1860s, described each district officer there as "a little king within his own domain" who administered the simple justice suitable to a "rough illiterate population."[23] Working in the Cis-Sutlej area of the Punjab in the same period, George Campbell depicted himself as "very nearly in the position of a benevolent despot" who "did pretty much what I thought right and just."[24] Arbitrary power, wedded to a rigorous sense of paternalistic responsibility, appealed to Campbell: "It suited my temperament to be a law giver as well as administrator on my own account, and to be thus thrown on my own resources, with a free hand."[25] Like the fictional civilians in Kipling's stories, these "Punjabis" responded imaginatively and energetically to their authority.

Even the most moderate and broad-minded members of the Indian Civil Service were not immune to the appetite for power. Writing at mid-century, Robert Cust described "the first sweet taste of unbounded power for good over others"[26]; Malcolm Darling, in an early experience of India in 1906, recounted that the natives responded to his advice "as if for a moment the fear of God had suddenly descended upon them."[27] It is the exercise of unlimited power, almost sensually experienced, that unites the period of imperial history bounded by these two statements.

If the British exaggerated the passivity of native life to enhance their own sense of unlimited authority, certain patterns in Indian magic and belief preoccupied the British and conspired to confirm this conviction. The Indian effort to manipulate the environment by magical means through spells, curses, or sacrifices was inspired, as the British saw it, by a supernatural rather than a naturalistic notion of cause and effect. Such manipulative use of magic was overshadowed by its opposite, an almost animistic sense of being controlled by nature, demons, and gods—forces that were thought to induce a profound fatalism, a feeling of literal possession by uncontrollable elements in the environment and the culture.

The British seized upon these "phenomena" and reported them extensively. In his *Cults, Customs and Superstitions of India*, J. C. Oman catalogued a number of instances of native witchcraft in which an individual was possessed by the curse of an enemy or a ghost, including that of a washerwoman who was taken ill by the spirit of a recently deceased husband whose funeral feast she had neglected.[28] Walter Lawrence noted of his experiences with natives in Kashmir: "The Kashmiris always gave me the impression that they stood in awe of their surroundings, and they certainly did not believe in the permanence of anything. To use an Oriental figure, they felt like an elephant when there is a *Dal Dal* (quicksand). When misfortune came, they would sigh and say it was due to the curse."[29] In popular Hinduism the dual character of Kali, whose demonic and destructive

traits alternated with nurturing maternalism, reduced her worshipers to impotent fear, or inspired them with the passive satisfac-
tions of primordial union.[30] J. C. Oman asserted that the British
represented the active principle in India and the natives the passive
one,[31] a view echoed by Steel, in her novel *Miss Stuart's Legacy*,
where she wrote that a native challenged by an Englishman always
flees.[32]

Robert Cust's portrait of a simple, submissive peasantry tended
by a paternalistic ruler remained the ideal image of the British officer into the twentieth century. The concern with absolute autonomy and control behind that ideal is reflected in Cust's account of
his first assignment on the frontier: "I had won it by energetic service. I had fought for it and held it, against all comers during a rebellion. Untrammelled by Regulations, unencumbered by domestic
cares, I had fashioned its institutions, had been led on by high burning, yet unflagging zeal."[33] Such zeal, like the effort and ingenuity
of Robert Bird and James Thomason in the Northwest Provinces in
the 1840s, and of Herbert Edwardes on the frontier a decade later,
also reflects the accomplishment and resourcefulness of the Indian
Civil Service and the military during the remainder of the nineteenth century.[34] The Punjab especially became at once a model
of British administration and economic progress and an arena in
which to test character.

Often, in fact, this passion for control extended by necessity to the
taming of the environment itself. The struggle against natural disas-
ters, and the famine and disease they brought with them, was a primary concern of the Civil Service in the post-Mutiny period. This
incessant struggle with nature was carried out imaginatively, in response to the extremes of heat, the seasonal danger of flood, and the
overwhelming scale of the mountain ranges in the north. In Diver's
novel, *Candles in the Wind*, her British officers thrill at the prospect
of harnessing one of the great rivers of northern India.[35] Flora Annie Steel said of a mountain scene in the north she was unable to
sketch, "The beauty of it all was, I think, rather oppressive. It eluded
my paint box and pencils; I was reduced to impotent admiration."[36]
She chastised the natives for their indifference to such a landscape,
for their inscrutable reluctance to engage in the struggles that pre-

occupied the British, and their willingness to eschew autonomy in favor of gratification through the agency of some higher power. Though baffled by these attitudes of indifference, passivity, and dependence, the British in India sought them out and exaggerated them in native character. The British determination to do the impossible symbolized the gap between East and West in India.[37]

These divergent attitudes to power reflected two distinct but related forms of magical thinking that dominated the imperial imagination. Although the British insisted on the rigid control of their own feelings, as well as of the environment, they perceived Indian culture as encouraging the display of violent or contradictory emotions. This contrast accounted for the strong lines of attraction and repulsion that linked the British to native India, and also suggests— from the object relations perspective—two closely connected stages of individual psychic development.

In struggling to maintain a coherent group identity in the face of challenges to their authority, the British focused on those aspects of Indian life that tapped their own vulnerability to be drawn to an earlier, more "primitive" stage of object relations.[38] The magic of this stage revolves around the infant's dependent ties to its primary love object, the mother. The infant experiences a chaotic "love" life, swinging between a magical identification with its seemingly omnipotent mother, and its desire to destroy both self and object in the face of sensual deprivation.[39] This mercurial stance toward the love object is played out in the infant's emotional extremes of rage or affection. The object is literally taken in or expelled, idealized or rejected.[40] The defensive mechanism of choice at this early stage is the relatively primitive one of splitting, in which the aggressive and libidinal components of drives are simply separated and attached to self and object images. Instead of such energies being bound and neutralized through fusion, repression, or sublimation, as they are in later psychic stages, they are simply expressed directly, or through the emotional "magic" of introjection and projection.[41]

The British saw as emotional anarchy religious rituals like the Hindu festival of Holi where the entire gamut of emotions, from destructive to orgiastic, were played out.[42] Of equal notoriety was the resort to bloodshed as a means of resolving disputes between rival Hindu and Moslem communities. Dramatic accounts of such "inevitable" confrontations became a favorite subject of Anglo-Indian novelists and political commentators by the end of the nineteenth century. In *Miss Stuart's Legacy* Steel describes one such imagined incident after a Moslem ceremonial tower toppled during a religious procession, "most likely from an inherent weakness of its architecture." The Moslems presumed it was the work of hostile Hindu onlookers. "The result was startling," Steel writes. "A sudden wave of passion swept along the Mahomedan line, and as a young man sprang to the pilaster of the mosque steps and harangued the crowd, every face settled into a deadly desire for revenge. 'Kill! Kill! Kill the idolaters—*Jehad! Jehad!*'—the cry of religious warfare rang in an instant from lip to lip."[43]

One of the stock figures in Anglo-Indian fiction, as represented by Roshan Khan in Steel's *Hosts of the Lord* or Wali Dad in Kipling's "On the City Wall," is the Western-educated native whose civility is stripped away at the first moment of crisis. Wali Dad is presented by Kipling as a spoiled, overeducated Indian who has discarded Islam for "books that are of no use" and the sybaritic pleasures of a prostitute's salon. Yet at the first outbreak of communal rioting between Moslems and Hindus, he becomes galvanized for action. As the narrator attests: "His nostrils were distended, his eyes were fixed, and he was smiting himself softly on the breast. . . . Wali Dad left my side with an oath, and shouting '*Ya Hasan! Ya Hussain!*' plunged into the thick of the fight, where I lost sight of him."[44] This figure has his fictional female counterpart in the Indian wife, described as victimized by uncontrollable rages and grasping possessiveness. In Perrin's *The Waters of Destruction* a native wife experiences a typical outburst after being unable to control her child.

There followed the sound of a smart slap, and then silence on the part of the victim, who was dumbly gathering strength for a howl that should eclipse all previous lamentations. Sunia flung herself from the bed. She shook with passion, her eyes blazed, her face was distorted and gray with anger. Epithets, to which the term used by the child were as nothing, poured from her mouth. She became almost unrecognizable with fury. Tulsi shrank into a corner and drew her *chudder* over her face. She had seen her mistress in many ungovernable rages, but none quite so diabolical as this. Even the child forgot his intention of surpassing his powers of noise, and stared openmouthed at the spectacle of his mother's violence. She tore hairs from her head, beat her breast, and actually bit her own arms till the blood flowed; she threw the brass cooking vessels across the room, rent her shawl and her clothes, and foaming at the mouth, struck her head against the wall as though possessed of a devil.[45]

The Anglo-Indian community demanded of its own members the containment or internalization of emotion. In object relations theory this attitude corresponds to the point in early emotional development marked by the wish to retain the love object, rather than simply to merge with it or to destroy it.[46] Although at this stage a greater capacity for separateness, autonomy, and self-discipline emerges, it is also a time of intense ambivalence and anxiety— reflective of the child's struggle to fuse its positive and negative feelings toward the love object into a more realistic and unified whole. When confronted with the prospect of object loss, the child is extremely vulnerable to regression. Unable to cope with such loss in reality, it is drawn to magical fantasies of manipulation and control.[47] These conflicts tend to correspond in time to the anal stage of psychosexual development, a time at which the infant's preoccupation with pleasure and unpleasure begins to shift toward a concern with strength versus weakness. Through this transition, in which the issue of interpersonal control is related to the control of the bowel, the infant's grandiose fantasies are often recaste in terms of anal concerns.[48]

Given their intense concern with power and control, the British preoccupation with sanitary conditions in India is hardly surprising—a kind of social manifestation, some psychologists might say, of the anal stage of infant development. No catalogue of native shortcomings was complete without discoursing on native indifference toward sanitation. No element in Indian society, from haughty Brahmin to the outcaste sweeper, was exempt from this criticism.[49] And even allowing that the English industrial cities of the nineteenth century were themselves far from models of cleanliness and sanitation, such criticism had its force. British administrators' accomplishments in creating hygienic conditions in this area were impressive.

The causal connection the Anglo-Indian often made between the malodorous native cities and the absence of character or political capacity of their residents was the metaphor on which Kipling constructed his caricature of municipal self-government in Calcutta. In disparaging nascent efforts at municipal self-government in the Punjab in 1888, the *Civil and Military Gazette* suggested along similar lines that Asiatic indifference to improving sanitation and supplies of fresh water had undermined the native community's claim to "the right to manage, or mismanage, their own and their neighbor's affairs."[50] In Steel's novel *Voices in the Night*, the pomposity and incompetence of the native municipal committee is characterized in terms of an indifference to sanitary measures that contribute to an outbreak of plague.[51] Native lack of concern for sanitation was symbolic not only of the cultural gap between Europeans and Indians, but also of the need of an inept and weak-willed people for continuing dependence on British rule.

British character is even more graphically presented in terms of its preoccupation with self-denial and self-control, a stoic ideal—exported from the public schools of Victorian England—that became the badge of the British administrator in India. The steel of character—calmness, determination, and consistency—not force, was the instrument with which they chose to conquer and cajole a passive peasantry.[52] The most conventional characterization of achievements in the Punjab—and in India as a whole—was expressed in the contrast between order and anarchy. Praising John Lawrence, head of the Punjab government, in 1859, Cust commented that "he had found the Punjab a den of wild beasts, and left it an orderly garden."[53] S. S. Thorburn, writing about thirty years later, attributed British success in the Punjab to persistent skill in harnessing Shiva, the Hindu god of destruction.[54] In A. E. W. Mason's novel *The Broken Road*, the British commander in Peshawur, a dangerous frontier outpost, insists that a British woman ride calmly through the city streets after she discovers a native thief entering her bedroom. As they set out he says, "Thank you . . . I know this can hardly be a pleasant experience for you. But it is good for these people to know that nothing they can do will make any difference—no not enough to alter the mere routine of our lives. Let us go forward."[55]

This idea of self-control was reinforced by personal asceticism, a British self-denial which had its parallel in Indian religious practices. In this vein J. C. Oman tried to distinguish the debased from the constructive elements in the practice of yoga, in comparing it to his own Protestant ideal of inner-worldly asceticism. He rebuked the native ascetic who "sits absorbed in the contemplation of the tip of his own nose, or wanders about the country living upon the credulity and fears of the ignorant." For him there was a heroic as well as a repulsive side of the yogi: "The ascetic's self-denial, his contempt of the world and worldly pleasures, his self-inflicted penances and mortifications . . . are indications of will-force, determination, tenacity of purpose and self-sufficiency, which attract and overawe the multitude. The ascetic, by his scornful renunciation of all they hold most valuable, asserts his superiority to and commands the homage of the vulgar, which in the case of the yogi is enhanced by the dread of his supposed power." To pursue Oman's line of reasoning, the "magical" power of the British was distinguished from that of the yogi only by the latter's failure to achieve "real (as distinguished from ceremonial) cleanliness, manly energy, and public spirit."[56]

Such examples self-consciously oppose the ideal of emotional reserve to violent and self-indulgent emotional expression, the fear of regression to a more primitive orientation. The British community, confronted by what they regarded as the behavioral extremes of Indian culture, sought to cope with the sense of threat. Its preoccupation with power and control reflected an underlying ambivalence over their position as rulers, and an acute vulnerability to the attraction of the more archaic fantasies they saw embodied in Indian life.

Because he exposed this critical conjunction between the magic of both communities, the "civilized" native became an object of caricature and condemnation in Anglo-Indian society. Diver's *Candles in the Wind* chronicled the disintegration of a half-caste doctor—with "the worst qualities of the two races" and "a want of grit" in his "constitution," both moral and physical[57]—who marries an attractive and virtuous Englishwoman and brings her out to India. Only in India itself does the impossibility of their marriage—the social and moral gulf between them—become apparent. Morally exhausted by the disintegration of his marriage, and by his wife's attraction to a vigorous English officer, Videlle decides on suicide and, as Diver points out, "he was Oriental enough to see neither shame nor horror in the idea."[58] Before he can take his own life, he succumbs to the plague while working in a stricken native village, thereby freeing his wife to marry more suitably.

A more dramatic form of regression occurs in *Voices in the Night*, in which the Western-educated Brahmin Chris Davenant (Khrishn Davenund) forsakes his religion and the customs of his caste to adopt English values and manners. Burdened by an ill-fated marriage to an Englishwoman, his Western persona drops away. One night he abandons his formal Western dinner clothes for a native outfit improvised from his wife's saffron colored shawl, and revels in the almost forgotten physical pleasures of his childhood, feeling "when the sun, now high in the heavens, smote on his bare limbs—so long unaccustomed to the warm stimulating caress—with all the intoxification of a new pleasure." As he drifts past the closed doors of the women's quarters, "another touch, still more stimulating"—made his brain reel with recollection, his heart leap with the possibilities it suggested."[59] In his excitement he presents himself as a "Brahmin of the Brahmins" at a Hindu temple until his mother, who symbolizes all that is unchanged and unchangeable in traditional India, exposes his apostasy and breaks the spell.[60]

From the British perspective Davenund's behavior was representative of that of Hindus generally. This sense of the regressive character of Hindu belief was reflected in the British absorption with the cult of Kali, especially marked during the first two decades of the twentieth century when "unrest" and "sedition" among the native population began to plague the Anglo-Indian ruling elite. Valentine Chirol's *Indian Unrest*, published in 1910, one of the most widely read accounts of the "seditious" *Swaraj* movement, pointed to buried elements in Hinduism as lying at the roots of dissent. It cited the cult of Kali and the cult of Durga, another incarnation of the bloodthirsty mother goddess, as its most fanatical expression:

. . . the constant invocation of the "terrible goddess," whether as Kali or Durga, against the alien oppressors, shows that Brahminism in Bengal is equally ready to appeal to the grossest and most cruel superstitions of the masses. In another of her forms she is represented holding in her hand her head, which has been severed from her body, whilst the blood gushing from her trunk flows into her open mouth. A very popular picture of the goddess in this form has been published with a text to the effect that the great goddess as seen therein symbolizes "the Motherland" decapitated by the English, but nevertheless preserving her vitality unimpaired by drinking her own blood. It is not surprising that amongst extremists one of the favourite euphemisms applied to the killing of an Englishman is "sacrificing a white goat to Kali."[61]

Chirol attributed "the blind hatred to everything English"—prevalent, he said, among the younger generation of Hindus—to such invidious influence.

In Steel's "On the Second Story," Kali's worshipers express "her" rage against a clique of Westernized Hindus who attempt to introduce sanitary measures in their neighborhood during a cholera epidemic. In response to the plan to distribute cholera pills and to circulate a pamphlet imploring people to filter their water, the intransigent populace declares: "'Jai Kali ma!' (Victory to Mother Kali!) . . . 'Such talk is pure blasphemy. If She wishes blood, shall She not drink it? Our fathers messed not with filters. Such things bring Her wrath on the righteous; even now in this sickness.'" Their acquiescence in the inevitability of the old ways is a "passivity . . . characteristic of the race, which yet only needs a casual match to flare into fanaticism."[62] The epidemic is brought under control, not by the sanitary precautions but, mysteriously, after the sacrifice of the group leader's betrothed to Kali's blood lust.[63] In her last novel of India, *The Law of the Threshold*, published in 1924, Steel tied the cult of Kali to the dissemination of Bolshevist teachings among Bengali students.

A similar theme dominates I. A. R. Wylie's *Daughter of Brahma*, in which Hindu fanaticism and the cults of both Kali and Durga are directly related to sedition and revolt. A secret Brahminical sect issues a manifesto that rouses a native army to demoniacal fury. "Arise," the manifesto proclaims, "and in the name of Durga use your weapons until no single demon defiles our holy soil! . . . Behold, the gods who witness our weakness and cowardice turn from us, but to every man who dips his hand in the blood of a white goat it shall be counted more than all the virtues."[64] Through such commentaries and accounts the cherished ideals of political progress and national liberation, then being articulated by Indian liberals and radicals, appeared as a fanatical doctrine of religious regression.

The Mutiny, in the works of British and Anglo-Indian historians, became a psychological drama in which the native propensity for sudden and violent expression was opposed by the iron will of their rulers. The frenzy of the mutineers was conventionally contrasted to the restraint and persistence of the masters they betrayed. This is one of the central motifs of John Kaye's monumental history of the Mutiny, *Sepoy War*, published during the following decade. At Kanpur, the scene of the notorious massacre of British women and children, Kaye contrasts the "steadfastness" and "settledness" of the British with the blind impulse of the mutineers.[65] Subsequent chroniclers borrowed both from the materials Kaye had collected and from his central theme. In T. R. Holmes's *A History of the Indian Mutiny*, published in 1883, the establishment of a rebel government in Allahabad quickly gives way to "lurid anarchy."[66] Ascott Hope's *Story of the Indian Mutiny*, published in 1896, disparaged the depravity and weakness of the mutineers: "Anarchy, as usual, sprang up behind rebellion. Debtors fell upon their creditors; neighbors fought with neighbors; old feuds were revived; fanaticism and crime ran rampant over the ruins of British justice."[67] Colonel G. B. Malleson testifies in his *Indian Mutiny of 1857*, published in 1893, that the British displayed "a stern and resolute character" when aroused by native antagonists.[68]

Under the stress of accumulating social and political agitation, the conflicts internalized by the British were threatened with diffusion into more primitive fantasies, fantasies that promised fulfillment of omnipotent wishes that had been repressed, compromised, or sublimated.[69] Indian culture—with its superstitions, magical rites, and emotional excesses—represented to the British a series of "regressed" images. This intense fear formed the center of a dialectic that divided yet linked Indian and British life; it lent emotional force to the argument for authoritarian policies. Some of these fantasies concerned the images of total fulfillment or total destruction embodied in the gods and demons of Indian culture. Others related to libidinal or aggressive drives. The Moslem practice of *purdah*, for example, was an endless source of fascination and condemnation, as was the practice of revenge murder among the northern tribes and peasantry. Through Indian life the British could view elements of their own instinctual lives—lives they denied in day-to-day existence.

## The Retreat to the Law

Both literally and metaphorically, British life became more isolated in the late nineteenth century. The Anglo-Indian compounds in the *Mofussil*—the Anglo-Indian term for the countryside—became increasingly self-centered and self-sufficient, and the opportunities for social intercourse with Indians, for those who wished it, diminished correspondingly. Administrative institutions like the jail and the treasury functioned not only as instruments of discipline and order, but also as refuges where the fear of loss of power could be symbolically allayed by the processes of calculation and control. After observing the panoply of native life in Benares, the holiest city of Hindu India, Malcolm Darling recalls: "It was my first contact with the mysticism of the East and superficial though it was, it fascinated me. It was perhaps as well that my brother, who had to deal with the problems of a famous pilgrim city, was there to draw my attention to the drains, the fountains and the police stations."[70]

In fiction such regressive fears were more self-consciously balanced against the saving conventions of British life. One striking instance is Kipling's "Without Benefit of Clergy," whose protagonist, a British civilian, has experienced native passion at first hand through a secret affair with a young Indian woman. After the birth of his son, Holden prepares to sacrifice a goat at a native servant's insistence.

"Strike!" said Pir Khan. "Never life came into the world but life was paid for it. See, the goats have raised their heads. Now! With a drawing cut!"

Hardly knowing what he did Holden cut twice as he muttered the Mahomedan prayer that runs: "Almighty! In place of this my son I offer life for life, blood for blood, head for head, bone for bone, hair for hair, skin for skin." The waiting horse snorted and bounded in his pickets at the smell of the raw blood that spurted over Holden's riding boots.

"Well smitten!" said Pir Khan, wiping the sabre. "A swordsman was lost in thee. Go with a light heart, Heaven-born." . . . Holden swung himself into the saddle and rode off through the low-hanging wood-smoke of the evening. He was full of riotous exultation, alternating with a vast vague tenderness directed towards no particular object, that made him choke as he bent over the neck of his uneasy horse. "I never felt like this in my life," he thought. "I'll go to the club and pull myself together."[71]

When Holden does arrive there—"eager to get to the light and the company of his fellows"—the club secretary notes that his boots are wringing wet with blood.[72] In such an experience the margin between civilized order and archaic fantasy, social convention and primitive ritual, is only tenuously maintained.

Writing some thirty years later, Edmund Candler in his 1922 novel *Abdication* invokes "the club" as a sanctuary against the teeming passions of native India. Though more sympathetic to native political ambitions, and more self-conscious about the narrowness of the Anglo-Indian perspective, Candler's hero Riley, a newspaper editor in "Thomsonpur," cannot help experiencing relief when he arrives at the club after a harrowing ride through the native city aroused by news of the arrest of their *avatar*, Mahatma Gandhi. "Half an hour after he had passed through the Baradar Gate the club received him, solid, homely, inviting, a fortress against the invasion of hybrid cares. Certain old stagers were already ensconced in their accustomed arm-chairs and hailed everybody who came into the room. . . . Others . . . would stay on and talk, disjointedly after the manner of their kind, until nine o'clock, discussing horses or motors or tennis or golf, deploring the good old days, and discovering again how Government had ceased to govern and how everything and everybody was going to the dogs. There were times when he hated the place; tonight he was conscious of its compensations."[73] Riley is depicted as the maverick Anglo-Indian who prefers the "frank squalor" of the native city to the "efficient" and "logically planned" English compound. He experiences "the guilty sense of prying" in first exploring the narrow alleys of the native city. As Candler makes clear, however, his newspaper editor is atypical. To others Riley's guilty "curiosity" is experienced as a chilling and oppressive fear. The physical distance between the orderly Anglo-Indian enclaves and the glutted, unsanitary native quarter was also expressive of a scrupulously maintained psychological distance.

As the nineteenth century advanced, the fear of regression, the instinctive retreat into sanctuaries of self-control, found conscious expression in the increasing identification of good government with the ideal of order. No tendency in British rule in this period is more obvious, or more widely acknowledged, than the gradual tailoring of imperial government to the dictates of order and efficiency—in a word, the stern rule of Law.[74] In the post-Mutiny period the beneficent rule of administrative efficiency and administrative reform was directed not only against the political ambitions and "seditious" attitudes of educated natives, but even against the paternalism and *esprit de corps* that had dominated the Punjab at mid-century. At least this seemed true to those civilians who struggled to maintain the tradition there in the 1870s and 1880s, in the face of complicated legal codes and burdensome paper work.

James Fitzjames Stephen was one highly respected commentator who saw little chance for a sympathetic relationship between the district officer and his native subject. Rather than relying on a paternalistic link between Prospero and Caliban, he posited a rigid adherence to law as the soundest approach to imperial administration. He described the establishment of such a system of law as "a moral conquest more striking . . . than the physical conquest which rendered it possible." He suggested that its impact was comparable to that of a new religion. It was nothing less than "the sum and substance of what we have to teach them . . . the gospel of the English." And, he added in an admonishing tone, "it is a compulsory gospel which admits of no dissent and no disobedience."[75] Along with his friend John Strachey, he believed that order based on unmistakable force was the *ultima ratio* of British rule in India. Furthermore he believed, like Strachey, that if Britain's grip on India were to relax, the consequence would be a massive retreat to the anarchic practices once tolerated there. Strachey concluded his own book on British India by quoting Stephen's conviction that if the vigor of the government should ever be relaxed, "if it should lose its essential unity of purpose, and fall into hands either weak or unfaithful, chaos would come again like a flood."[76]

As many historians of British India have noted, such an outlook must be credited with many practical achievements. What has gone unacknowledged, however, is the emotional force behind this ideal. The devotion described by A. E. W. Mason to the "daily routine of life" and the homage generally paid to "the day's work," however austere and uningratiating these doctrines may have seemed to Indian subjects, were designed to arouse their enthusiasm and even their affection. Paradoxically, order and stability were not merely the practical benefits of British rule brought to the countryside by the district administrator, but the emotional medium through which he tried to communicate his paternalistic ideology. Regulations and procedures that seemed intrusive and absurd to the native had a magical meaning to the British civilian that often transcended their practical importance. Such formulaic attachment to the law and to the force behind it reflected emotional conflict. His love, all too often, was dependent on his absolute power.

From this perspective the native states—those enclaves of traditional "misrule" within British India—became identified with lawlessness. A pejorative comparison between the chaos and immorality of the native-governed states and the well-ordered areas under British control is a universal theme in official correspondence and political memoirs. The native prince is repeatedly portrayed in Anglo-Indian literature as the epitome of the Oriental character—a voluptuary, a sadist, a tyrant, and a habitual liar—all of whose depraved and despotic tendencies, as we have seen, were reinforced and regenerated through the institution of the harem. In typical fashion Colonel A. G. Durand, on a military and diplomatic mission to the frontier in the late 1880s and early 1890s, described the two-sided prince of a frontier state who was "bright, cheery, of an enquiring turn of mind, . . . courteous to all," yet "at heart he was a pure savage, a mixture of the monkey and the tiger. . . . Under his cloak of open bonhomie, generosity, and transparent honesty . . . he was . . . the most persistent plotter, and the most treacherous and ruthless foe."[77]

As the more candid observers conceded, Indian subjects usually felt more affection for their kindred rulers, however decadent and unscrupulous, than for their honest British counterparts. Strachey suggested that the popularity of a government in India seemed in inverse proportions to the degree of its ruler's "enlightenment."[78] Walter Lawrence, among others, was responsive to the divided feelings at the roots of this issue. "The Indian States . . . were to me the

# INDIA

The Himalayas from Nakanda
*From W. L. L. Scott,* Views in the Himalayas, *1852, Harvard College Library*

The Mall in Simla
*Courtesy of the India Office Library, copyright The British Library*

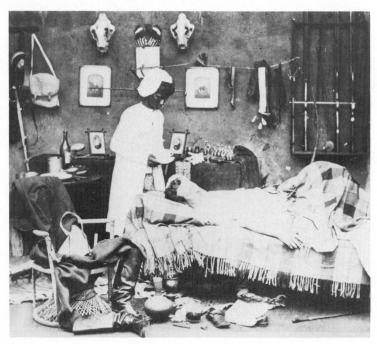

Englishman being served coffee in bed
*Copyright 1976 by Aperture, Inc., as published in* The Last Empire: Photography in British India, 1855–1911, *Aperture, Millerton, 1976.*

An afternoon tea
*Copyright 1976 by Aperture, Inc., as published in* The Last Empire: Photography in British India, 1855–1911, *Aperture, Millerton, 1976.*

Mess Room, Wiltshire Regiment, Peshawur, 1886
*Courtesy of the India Office Library, copyright The British Library*

"Our Magistrate"
*From G. Atkinson,* Curry and Rice, *1859*

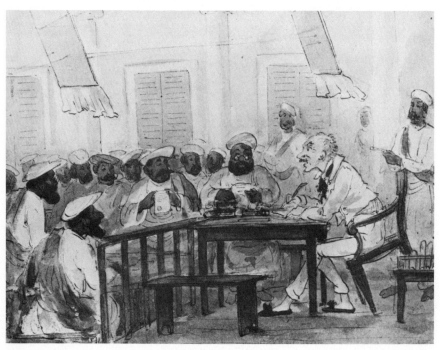

"Our Judge"
*From G. Atkinson,* Curry and Rice, *1859*

"Our Magistrate's Wife"
*From G. Atkinson,* Curry and Rice, *1859*

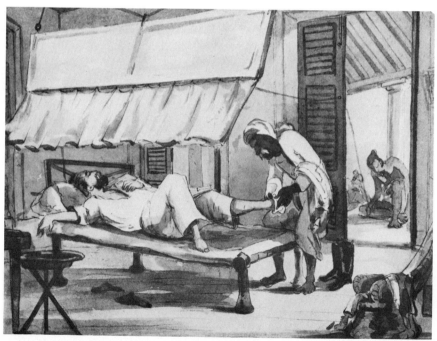

"Our Bedroom"
*From G. Atkinson,* Curry and Rice, *1859*

Sikh ruler of the Punjab, Ranjit Singh
*Courtesy of the Victoria and Albert Museum*

Fateh Singh, Maharana of Mewar, with Lord Elgin
*Copyright 1976 by Aperture, Inc., as published in* The Last Empire:
Photography in British India, 1855–1911, *Aperture, Millerton, 1976.*

Khyber Chiefs and Khans,
1878–1879
*Copyright 1976 by Aperture,
Inc., as published in* The Last
Empire: Photography in Brit-
ish India, 1855–1911, *Aperture,
Millerton, 1976.*

John Nicholson
*From a portrait at the East India Club, London*

Lord Lytton, Viceroy 1876–1880
*Courtesy of the India Office Library, copyright The British Library*

Henry Lawrence
*Courtesy of the India Office Library, copyright The British Library*

John Lawrence as Viceroy
*Courtesy of the India Office Library, copyright The British Library*

Lord Curzon as a young man
*From* Vanity Fair, *1892*

Lord Curzon, "The Old and the Young Self"
by Max Beerbohm
*Courtesy of Eva G. Reichmann*

Lord and Lady Curzon in fireworks, Delhi Durbar, 1902–3
*Courtesy of the India Office Library, copyright The British Library*

real India, rich in variety, types and contrasts," he wrote. He seemed to feel that he passed into a new world when he left British India "for the country of chance, colour and charm. . . . The dweller in British India, wherever he may go, will find the same lawcourt, the same school, and the same gaol, all of the same pattern. If he likes monotony, it is there. But the Indian dislikes monotony in excess," Lawrence reminded his readers, in an effort to explain the failure of natives to respond imaginatively to British rule.[79] Theodore Morison was one of several British officials—Lord Curzon among them—who believed that imperial administration required monarchical pomp and circumstance to make a lasting impression on native subjects.[80] But the gap between the methodical British lawgiver and such flamboyant devices was too great. In any case, neither administrative fiat nor "Oriental" posturing could by this time have satisfied India's articulate middle classes.

## The Fear of Loss

The British Raj inspired the fear and respect of Indians, but rarely their affection. Although the affection of the British for India and for their native subjects was often real, all too frequently it revolved around the need to control their possession with an emotional absolutism akin to that directed at a primary love object. Like the obsessive who creates rigid formulas to maintain order in his life, the British affection, expressed in abstract ideals like justice and order, was implemented through administrative decree. When the hopes placed in their native subjects seemed to be betrayed, or their efforts failed to strike a responsive chord, the British reacted with deep distrust. C. T. Buckland, in his book on social life in India, quoted from Cicero's disparaging comments on the Greeks: "Where can you find one who will sincerely love you," Buckland asks, "a mere stranger to them, and not merely pretend to do so for his own advantage? . . . If amongst such men you should find one . . . who loves you more than he does his own interests, enroll him as a friend; but if you do not perceive this, there is no class of acquaintance more to be avoided; because they know all the arts of getting money, they do nothing but for money, and they are indifferent about the opinion of any man with whom they are not to continue to live."[81]

The complaint almost invariably arose that the Indian population lacked gratitude for all the British had given them. They could underscore that point with all the churlishness of a rejected lover. Occasionally such a notion was directly related to the fear or pain of loss, as in S. S. Thorburn's fictional account of a deserting wife.

When he had collected all the meagre details of the supposed flight, Leslie went back to his bungalow in a state of the wildest grief. She, his little waif, his treasure-trove, his own pupil, his pet, his Aimana had gone, had left him, had *deserted* [his emphasis] him. That was the blow which tore his bleeding heart the most, and made him like a maniac. He had saved her from starvation, had fed her, had clothed her and educated her for more than three years, and this was her return, this was her gratitude.[82]

More often, as in Steel's story "Little Henry and His Bearer," the theme of gratitude crops up in a *memsahib*'s comment on the basic selfishness of Indian servants despite their apparent devotion.[83] This was no less a problem from the point of view of the Civil Service. In assessing the deteriorating relationship with natives in the Punjab, H. W. H. Coxe complained that "we might claim a modicum of gratitude from the people of India for much good intention, and for a considerable measure of benefits actually conferred." He asked rhetorically, "Is there any significance in the fact that there is no word for gratitude in the Hindostanee language?"[84] The need for control was indistinguishable from a deep-seated desire for recognition.

It seems clear that at an intrapsychic level the British were unable to separate their possession of India and control of its population from an erotic involvement with native life. When faced with the threat of loss—in the form of native demands for political recognition and eventual self-government—they responded defensively. They denied these pressures by ignoring them, as they did initially with the Indian National Congress; by denigrating the groups who demanded reform; and by invoking a mythology of imperial rule patterned on their earlier experience in the Punjab. Such an emotional investment reinforced their political incapacity to view the Indians as potentially equal to and independent of them. The threat of loss can be understood literally in political terms; it can also be viewed metaphorically as a loss of cultural identity or psychic structure that conferred meaning on everyday situations.[85]

The impact of the Indian Mutiny, for example, must be seen within this context. Although the political aspirations of the Mutineers were contained, the emotional meaning of their revolt was deeply ingrained in the imperial imagination of post-Mutiny India. Through the 1880s and 1890s the Mutiny remained a favorite topic of writers on India and the British Empire. One central theme emerges from these accounts: the fickleness, inconsistency, and weakness of native character and behavior, measured against the steely control of the British. Yet the dread of rejection represented by the insurrection was always present in post-Mutiny India, and rationalized the iron grip—the ideology of permanence—of the period.

This process was clearly reflected in the eruption of feeling over the Ilbert Bill in 1883. Many of the attacks against the proposed reform of the courts were blatantly racist, denouncing the Viceroy and the entire class of educated Indians, and threatening the armed resistance of the white community. Yet in his more closely reasoned repudiation of the bill, Fitzjames Stephen cut to the core of the anxiety it had aroused: "it is impossible to imagine any policy more fearfully dangerous and more certain to lead to results to which the Mutiny would be child's play."[86] The specter of sweeping rebellion was an unspoken reality of post-Mutiny India. During the next two decades similar anxieties focused on outspoken and occasionally violent Indians who were castigated as radicals and seditionists. Native proposals for reform in India became equated with sedition and revolt, violence and loss.

During these years the defensive maneuvers of the British might be described as increasingly characterized by masochism and paranoia. The psychologist Jules Nydes has written: "The masochist appears to renounce 'power' for the sake of 'love'; and the paranoid character appears to renounce 'love' for the sake of 'power.'"[87] The masochistically inclined individual imagines that he must continually sacrifice himself to others to retain their affection, while the paranoid imagines that others are constantly trying to sacrifice him to their own designs. As psychoanalysts have suggested, these two fantasies often function in phase with one another in the dynamics of individual mental life. In the masochistic phase the individual introjects or incorporates the love object in order to ward off a sense of loss; but with the failure of this device he angrily projects the object—and the intolerable feelings bound up with it—onto others.[88] Such primitive mental functioning, under the power of the paranoid delusion, can produce a mercurial shift from a sense of self-sacrifice to a preoccupation with persecution and betrayal. The British attitude toward native India seemed increasingly and more rigidly defined in terms of two such dynamically related group fantasies, as the pressure on British rule intensified by the end of the nineteenth century.

A British officer in Diver's *Candles in the Wind*, struggling to construct a road under debilitating conditions, consoles himself with the thought that he is one of an army of selfless workers scattered throughout India.

With every mile of descent towards Ramghat the sun smote more fiercely upon bare rock, and bare bodies of long-suffering men. The mercury in Alan's tent rose daily, till it touched 125°—which sufficed! There were moments of inevitable despondency when heat disintegrated nerves and muscle, when stone showers swept away the work of days, or a crumbling foothold flung a couple of coolies shrieking into the void. But thought of the campaign, of the Colonel's reliance on his progress, heartened him unfailingly; and he braced himself with the reminder that he was but a unit in the battalion of lonely workers scattered broadcast over India's colossal emptiness; lonely planters among the foot-hills; District Officers in the salt ranges, counting camels and weighing salt, year in year out; Civil Engineers, encamped on glaring reaches of river or canal; and scores of others, whose conditions of life and work were infinitely harder than his own.[89]

Diver's admiring biography of Honoria Lawrence, Henry Lawrence's wife, said of the Lawrences' devotion to their work: "In their eyes it was expedient that a few white men should suffer—and if need be—die for the dusky millions of the Punjab. Without any tall talk of the white man's burden, they shouldered it as a matter of duty."[90] George Steevens concluded that it was precisely such unselfish dedication that made British rule unpopular with the natives.[91] Underlying the celebration of self-sacrifice to empire as a political ideal was the personal and communal fear of the loss of empire.

The anger of the British over "Indian unrest" and "sedition" was expressed most often in a painfully felt sense of betrayal. In the Punjab especially where paternalistic rule was predicated on native loyalty, civil servants like Darling responded with disbelief to open political agitation. Rather than question the loyalty of the Punjabis themselves, Michael O'Dwyer, who became Lieutenant-Governor there in 1913, denounced the seditious elements in the Punjab as "outside agitators." In his memoir of his service he describes all educated Indians in the Punjab as actual or potential conspirators.[92] George MacMunn, who served as an army officer in the Punjab in this period, wrote with obvious distress of youthful disloyalty in the province. Speaking through the voice of a police officer in his book, *The Underworld of India*, he describes the sedition of the son of a loyal Sikh, Ganesha Singh, who had been a devoted soldier in the British army years before. "D—n it man what tomfoolery this is," complains the officer. "This good university here with all these fine lads has got the Bengal sedition poison running wildfire, for no reason whatever. . . . I've always wanted to bring this country on fast but not in a way that it would run away from itself and us. You can't play games here. . . . You know as well as I do how this country has been saved and helped, and how we are always teaching, helping, building, but always watching some wild devils. Always have, but we never expected some ass would let the intelligentsia go mad."

In MacMunn's political fantasy the old Sikh soldier himself denounces his son, asking, "Who has brought the whole Punjab to wealth and prosperity, who treats me as I've never been treated before. Who has saved your mother's life when she was ill . . . you worm you, you swine's offspring, not my son."[93] MacMunn's solution is to give the rebellious boys a sound beating and replace them safely within the ranks of Ganesha Singh's old regiment: "It was a big thing taking young fisad-wallahs (rebels) into a regiment like the Doabas, or indeed any of his Majesty's Indian Corps which the sedition-mongers were so anxious to turn into political machines like the old Sikh army and break the great tradition of camaraderie. But the stock was good, the lads had learnt their lesson, and Ganesha Singh had a claim."[94] This hope of political regeneration reflected the sadness and bewilderment the British felt in confronting Indian political demands. Alice Perrin's observation that "it is the Westerner who has to venture over to the other side for there is never a meeting half way," echoed this emotional confusion.

The image of the unappreciated administrator carrying out his duties in some remote outpost, which Rudyard Kipling popularized in the 1890s, captured not only the manifest content of imperial government, but also the less clearly perceived sense of emotional impoverishment that accompanied it. It is no coincidence that many of Kipling's lonely administrators became suicides or contemplated suicide.[95] Kipling's father, Lockwood Kipling, who was an art teacher and museum curator in India, characterized British rule in these terms: "Like a strong ass between two burdens, the British government has been beaten with many staves, and also with fools' truncheons of pantomime paper."[96] Such an image of imperial rule reflects the vulnerability of the magic on which it was based—a fear of loss rooted in archaic fantasy as well as in political reality.

## Chapter Three

# British Heroism in India:
# History as Mythology

*Go to your work and be strong, halting not in your ways,*
*Balking the end half-won for an instant dole of praise.*
*Stand to your work and be wise—certain of sword and pen,*
*Who are neither children nor Gods, but men in a world of men.*
—*Rudyard Kipling*

Writing in 1889 in an admiring biography of his friend and mentor John Lawrence, Richard Temple commented:

After the lapse of just one generation, time is already beginning to throw its halo over his deeds in 1857; the details are beginning to fade while the main features stand out in bolder and bolder relief. There is a monument to him in the minds of men.

> 'And underneath is written,
>    in letters of gold,
> How valiantly he kept the Bridge
>    in the brave days of old.'[1]

If the impulse behind British rule in India was informed by magic—by the desire for omnipotence, and by the need to ward off the threat of loss—then such magic most often took the shape of myth. As the intermediary between culture and the unconscious, the mythology of British heroism in India provided a communal focus around which these magical aspirations could crystallize, and a means of adapting these fantasies to the historical constraints of time and place. Temple's image of time throwing "its halo over his deeds in 1857" epitomizes the link between history and mythology.

79

### The Mythological Present

Joseph Campbell, perhaps the most psychologically attuned inter-
preter of myth, has suggested that mythological thinking is characteristic of societies under stress or in a state of disintegration, an
"ideological" alternative to the prospect of unwanted or unacceptable change.[2]

The British Raj maintained a dignified face in the half century
after the Indian Mutiny, yet its militant style and paternalistic policies constituted a defensive response to increasingly threatening,
anxiety-inducing conditions. In the Punjab, this response was more
deeply felt because of the dramatic change, since mid-century, in the
administrative role of the British and in their relationship to their
native subjects. The Punjab, after all, was a model province in the
years after its incorporation into the Raj, both in material progress
and in the relationship initially established with its native population. At its height the Punjab Style best embodied the aims of the
British rulers and the "real India" of sturdy peasants and unruly
tribesmen. This tradition remained alive into the last decades of the
century, but only in attenuated form. The introduction of more formal administrative and judicial procedures undermined the autonomy of the district officer, and the growth of a money economy and
the consequent rise in the value of land threatened the stability of
rural life on which the Punjab system was based. Despite legislative
efforts and literary encouragement, the British were powerless to reverse these trends.

The anxiety engendered by these trends was, from the 1880s onward, reflected in the celebration of the heroic achievements of the
British in the Punjab and the northwest frontier at mid-century.
The accomplishments of the Lawrences and their assistants in domesticating the Punjab and in containing the Mutiny reached
mythic stature. At its least self-conscious level this process was reflected in a wistful regard for the "old days." Recalling his experience in Lahore in the 1880s, Walter Lawrence wrote that he was told
"that I had come twenty years too late. The golden age of Anglo-
Indians was before the Mutiny."[3] Although he was no relation to
the great Lawrences, John and Henry, he remembered that Lock-

wood Kipling insisted on calling him "young Lawrence," after his great predecessors. [4]

In the genres of fiction and historical biography such incidental recollections were shaped into a mythology of British character and authority. The novels and stories produced by Anglo-Indian writers in this period that took northwest India as their locus—and most did—indulged in an unqualified celebration of heroic action and achievement on the frontier. Kipling was a salient exception to this trend, but his work was far from untouched by it. In his picaresque novel *Kim*, the young protagonist, while a student at St. Xavier's— a special school run by the British at Lucknow—wins as a prize for achievement in mathematics and mapmaking, "*The Life of Lord Lawrence*, tree-calf, two vols., nine rupees, eight annas." Also in the novel Kipling describes "an old man's high, shrill voice ringing across the field, as wail by long-drawn wail he unfolded the story of Nikal Seyn (Nicholson)—the song that men sing in the Punjab to this day. . . . 'Ahi! Nikal Seyn is dead—he died before Delhi! Lances of North take vengeance for Nikal Seyn.'" [5] S. S. Thorburn, one of the most outspoken critics of the economic transformation of the Punjab, wrote a number of novels, including *David Leslie* and *Transgression*, which portrayed the traditional Punjabi values of initiative, independence, and moral tenacity.

Writing after the turn of the century, I. A. R. Wylie and Maud Diver named their characters after earlier heroes such as Nicholson and Lawrence, invoking their virtues for a lesser generation of soldiers and civil servants. [6] In the frontier fiction and historical novels of Diver, especially, this purpose was explicitly pursued. In 1909, in *Candles in the Wind*, she commented that "the increasing burden of officialism has loosened the ties that bound the Anglo-Indian of fifty years ago to the country and the work; but in a lesser degree men still feel the magnetism of the Punjab." [7] Despite the materialism and parochial party politics of turn-of-the-century Britain, the northwest frontier continued to provide a refuge "where, alone, strong natures can grow up in their own way." [8] Heroes like Desmond and Meredith in the *Great Amulet* are molded as the reincarnation of an earlier generation of Punjab heroes: "It is to the Desmonds and Merediths of an earlier day that we are indebted for the sturdy loyalty of our Punjab and Frontier troops." In the society of her day, "individual aspiration and character are cramped, warped, deadened by the brute force of money." She still looked out to "the vast spaces and comparative isolation" of the empire. Only by failing to inculcate the virtues by which the Punjab was initially governed, "will power pass out of our hands."[9] This same theme informs Diver's historical novel of 1913, *The Hero of Herat*, in which she chronicles the exploits of Eldridge Pottinger, a principal in Britain's ill-fated military mission in Afghanistan in the late 1830s. In praising Pottinger's "innate, self-sacrificing heroism" and his "large nobility of soul," she connected him directly to "Nicholson, Outram, the Lawrences . . . who established also an ideal of British character that remains unshaken to this day."[10]

Such self-conscious mythmaking was initiated even earlier through the medium of historical biography, and often by men like Temple who had themselves served under the Lawrences in the Punjab. A series of such works appearing in the 1880s and 1890s tied the heroic achievements of British officers in the Punjab to the salvation of British India itself at the time of the Mutiny. Like Temple's biography of Lawrence, such books were designed to portray these accomplishments "in letters of gold." A classic example of such hagiography is found in Bosworth Smith's portrait of John Lawrence.

No Samson, no Hercules, no Milo, no Arthur, can have had more stories of personal prowess, of grim humour, of the relief of the distressed to tell than he. Physically he was a Hercules himself. . . . And when these physical characteristics are combined with others, moral and intellectual, which are conspicuously wanting in most Indian races—with absolute truthfulness in word and deed, with active benevolence, with sagacity which is the result not of mere shrewdness, but of untiring honesty of purpose, with boundless devotion to duty and hard work—their possessor becomes a power indeed in the land.[11]

He compared Lawrence to Oliver Cromwell. Like Cromwell, "John Lawrence was rough and downright," and "cared nought for appearances. . . . His voice was loud, his presence commanding; his grey eye, deepset and kindly as it was, glared terribly when it was aroused by anything mean or cowardly or wrong."[12] By stressing both the purity and power of British rule, works like this removed the Punjab Style from the historical past to the mythological present. A figure like John Lawrence functioned as a touchstone for the omnipotent magic that helped to unite the Anglo-Indians against anxieties and impulses that were forbidden public expression in their own lives, and against those emotions they saw embodied in the character and behavior of their native subjects.

## The Lawrence Brothers: Poetry versus Prose

In forging a compromise between the omnipotence of magical thinking and the persistent pressures of reality, mythology—especially the myth of "the Giants of the Punjab"—served as a mediating force in the history of post-Mutiny India. The adaptive function of myth, its effort both to shape history and to make sense of it, is graphically represented in one significant fragment of this mythology, the celebration of the fraternal rivalry between the two great Lawrences, John and Henry.

The Lawrence brothers came from a Protestant family from Northern Ireland. Their father, Alexander, had served in the British army in India, where he earned a commission. Henry Lawrence, the elder and more flamboyant of the brothers, was the first to come out to India with a military commission in 1822. John Lawrence followed in 1830 with an appointment to the Civil Service. Both men were forceful individuals, devoted to their professions and at their best under conditions of crisis. The opportunity to display these gifts came first to Henry in the 1830s and 1840s when he rose in rank to command the British forces in a series of wars against the Sikh rulers of the Punjab. The British defeated the Sikhs decisively at the battle of Sobraon in February 1846 and held the Punjab at their mercy. At this time, however, neither Henry Lawrence nor the Governor-General, Lord Hardinge, favored outright annexation of the Punjab into the sphere of British Indian administration. Nor was the corrupt and divided Sikh ruling class, headed by a maharajah in his minority, capable of maintaining independent rule there. As a compromise the British established themselves as guardians of the Sikh government in the Punjab, with Henry Lawrence as resident. Under this arrangement Henry ruled the province as a virtual autocrat, pursuing a vigorous administration in the Punjab Style. He was favorably inclined to the traditional Sikh ruling elite and tried to foster its political potential. During this same period Henry's younger brother John had enjoyed a steady but much less spectacular rise through the ranks of the Civil Service in northern India. He served initially as a district officer in the vicinity of Delhi, and first distinguished himself in the eyes of Hardinge in 1845 for his work in organizing military transport for the campaign against the Sikhs. After their defeat in 1846 John was established as commissioner in the Trans-Sutlej Territory, and substituted periodically for his brother Henry as resident at the Punjab capital, Lahore.

In 1848 two events initiated a chain of developments that eventually brought the brothers into conflict: the Sikh nation rose up in a last bid for independence from their British rulers; and Lord Dalhousie, an aggressive and autocratic administrator, replaced Hardinge as Governor-General. Although Henry Lawrence had been on intimate terms with Hardinge and had enjoyed a free reign in the Punjab under his rule, he found Dalhousie personally cold and jealous of the prerogatives of his office. Lawrence returned to the Punjab from a trip to England in time for the final defeat of the Sikhs at Chilianwala in January 1849, but shortly afterward he was sternly rebuked by Dalhousie for assuming to speak for British policy in the Punjab. In fact, two major policy issues separated these men. First, against Lawrence's desire to maintain the political power of the Sikh Sirdars, Dalhousie insisted that the instability of native rule necessitated outright annexation of the area. Second, on the vital question of land settlement in the Punjab, Henry Lawrence leaned toward the economic as well as the political claims of the Sikh aristocracy, while Dalhousie was determined to strengthen the landed position of the Punjab peasantry.

When annexation became a fact in the ensuing months and a provincial government was set up, Henry Lawrence was regarded as the natural man to lead it. Yet Dalhousie distrusted not only Henry's policy toward the Sikh leadership, but also his administrative skills. Instead of a single administrator in the Punjab, Dalhousie appointed a troika dominated by Henry and his younger brother John. The third member was Charles Greville Mansel, who served largely as a mediator between John and Henry. John Lawrence had favored annexation, and was expected to balance his brother's dyna-

mism with his administrative abilities and his peasant-oriented political views. As measured in terms of material progress and domestic peace within the province, the troika arrangement worked
well enough. But even though the brothers genuinely admired each
other, the friction between them over policy issues gradually intensified. Henry believed that his position of trust with the Sikh aristocracy was being systematically undermined by the nature of the
land settlement. John felt equally intensely the fundamental justice
of the government policy and chafed under the burden of what he
regarded as an unequal share of administrative work left to him by
his brother. By the end of 1852 their disagreement had reached a
breaking point. Dalhousie felt he had no alternative but to intervene and side with John Lawrence. He appointed him Chief Commissioner of the Punjab and offered Henry Lawrence the post
of political agent to Rajputana, an area of native-governed states.
Henry left with great bitterness and great regret. He was killed during the Mutiny while defending his quarters at Lucknow, where he
was serving as Chief Commissioner of Oudh. John Lawrence was in
process of becoming the greatest hero of British India by thwarting
the native revolt in the Punjab, and by helping to break the back of
the Mutiny in the siege and conquest of Delhi. In the 1860s he succeeded to the highest post in the Indian administration, that of
Viceroy; he was the only member of the Civil Service to attain it.

In the heroic tradition of the protagonists, and in the tragic inevitability of their struggle, this story of fraternal conflict possesses
both the directness and simplicity of myth. In its delineation of the
clashing personalities of John and Henry, it is a deeply revealing
narrative of the vicissitudes of the Punjab Style as a historical phenomenon. In her admiring biography of Honoria Lawrence, Henry's wife, Maud Diver characterized the difference between the two
men: "To those who knew and admired both he [Henry] seemed to
present the poetry of Indian statesmanship; John, its clear, forceful
prose."[13] Both brothers are consistently treated as giants within the
conventions of charismatic leadership: Henry Lawrence as the heart
of British government in the Punjab, John Lawrence as its sober
head; Henry as a benevolent despot, John as the tireless bureaucrat;[14] or in the light of their mixed Celtic blood, Henry as the romantic Irishman, John as the doughty Scot.[15] These contrasting

traits came to symbolize the changing character of British rule in India.

To his biographers Henry Lawrence was introspective, impulsive, and romantic. In spite of "a spare, gaunt frame" and "a worn face," the initial impression he conveyed was "of masculine energy and resolution."[16] He opposed the introduction of too much administrative routine into the Punjab, preferring men "who will not spare themselves, and will do prompt justice in their shirt sleeves, rather than profound laws."[17] As a soldier he much preferred the military campaign or a horseback tour to the sedentary rigors of office work. As an administrator he relished the scope and power of autocratic rule. One of his biographers, J. L. Morison, characterized his governance of the Punjab as that of a "just and humane Oriental king" with a gift for decisive action and warm personal relationships.[18] He was depicted as by far the most loved man in the Punjab, both among his British subordinates and among the native chiefs with whom he fought, negotiated, and governed. In their work on Henry, Herbert Edwardes and Herman Merivale record this eulogy by a noted subordinate, Major James Abbott:

> He was the spirit which inspired every act of the local government, which touched the heart of all his subordinates with ardour to fill up each his own part in a system so honourable to the British name. All caught from him the sacred fire; his presence seemed all-pervading, for the interests of the meanest were dear to him as those of the most powerful; and goodness and greatness were so natural wherever he came that other fruits seemed strange and impossible.[19]

As Bosworth Smith wrote of Henry Lawrence in 1885, "nobody has ever done so much for bridging over the gulf that separates race from race, colour from colour, and creed from creed; nobody has ever been so beloved, nobody has ever deserved to be so beloved, as Sir Henry Lawrence."[20] And in Henry, as the story goes, this love was returned in full measure. His policies emphasized kindness and conciliation, and his romantic imagination responded to the forceful qualities of the native chiefs and aristocrats. His support of the privileged classes and their political leadership made him reluctant to expand British rule in the 1840s, and extremely conciliatory when that rule became an established fact. Indeed, it was Henry's insistence on dealing generously with the Sikh chiefs in defeat that brought him into direct conflict with his brother John and with the Civil Service. More than Henry, John and other civilians tended to identify their own rule with justice, and to see their primary role as that of defender of the native peasantry.

In his sketch of the elder Lawrence, John Kaye quotes from a letter from Herbert Edwardes, composed in the aftermath of Henry's death in 1857: "how much of the *man* there was left in him; how unsubdued he was; how great his purposes . . . and fiery will . . . and strong passions. . . . He had not been tempered yet as it was meant he should be."[21] This warm and impulsive temperament was also recognized as Henry's Achilles' heel. In his biography of Lawrence, Edwardes described him as "by nature headstrong and opinionated, intolerant of opposition and of contradiction."[22] From the perspective of the evangelical Edwardes, Lawrence engaged in a constant struggle—fortified by his ardent Christian faith—to keep these violent tendencies in check. Yet even the admiring Edwardes recognized a tendency on Henry's part to personalize his political struggles, a tendency toward moodiness that was quick to ignite into anger and difficult to domesticate to the routines of bureaucratic procedure.[23] His morbid sensitivity crippled him in his struggle with his brother and the Governor-General.

As the analogy with Cromwell suggests, the balance in John Lawrence's character comes down unmistakably on the side of justice against liberality, of rigid self-control against spontaneity. "To do the thing that lay before him, to do it thoroughly, to do it with all his might, not regarding the consequences and not turning either to the right hand or to the left," Smith tells us, "this was henceforward the ruling principle of his life."[24] John was motivated by a practical concern for the native peasantry and for the introduction of orderly administration along Western lines, rather than admiration for the Sikh nobility or a romantic attachment to native life in general. He tailored his administration to the demands of cost and efficiency, and took pride in producing a surplus of revenue in the Punjab. John depended on commanding the respect and fear of his native subjects, not their love. He was depicted as a blunt man who could be extremely direct in the pursuit of his objectives. "If he thought a man a knave or a fool," Smith writes, "he generally called him so to his face. If he had to strike at all, he struck a knock-down blow."[25] Charles Aitchison wrote in 1892 that John possessed a straightforwardness and penetration that overmastered "Oriental artifice."[26]

To his biographers, his most characteristic dedication was to work. "No old bullock," Aitchison remarked, "is worked harder."[27] Despite exhaustion and increasing fragility, Lawrence chose "to work on in the Punjab with increased responsibility and power, not merely for three or four, but for seven years, doing each day as much as most men do in a dozen days." When Lawrence was called upon to be Viceroy in the 1860s, in the aftermath of the Mutiny, "when his health had finally broken down, when his sight was nearly gone, and when he seemed to have set his face towards the grave, he was to rouse himself again at the trumpet call of duty. . . . If any life was ever dignified from first to last with that kind of dignity which nothing but labour—honest, unsparing, unselfish labour—can give, that life was John Lawrence's."[28]

It was, essentially, Lawrence's role in suppressing the Sepoy Revolt that served to enshrine these qualities of character in the annals of British India. While Hindustan, the heartland of the Raj, was reeling from the blows inflicted by the Mutineers in the summer of 1857, John Lawrence and his lieutenants worked with calmness and vigor to contain any instances of revolt in the Punjab, and then to relieve Delhi itself. Precisely this emergency, his biographers agreed, brought out John Lawrence's best qualities. Smith praised his decisiveness and deliberate courage while looking in the teeth of chaos, "quite above any feeling of physical fear."[29] Richard Temple, who had served with Lawrence in the Punjab, described him in these days as a protean figure.

It is hard to paint the picture of his work in these days, because the canvas has to be crowded with many diverse incidents and policies. At one moment he cries in effect—disarm the rebel Sepoys, disarm them quick, inflict exemplary punishment, stamp out mutiny, pursue, cut off retreat—at another, spare, spare, temper judgment with discriminating clemency— at another, advance, advance, advance, raise levies, place men wherever wanted—at another, hold fast, don't do too much, by an excessive number of new men a fresh risk is run—at another, seize such and such strategic points, guard such and such river-passages. . . . He unravelled the threads of countless transactions, collated the thick-coming reports from all the districts, and noted the storm warnings at every point of his political compass. . . . His word always was, attack, attack, so that the people, seeing this aggressive attitude, might not lose heart. His energy in these days might be called resplendent, as it was all-pervading, life-infusing, and ranged in all directions with the broadest sweep.[30]

In his Old Testament zeal, his capacity for self-sacrifice, and his unflinching devotion to duty, John Lawrence was celebrated as the very incarnation of the Punjab Style.

The struggle between the two brothers—invoked as a myth of tragic conflict—encapsulated much of the history of British India in the fifty years after the Mutiny. Their conflict had corresponded in time to the most traumatic event which the British endured in nineteenth-century India—the Mutiny, to which Henry was a martyr, and through which John's reputation reached its pinnacle and spread to India as a whole.

The underlying theme of the myth of the Lawrences is the transmission and perpetuation of authority. The emotional balance of contrasting personalities corresponded to a political balance that fostered peace and prosperity in the Punjab—a balance perpetuated, we are told, even after Henry's departure in 1853. Although John, Richard Temple informs us, was now left "to walk alone" in the Punjab, "he ever remembered his absent brother."[31] In Bosworth Smith's biography, Henry's personal qualities are magically maintained in John.

In personal character too, I think I am not wrong in saying that John Lawrence bore, henceforward, a greater and constantly increasing resemblance to his brother. Without losing a particle of his energy, his independence, his zeal, he did lose, henceforward, something of his roughness, something of that which an outsider or an opponent might have put down as harsh. "The two Lawrences," says one who knew them equally, General Reynell Taylor, "were really very much alike in character. They each had their own capabilities and virtues, and, when one of them was removed from the scene, the *frater supertes* succeeded to many of the graces of his lost brother." In this sense it is, I believe, true that the influence of Henry Lawrence was greater on his brother, and was even more felt throughout the Punjab administration when he had left the country forever, than while he was living and working within it; just as the words, the looks, the memory of the dead have often a more living influence on the survivors than had all the charms of their personal presence.[32]

Thus Henry Lawrence was assimilated to the harsher contours of the Punjab Style. None of Henry's biographers, incidentally—not even his closest friend, Herbert Edwardes—maintained that he was unjustly treated by Lord Dalhousie; none seriously defended his anti-annexationist attitudes.[33] Although mourning his loss, they ultimately identified with the policy of imperial expansion and with British administration personified by his brother.

Both Henry Lawrence's death and John Lawrence's conquest in the Sepoy Revolt take on symbolic scope through the elements of continuity and change in pre- and post-Mutiny policy. Henry Lawrence loved and admired native society, yet died at the hands of the natives themselves, a martyr to the ingratitude, vengefulness, and emotional excess that the Mutiny signified to most Anglo-Indians. In this sense his death symbolized the collective mastery of emotional excess—that aspect of native personality which he clearly embodied.

With the authority—in fact, the personality—of his brother vested in him, John Lawrence was free to establish his own patriarchal presence, a presence which embraced the emotional conflicts at the heart of the British identity in India in the post-Mutiny period. Only his stern figure, the embodiment of omnipotent self-control and self-sacrifice, could provide protection from the regressive pull of such primitive emotional expression, and from the prospect of loss. He symbolized the victorious and repressive strain in Anglo-Indian identity that dominated at the expense of the Indians and of the British themselves.

## John Nicholson: The Avenging Angel

The legend of one other figure loomed as large as that of the Lawrences in the Punjab, and carried an equal symbolic weight in Anglo-Indian mythology in the post-Mutiny period. This is General John Nicholson, who died in 1857 at the age of thirty-five of wounds suffered in leading the successful assault against Delhi. He was from an Anglo-Irish family situated in Dublin, where his father worked as a physician. Nicholson first arrived in India in 1838 with an army commission, and a few years later was involved in an incursion into Afghanistan which led to his capture there, along with a group of British soldiers, in 1842. Before leaving Afghanistan he met Henry Lawrence in Kabul, and Lawrence was apparently impressed with the young man's enthusiasm and soldierly qualities.[34] When Lawrence assumed charge of the political administration of the Punjab later in the 1840s, Nicholson was one of the lieutenants he hand-picked to assist him. Nicholson distinguished himself for his calmness and courage on the northwest frontier in the final confrontation with the Sikhs in 1848. After a furlough in England he returned to the Punjab to administer the frontier district of Bannu, where he enhanced his reputation with his work in subduing and domesticating the fiercely independent Pathan tribes.[35] Although angered and saddened by Henry Lawrence's departure from the Punjab in 1853, he continued, somewhat reluctantly, to serve under his brother.

It was the Mutiny itself that sparked Nicholson's brief and meteoric ascent during the trying summer months of 1857. He was placed in charge of a column of cavalry entrusted with the critical task of suppressing any rebellion among the native troops stationed in the province, and when that work was accomplished he was selected to command the troops Lawrence dispatched to relieve Delhi. He carried out these tasks heroically, and consequently surpassed his senior officers in authority, reputation, and rank. With the British troops ranged before Delhi in September 1857, Nicholson was given the honor of leading the assault.

As the greatest military hero of the Mutiny, and one of its foremost martyrs, John Nicholson became the incarnation of British strength in India, a strength that could barely be constrained by the broader mandates of civility and self-control. He became a mythic figure both in his own time and in the novels of Steel and Wylie at the turn of the century. "If there is ever a desperate deed to be done in India," Herbert Edwardes suggested to the Governor-General, Lord Canning, shortly before the outbreak of the Mutiny, "Nicholson is the man to do it."[36] Recalling a meeting with Nicholson in 1857, Lord Frederick Roberts, who was to become Commander-in-Chief of the Indian army in the 1880s, records in his memoirs that "Nicholson impressed me more profoundly than any man I had

ever met before, or have ever met since. I have never seen anyone
like him. He was the *beau idéal* of a soldier and a gentleman. His
appearance was distinguished and commanding, with a sense of
power about him which, to my mind, was the result of his having
passed so much of his life among the lawless tribesmen with whom
his authority was supreme."[37]

So commanding was Nicholson's presence, John Kaye reported,
that the frontier tribesmen under his charge came to fear and admire him literally as a demigod. Among a group of Moslem fakirs in
the frontier district of Hazara, a cult of "Nikkul Seyn" worship
grew up that not even flogging and imprisonment could discour-
age.[38] Nicholson's personal strength was conveyed through his features which, one British officer observed, "made an impression
upon my mind, and doubtless upon others who had not met him
before, which could never be effaced. No pictures that I have ever
seen could do him justice. His face was full of power, and no one
could look on him without feeling that he was a man of mark, and
no ordinary character."[39] William Wilberforce, in his *An Unrecorded
Chapter of the Indian Mutiny*, reported that Nicholson possessed a
colorless face "over which no smile ever passed," and dark gray eyes
with black pupils which "under excitement of any sort . . . would
dilate like a tiger's."[40]

His biographers say that Nicholson could barely contain a violent
and brutal temperament. Bosworth Smith described Nicholson as
being driven by "ungovernable restiveness."[41] John Trotter reports
that in 1849 Henry Lawrence—who had his own problems with
temperament—wrote his trusted subordinate a letter in which he
appealed to Nicholson to curb his violent temper. "Bear and forbear
with natives and Europeans," Lawrence suggested. "Don't think it
necessary to say all you think to every one. The world would be a
mass of tumult if we all gave *candid* opinions of each other. I admire
your sincerity as much as any man can do, but so this much as a
general warning."[42] Nicholson recognized "the faults of my temper,"
but could not restrain them.[43] When one insolent native chief spat
in his presence, Nicholson forced the proud chief to lick up his spit-
tle while his face was ground into the earth.[44] Olaf Caroe likened
Nicholson to Achilles angry in his tent, and he echoed Lord Roberts in comparing him to a Pathan warrior in his ferocity.[45]

To the chroniclers of British heroics in the Punjab, Nicholson's willfulness brought him almost ineluctably into conflict with John Lawrence. Trotter described Nicholson as possessing "a nature as masterful and more stubbornly self-reliant" than that of the Chief Commissioner.[46] And in the heat and dire uncertainty of the first months of the Mutiny he proved impossible to subordinate, even to Lawrence's iron will. Nicholson's attitude to Lawrence's commands in the summer of 1857 has been variously described as a "heroic disregard for orders" or a "contempt of all authority and rule."[47] He withdrew a column of European troops from Rawal Pindi in June 1857 to supplement his own force, which was pacifying the Punjab. Only Lawrence's "magnanimity and forbearance" could have absorbed so insubordinate an action, Bosworth Smith assures us.[48] It was Nicholson's success in foiling every potential revolt in the Punjab that ultimately sanctioned his insubordinate behavior. "I fear that you are incorrigible," Lawrence wrote to Nicholson in August 1857, when against orders he had carried off a body of European gunners from a fort in the Punjab, "so I must leave you to your fate."[49]

Yet in the mythology of the Punjab the most pivotal division between Lawrence and Nicholson centered on the treatment of the defeated Mutineers. Lawrence urged that justice be tempered with restraint; Nicholson is portrayed as the avenging angel of British India, symbolizing the relentless demand for revenge that the British identified with the Pathan warriors they both hated and admired. After being freed from Afghanistan in 1843, Trotter reports, Nicholson wrote his mother complaining that British retribution had not been heavy enough and that "he was sorry to leave Kabul while one stone of it remained on another."[50] In confronting the rebellious Sikhs on the northwest frontier in 1848, Nicholson's name became a "word of fear," and his threats were often sufficient to cajole the enemy into submission. "He stalked among them like an avenging deity," and "dared them to lift a finger against him."[51] Nicholson appealed for unbridled revenge in dealing with Indians responsible for atrocities against British women and children during the Mutiny. In a letter from the frontier to the more moderate Edwardes, he appealed for "a Bill for the flaying alive, impalement . . . of the murderers of the women and children at Delhi. The idea of simply hanging the perpetrators of such atrocities is maddening. I wish that I was in a part of the world that I might if necessary take the law into my own hands."[52] In Steel's fictional account of the Mutiny fifty years later, Nicholson is still depicted as the belligerent spirit who embodies Britain's outraged sense of justice.[53]

By contrast, John Lawrence's strength finds its most mature expression, in the historical accounts, in mastering the temptation to indiscriminate revenge. As Smith comments:

> It may have been observed that I have repeatedly quoted letters in which Sir John Lawrence advocates strong measures in dealing with the mutineers. And I have done so purposely, in order that I may now lay all the more stress on what implies the possession of much rarer and more admirable qualities, and marks him out pre-eminently the man to have held the reigns of power at such a crisis—I mean his rigid sense of justice, and his determination, while he was for severity so long as severity was necessary or was likely to prove mercy in the end, not to allow a drop of blood to be shed in the mere luxury or wantonness of revenge. Unlike some of his subordinates, and unlike, it may be added without injustice, too many of our countrymen, at that terrible time both in India and at home, he kept his head throughout. He never joined in the cry for indiscriminate vengeance, a cry which he thought to be as impolitic as it was un-Christian and unjust, and which was sometimes heard most loudly in quarters where it was least to be expected or excused.[54]

The Chief Commissioner tirelessly pursued a restrained justice, "judicial calmness" balanced with "irrepressible energy, which marked him throughout, which made him head and shoulders taller than even the ablest and most energetic of his subordinates." In contrast to the courage informed by obliviousness to danger and inflamed passion, such a leader "is determined to shut his eyes to nothing, to explore all the ramifications of the danger, and then, having counted the cost beforehand . . . sits down, determined, by every means in his power to make the improbable, probable, and the impossible, possible." Smith described this more deliberate and self-conscious bravery as the "higher courage . . . of the responsible ruler."[55]

Nicholson died in the Mutiny of wounds suffered at the conclusion of the first day's assault on Delhi, after he and his forces had penetrated the city walls. He was martyred by his own supernal powers, insisting on one final charge when his troops were exhausted from the day's fighting.[56] Like Lawrence, he became a martyr to the native passions kindled in 1857 and then contained by the irresistible force of British character. John Lawrence, who set the tone for post-Mutiny India, embodied Nicholson's power and sense of justice, muted by a "higher courage."

If one were to represent in schematic form the shape of the communal psyche represented in the mythology of the Punjab Style, John Lawrence might be viewed as its ego ideal, John Nicholson as its sometimes sadistic superego, and Henry Lawrence might be identified with the erotic strivings that underlay its accepted social values.

The lionization of John Lawrence at the end of the nineteenth century gave both emotional and moral sanction to the repressive policies pursued by the British. In the face of the related threats of regression and object loss, he became a communal symbol of the need for ascetic self-control and of omnipotent political authority.[57] From the perspective of an object-relations or self-object psychology, Lawrence's idealized image met the narcissistic needs of the Anglo-Indian community for a source of internalized authority with which to identify.

## The Conquest of Character

The historiography of the Indian Mutiny revolved around the dichotomy between emotional expression and emotional control, an all but universal contrast that lent these accounts a mythical quality of their own. One major theme of such writing was, of course, the conflict between the restrained strength of the British and the uncontrolled passion and depravity of the rebellious natives. At a more fundamental level this same conflict raged within British character itself.

The heroic literature of the Mutiny saw the British victory as one of personal rather than military strength. From the first explosion of violence at the British garrison in Meerut, the native rebels were depicted as furies, transformed suddenly from docile children into deadly assailants.[58] Like children their rebellion quickly disintegrated into anarchy—impulsive, mercurial, and all the more dangerous for its lack of control or consistency. As Ascott Hope wrote: "Many [mutineers], if not most, were hurried into it by panic or excitement, or the persuasion of the more designing, and their hearts soon misgave them when they saw the fruit of their wild deeds, still more when they considered the punishment likely to follow. . . . Towns were sacked, jails broken open, treasuries plundered. Broken bands of Sepoys and released convicts roamed about the country, murdering and pillaging unchecked."[59] By contrast, even in its initial defeat the small British garrison at Delhi displayed the qualities that spelled ultimate doom for the mutineers. "It was the first reply to the general revolt," wrote G. B. Malleson in his history of the Mutiny in 1891, "it was the first warning to the King and to the sepoys of the nature of the men whose vengeance they had dared; the first intimation to the rebels of the stern and resolute character of the Englishman when thoroughly aroused."[60]

For T. Rice Holmes, whose history was first published in 1883 and reprinted five times in the next twenty years, "at no epoch of history has individual character achieved more extraordinary results than in the course of the Indian Mutiny."[61] In these terms he celebrated General James Neill's accomplishments in Benares and Allahabad in 1857.

Within a few days he had paralyzed the insurgent population of a crowded city and a wide district, and had rebuilt the shattered fabric of British authority. He had done this while labouring under a physical weakness that would have prostrated many energetic men. But nothing could overcome the resolute heart of Neill. When he arrived in Allahabad, after a week of ceaseless activity and anxiety at Benares, he had felt almost dying from complete exhaustion; but "yet," he wrote to his wife, "I kept up heart." Unable to move, barely able to sustain consciousness by taking repeated droughts of champagne and water, he had had himself carried into the batteries, and there, lying on his back, had directed every operation. And now he felt that his work was only begun.[62]

The celebrated historian of the Mutiny, John Kaye, saw British power as best expressed in "that calm confidence which betrays no sign of misgiving, and the very quietude that indicates a consciousness of strength."[63]

Kaye and many others acknowledged that such qualities of character were strained to their utmost in the tempest unleashed by the

Mutiny. The success of the sepoy uprising at Meerut, one of the strongest British garrisons in India, was universally attributed to a deplorable failure of leadership on the part of the British officers stationed there. These officers were characterized as negligent in their failure to perceive a threat, and then apathetic in their own defense and in the defense of the smaller British force in nearby Delhi.[64] This may fairly describe the British leadership at Meerut, but it was an interpretation tailored to the tutelary purposes of those historians who regarded the ultimate British victory as an expression of renascent courage and fortitude.

Perhaps just as threatening as evidence of weakness were those expressions of aggressiveness that to one degree or another soon inspired such stern resistance to the rebellious sepoys. Kaye placed this in a scriptural framework, citing those Englishmen who, as early as May 1857, were prepared "to strike at once, smiting everywhere, hip and thigh, like the grand remorseless heroes of the Old Testament."[65] Smith struck closer to the unconscious fantasies behind such an image when he wrote, in discussing the British treatment of a vanquished Delhi, that "in the English, as well as in all Imperial races, there is an element of the wild beast. There is a disposition which has shown itself, once and again, in the hour of provocation or of panic to indulge in wild reprisals or even in deliberate revenge long after all justification, or even excuse for it, has ceased."[66]

Such moral weakness was mitigated in Smith's mind by the pressures of Britain's imperial mission, where "England in her worldwide rule is brought into contact with so many weaker races, her officers may be so often tempted in the hateful pride of blood, of colour, or of empire to forget that the obligations of humanity are thereby not weakened but intensified."[67] Indeed, to Smith and his contemporaries, British action in the Mutiny revealed their self-control and moral superiority as imperial rulers. In this respect the British capacity for restraint distinguished them from earlier conquerors like the Turks and Persians. These "lesser breeds" yielded to the destructive instincts unleashed "in the fury of the hour." Had the British yielded to such temptation in their assault on Delhi, Smith reminded his readers, they would have undermined their moral claim to hold India. "All honour, then," Smith proclaimed, "to those who, in the exasperating conflict of the Mutiny, lost neither head nor heart, but saved us from our baser selves, saved us from the brief delerium of a revenge which must have been succeeded by a long and unavailing repentance!"[68]

Even in describing those instances where retributive violence seemed to get out of hand—as in the indiscriminate slaughter of natives by the British forces under Neill in the districts around Benares—it was necessary to establish some moral justification. Holmes, in citing the indiscriminate burning of native villages and the arbitrary killing of old men, mothers, and infants, writes that, "to the honour of Neill . . . the infliction of punishment was not a delight, but an awful duty."[69] Kaye reminded his readers of the need to be "sternly, rigorously just against all treason, violence, and treachery, and hand down a tradition of our severity." He wrote: "What is dreadful in the record of retribution is, that some of our people regarded it not as a solemn duty or a terrible necessity, but as a devilish pastime, striking indiscriminately at the black races, and slaying without proof of individual guilt." That Neill "was fully assured in his own mind that the men, on whom he had inflicted the terrible punishment thus described in his own words, were among the actual perpetrators of the great crime which he was called upon to punish, cannot be questioned; and we must all devoutly hope that he was right."[70] To place this line of argument in psychoanalytic terms, the violence of the id had to be carefully distinguished from that of the superego. Such a stern sense of awful duty, presumably turned against the imperial self, provided the foundation of British identity in the post-Mutiny period.

One model of self-restraint was of course the Governor-General, Lord Canning—"Clemency Canning," as he was called derisively by those critics who wished harsher prosecution of Mutineers. Canning, with "his still face of marble and his tranquil demeanor," remained "firm as a rock" and a model of outward calm to the British community in Calcutta.

Still, John Lawrence was most representative of the Anglo-Indian ideal. He was regarded as perhaps the purest embodiment of the cult of character that was subscribed to by both Anglo-Indians and middle-class Britons in the Victorian period. His strength and virtues had been bred in India, and his entire career was identified with the authority of the British Raj. He had proven his capacity for decisive and courageous action, as well as for judicious restraint. Bosworth Smith, in emphasizing Lawrence's uniqueness even among his brilliant subordinates in the Punjab, writes: "Which of them struck harder while it was necessary to strike, or was more resolute to withhold his hand at the moment it was possible to do so?" Though "he had proved that he had the strength and grip of a giant," he was prepared to use it with restraint.[71]

One further aspect of John Lawrence's appeal was presented in contrast to his brother. Whereas his brother Henry had risen quickly through the ranks of the British army in India thanks to his flamboyant brilliance and to the patronage of his superiors, John Lawrence's success was depicted as a triumph of patience, endurance, and superhuman effort.[72] Temple noted that "as a young man he was never deemed remarkable, and almost up to his middle life he was not expected by his best friends to acquire greatness. When the hours of difficulty came . . . he was found more and more to be the man for them all . . . he was overtaken by the desperate tempest of the Mutinies, and he rose on the crest of every wave. . . . Thus he rose not by assumed antecedants nor by collateral advantages, but by proved merit in action."[73] This description was intended by Temple to "have a spirit-stirring effect on the middle class."[74]

Henry Lawrence had associated himself with the aristocratic tradition, both through his personal romanticism and his political endorsement of the Sikh aristocracy, whereas John Lawrence was consistently depicted as a staunch defender of the common people. "All through his public career he was the plain Englishman," Aitchison assures us, "as simple in his ways when he was a Viceroy as when he was a District Magistrate."[75] In their history of the Mutiny, published in 1895, Alfred Miles and Arthur Pattle expound the popular lesson expressed in Lord Lawrence's life.

The display of great gifts often discourages as many as it inspires, but the record of high achievements made by ordinary men under extraordinary circumstances is an unfailing stimulus to all. Brilliant powers are the coveted possessions of the few, and genius often dismays as well as dazzles; character, integrity, and sound sense are among the common possibilities of the many, and triumphs wrought by plain men of high principle are of universal inspiration and appeal. The career of Lord Lawrence presents a wholesome example which stimulates without discouraging, for though he can scarcely be called an ordinary man (genius other than that of hard work has never been claimed for him), his distinction was due to the possession of ordinary qualities in an extraordinary degree of development, and efficiency, based upon fine character, unswerving integrity, and an energy which was little less than magnificent.[76]

Within the Anglo-Indian context itself these qualities of character were narrowly associated with the symbol of the Law as the incarnation of British authority. This idealization of the law embodied the moral force of the evangelical and utilitarian doctrines, now invested in the notions of order and efficient administration as ultimate political ends.[77] In externalizing and historicizing internal conflict, the myth of John Lawrence and his struggles in the Punjab might be said to have rationalized the authoritarian "magic" apparent in post-Mutiny policy. Insofar as he became identified with the rigid repression of affect and energetic devotion to duty, Lawrence was incorporated into the ego ideal of the Anglo-Indian official. His role in the Mutiny—both in repressing the Mutineers and in restraining himself—helped to rationalize Britain's imperial posture in the closing years of the nineteenth century.

If the need for control, more rigid and more mechanical than ever, dominated every softer impulse in late nineteenth-century India, the tension between involvement with Indian life and narrow identification with British values was never fully resolved by the Punjab Style. No one can read Kipling's writing on India without sensing this conflict as basic to the power and appeal of his work. Yet the recourse to authority, as an end in itself rather than an instrument of reform, undoubtedly became more characteristic of British rule in India by the end of the nineteenth century, and in this regard the myth of John Lawrence's rise to power validated a historical process that was responsive to both political and emotional needs. Only through his "prose" could the magic of British rule be perpetuated.

## Chapter Four

# Kipling's India: In Black and White

*To our dear dark foster-mothers,*
*    To the heathen songs they sung—*
*To the heathen speech we babbled*
*    Ere we came to the white man's tongue.*
                                    *—Rudyard Kipling*

*The Black and White mix very quaintly*
*in their ways. Sometimes the White shows*
*in spurts of fierce, childish pride—*
*which is Pride of Race run Crooked—*
*and sometimes the black in still fiercer*
*abasement and humility, half-heathenish*
*customs, and strange unaccountable*
*impulses to crime.*
                                    *—Rudyard Kipling*

"*O*n the City Wall" is one of the last stories Kipling wrote in India, and one of the most revealing. It is made up of all the elements that mark the turbulent life of Kipling's Lahore: religious discord between Hindu and Moslem; the ubiquitous but somehow superficial presence of the Sahib; and the canker of "Oriental" intrigue that gradually permeates the action of the story. Structurally, "On the City Wall" is divided into "black" and "white," native society and European power. On one side is ranged the "supreme Government" and its hirelings, treated by Kipling with relentless irony.

Year by year England sends out fresh drafts for the Indian Civil Service. These die, or kill themselves by overwork, or are worried to death or broken in health and hope in order that the land may be protected from death and sickness, famine and war, and may eventually become capable of standing alone. It will never stand alone, but the idea is a pretty one, and men are willing to die for it, and yearly the work of pushing and coaxing and scolding and petting the country into good living goes forward. If an advance be made all credit is given to the native, while the Englishmen stand back and wipe their foreheads. If a failure occurs the Englishmen step forward and take the blame. Overmuch tenderness of this kind has bred a strong belief among many natives that the native is capable of administering the country, and many devout Englishmen believe this also, because the theory is stated in beautiful English with all the latest political color.[1]

By contrast, the values of native life are embodied in Lalun, a courtesan who presides regally over her salon nestled on the city wall.

Lalun has not yet been described. She would need, so Wali Dad says, a thousand pens of gold and ink scented with musk. She has been variously compared to the Moon, the Dil Sagar Lake, a spotted quail, a gazelle, the Sun on the Desert of Kutch, the Dawn, the Stars, and the young bamboo. The comparisons imply that she is beautiful exceedingly according to the native standards, which are practically the same as those of the West. Her eyes are black, and her hair is black, and her eyebrows are black as leeches; her mouth is tiny and says witty things; her hands are tiny and have saved much money; her feet are tiny and have trodden on the naked hearts of many men. But, as Wali Dad sings: "Lalun *is* Lalun, and when you have said that, you have only come to the Beginnings of Knowledge."[2]

Lalun is not only an ardent lover who "knew how to make up tobacco for the *huqa* so that it smelt like the Gates of Paradise." Her professional heritage goes back "before the days of Eve," symbolized by her marriage to a "jujube-tree" in the custom of the East. She is both mother and seductress who "knew the hearts of men, and the heart of the city."[3]

Through her intrigues, Lalun's authority rivals that of the British, as measured by the reality of her power in Lahore, and by her place in the fantasies of the narrator. "By the subtlety of Lalun the administration of the Government was troubled,"[4] he tells us, and she knew "more of the secrets of the government office than are good to be set down."[5] On the eve of an outbreak of native violence, the narrator daydreams that he is made vizier in Lalun's "administration," with Lalun's silver *huqa* for a mark of office.[6] And in the midst of religious rioting the narrator is literally seduced into leading an important political prisoner to his freedom, unknown to him or to the British troops trying to quell the outbreak. As the narrator realizes at the end of the story, he has "become Lalun's Vizier after all."[7]

Kipling's view of India—from a psychological perspective or any other—must encompass the native prostitute as much as the ascetic administrator. Kipling's self-image was deeply invested in both figures. Although he associated almost reflexively with the rigid values of the military caste, his curiosity about native life was equally instinctive, drawing on a personal reservoir of primitive fantasy. His social and political views cannot, of course, be reduced to a set of psychological determinants; nonetheless, his power and appeal as a writer—the "magical" character of his work—depended to a large degree on the ability to draw on his own experience in dramatizing the oppositions inherent in Indian life. These oppositions were expressed in the symbolic language of colonial conflict—between black and white, between light and darkness. "Let the White go to the White and the Black to the Black," Kipling warned, in his first collection of Indian stories.[8]

Family romance and political mythology converge in Kipling's view of India. In trying to disentangle the personal and political elements in the image of India which Kipling portrayed in his fiction, it is useful to keep in mind how that image altered with time and with personal growth. Critics have tended to associate Kipling with a fixed or inflexible heroic ideology of imperialism. Yet like any other writer, Kipling's views evolved over time along with his personal and political experience. His earlier stories were taut and abrasive. But he had not one "vision" of India but several. These visions altered with his increasing maturity and his geographical and temporal removal from his subject matter. The process of evolution is apparent by the mid-1890s, after he had been out of India for several years. His Indian stories such as "William the Conqueror" and "The Tomb of His Ancestors" possess a greater distance and a broader sense of the imperial context. The difference is most sharply felt in *Kim*, published in 1901, with its panoramic view of Indian life on the Great Trunk Road, its immersion in Buddhist philosophy, and its sympathetic treatment of so many different types of Indians.

*Kim* includes what is virtually the only positive portrayal of a Bengali *Babu* in Kipling's writings on India. Hurree Chunder Mookerjee is one of Kim's mentors and collaborators in intelligence work. The "hulking obese Babu," so incongruous in the context of the Great Game, is presented as one of its most skillful practitioners and teachers. His instruction to Kim is rich not only in historical allusion and literary reference—in the style of the Babu—but also in the practical arts of survival.[9] For all the story's frenetic action—through which Kim, an orphaned, street-wise British boy, leads an ancient monk on both a political and spiritual quest—it is pervaded with an aura of philosophic calm. Kipling wrote the book in England in 1899–1900 after recovering from a nearly fatal attack of influenza, and from the loss of a daughter to the same disease. In a letter to Charles Eliot Norton in January 1900 he said of it, "I've done a long leisured asiatic yarn in which there are hardly any Englishmen. It has been a labor of great love and I think it is a bit more temperate and wiser than much of my stuff."[10]

Kipling's early Indian stories, by contrast, were written while he still worked there, or while the experience of India was still fresh enough to be felt as well as reflected on. His location in the Punjab had provided him with direct access to the models which best embodied the heroic British presence in India. He had imbibed the special pride and *esprit de corps* that set that area off from other parts of British India, and as a consequence his fictional creations—the soldiers and officers of his military tales, and the savage tribesmen of the hills—became identified in the mind of the reading public and in those of Anglo-Indians for decades to come with what was most ennobling and most intriguing in Indian life. The contrapuntal appeal of India, both as a bastion of British authority and as an underworld of erotic interest, emerges from these stories in its most beguiling form.

### The Family Square

Rudyard Kipling had rejoined his parents in India in the autumn of 1882. His father Lockwood was serving as curator of the art museum in Lahore, the capital of the Punjab, and he had arranged a job for Rudyard as a reporter for the local newspaper. His arrival constituted a long-awaited reunion both with his parents and with India itself. Rudyard's father had served in India since 1865—the year of his son's birth—and Kipling had spent his first five and a half years in Bombay, where Lockwood Kipling worked as a teacher at an art school. Like other Anglo-Indian children, Rudyard and his younger sister Trix had then been sent to England for their education, and the ensuing separation had proved an extreme hardship to both children and parents. These intervening years—years of apparent emotional privation—have been memorialized in Kipling's fiction and in the commentaries of his biographers. That period lies outside the scope of this essay, but it provides a bleak background against which the warmth of Kipling's return can be better appreciated.

Within the framework of his family Kipling was able to take up both of the broken threads of his childhood experience: direct contact with sympathetic and supportive parents, and reimmersion into the Indian environment in which he had been nurtured as a child. Kipling described the pleasure of returning to his parents' house:

That was a joyous home-coming. For—consider!—I had returned to a Father and Mother of whom I had seen but little since my sixth year. I might have found my Mother "the sort of woman *I* don't care for," as in one terrible case that I know; and My Father intolerable. But the Mother proved more delightful than all my imaginings or memories. My Father was not only a mine of knowledge and help, but a humorous, tolerant and expert fellow-craftsman. . . . I do not remember the smallest friction in any detail of our lives. We delighted more in each other's society than in that of strangers; and when my sister came out, a little later, our cup was filled to the brim. Not only were we happy, but we knew it.[11]

Yet their happiness, though genuine, was not without a suggestion of guarded or grasping love. In India, as Kipling himself would recognize, it could hardly have been otherwise. They came to adopt one of Mrs. Kipling's phrases to identify themselves as the Family Square, a term taken from a defensive formation employed by the British army.[12] Thus Kipling commented on the danger of swift death in India from infectious diseases: "As regarding ourselves at home, if there were any dying to be done, we were four together. The rest was in the day's work, with love to sweeten all things."[13]

Beyond intimacy and affection, the Family Square provided a critical and empathic center for Kipling's creative work. All his life

Kipling insisted—and often acted as though it were true—that his parents were the only critical audience he cared about.[14] Together, in 1885, they collaborated on a family magazine entitled *Quartette*, which contained two of Kipling's early tales of the strange and supernatural, "The Phantom Rickshaw" and "The Strange Ride of Morrowbie Jukes." The magazine was the product of a leisurely season the Kiplings spent together in the Punjab hill station of Simla, the cool summer capital of British India.[15]

Though not included in either the Civil Service or the military hierarchies in a status-minded society, the Kiplings established a place for themselves in the round of social occasions that typified Anglo-Indian society, and especially that of the hill station.[16] Lockwood Kipling had a reputation for good character and good nature, and for his knowledge of native arts. At his post in Bombay and later at the art museum in Lahore—the "Wonder House" of *Kim*—he was acknowledged as a leading expert on Indian crafts. He was almost universally admired, as much for his warmth, curiosity, and wide-ranging intelligence as for his artistic talents. He could also be severely moralistic. He seems to have drifted from his Methodist upbringing almost into agnosticism,[17] but he retained his Victorian zeal for honesty and accuracy unimpaired. He formed an extremely close bond with his son, as a trusted critic and as a figure for emulation. In retrospect he seems to have been formidable but not overbearing.

Rudyard's mother Alice made a reputation in her own right for her conversation and her rapid, sometimes hard-edged wit. Her older brother Frederic remarked, "When she was at her ease and the subject was to her mind she was very brilliant, and her felicities of speech and illuminating epigrams were a delight to us all. . . . Her wit was for the most part humorous and genial, but on occasion it was a weapon of whose keenness there could be no doubt, and foolish or mischievous people were made to feel it."[18] As for Rudyard's sister Trix, when she came out to India a year after him, she quickly established herself as one of the reigning beauties of the Simla season—"the ice-maiden," her brother sometimes called her.

In many respects the youthful Rudyard was the least impressive of the four. In his first meeting with the Kiplings in 1886, the journalist Kay Robinson, who became Kipling's admired editor and friend at the *Civil and Military Gazette*, said Lockwood was "the most delightful companion he had ever met," noted Alice's brilliant "if occasionally" caustic wit, Trix's beauty, and saw Rudyard first only as a boy, stooped, with heavy eyelids and a sallow complexion. He spoke jerkily, thought Robinson, with abrupt and awkward bodily movements. After ten minutes of conversation, however, he became aware of the boy's brilliance.[19]

Kipling embraced the native India he had known as a child just as he did his family. He later recalled, disembarking at Bombay, how he moved "among sights and smells that made me deliver in the vernacular sentences whose meaning I knew not. Other Indian-born boys have told me how the same thing happened to them. . . . my English years fell away, nor ever, I think, came back in full strength."[20] In his autobiographical writings Kipling's first encounters with native India enjoy an especially prominent place. His parents remained a gray presence compared to the vivid recollections of India in his first years in Bombay, and especially the retinue of native servants—above all his nursemaid or *ayah*—who surrounded the young Sahib. Of course the isolation of the nursery from the adult world was an accepted fact of Victorian middle-class life, an isolation which seemed to magnify the authority vested in parental figures.[21] In India this distance was increased by the multiplicity of native servants, by their apparent devotion to their fair-skinned charges, and by the racial and linguistic barriers that divided native life so graphically from Anglo-Indian society. Kipling recollected that "in the afternoon heats before we took our sleep, she (the ayah) or Meeta would tell us stories and Indian nursery songs all unforgotten, and we were sent into the dining-room after we had been dressed, with the caution 'Speak English now to Papa and Mama.' So one spoke 'English,' haltingly translated out of the vernacular idiom that one thought and dreamed in."[22] The first pages of Kipling's memoir, *Something of Myself*, are suffused by a sense of intimacy with his half-caste Portuguese *ayah* and his Hindu bearer Meeta. In his Indian stories—such as "Tod's Amendment" and "Wee Willie Winkie"—one stock figure is the fair-haired young Sahib whose authority is derived from an intimate knowledge of native life and from the devoted affection of admiring natives.[23] The feeling of omnipotence drawn from this source enable these children to make conquests in the more hazardous white world of soldiers and bureaucrats.

These native figures serve as a link to the sensuality and danger with which Kipling endows the Indian environment, a quality which comes through in these recollections with a certain elemental force. "My first impression," Kipling tells us of early morning walks with his *ayah*, "is of daybreak, light and colour and golden and purple fruits at the level of my shoulder."[24] And in this recollection the "menacing darkness" and death are tied to his intimate relationship to his native nurse.

> . . . near our little house on the Bombay Esplanade were the Towers of Silence, where their Dead are exposed to the waiting vultures on the rim of the towers, who scuffle and spread wings when they see the bearers of the Dead below. I did not understand my mother's distress when she found "a child's hand" in our garden, and said I was not to ask questions about it. I wanted to see that child's hand. But my *ayah* told me.[25]

The India of "strong light and darkness" which he experienced as a young child reinforced the intimate link between "black" and "white" that marked his later literary work.

On his return to India Kipling actively sought after native life in Lahore at a time when the Anglo-Indian and native communities were drifting apart and such contacts were generally frowned on. Undoubtedly, Kipling's rather nebulous social position as a journalist made his passage into the underworld of a city such as Lahore less difficult. Sketches like "The Gate of the Hundred Sorrows" were based on wanderings such as this during sleepless nights in the hot weather. In *Something of Myself* he described his nocturnal explorations into "liquorshops, gambling and opium dens . . . or in and about the narrow gullies under the Mosque of Wazir Khan for the sheer sake of looking." And he told of his return home from these escapades "just as the light broke, in some night-haw, of a hired carriage which stank of Hookah-fumes, jasmine flowers, and sandalwood; and if the driver were moved to talk, he told one a good deal. Much of real Indian life goes on in the hot weather nights."[26] Doubtless Kipling employed his license as a writer to embroider these adventures. But by the end of his stay in India Kipling was known for his unusual knowledge of native life, and for his intimacy with "wild" or "filthy" Indians from the frontier regions at the borders of the Punjab. Kipling, according to Robinson, was familiar with natives and their customs, and was constantly holding chats with "filthy" tribesmen who regarded him as a "Sahib apart."[27]

The link between these two worlds was provided by Kipling's journalistic apprenticeship, the testing experience through which he earned a sense of independence and self-respect. In *Something of Myself* Kipling described his experience as "fifty percent of the editorial staff" at the *Civil and Military Gazette* as a struggle with the editor whom he "loathed" and who "had to break me in," and with the conditions in which he worked. "I never worked less than ten hours. . . . I had fever, too, regular and persistent, to which I added for a while chronic dysentary. Yet I discovered that a man can work with a temperature of 104, even though the next day he has to ask the office who wrote the article."[28]

Some of the strain of those first years was relieved by the replacement of his first editor, Stephen Wheeler, with the more congenial Kay Robinson, who recognized Kipling's talents and gave them greater scope than the editorial desk had. Robinson's confidence was confirmed in 1887 when Kipling, at twenty-two, was promoted to the more important *Pioneer*, the parent paper of the *Civil and Military Gazette*, located in Allahabad. Kipling now had a chance to break away from the Family Square and to observe a predominantly Hindu city at first hand. Perhaps his rather brittle sense of independence, the icy cynicism of the outsider, was fostered by his work as a journalist. His experience of being approached with bribes, of "visits with Viceroys to neighboring Princes on the edge of the great Indian desert," and of "murder and divorce trials,"[29] gave him a solid claim to maturity consistent with his own mature appearance at twenty-two.

The literary style Kipling brought to India was imitative and romantic. In a few years there he developed the taut, laconic, journalistic prose on which he made his early reputation. The sketches that constitute his first mature book, *Plain Tales from the Hills*, were produced to order for Robinson in 1886–87 as newspaper "turnovers," restricted to about two thousand words.[30] Their subject matter was drawn from the journalist's experience of civilian and military manners in official India, and from his unofficial but acute observations of Anglo-Indian and native social life. When Kipling moved on to Allahabad he would write at greater length, but these subjects remained his principal concerns. After *Plain Tales* was published and later stories began appearing in collected versions—the so-called Railway Editions first issued in 1888—Kipling established a reputation in India on the strength of which he soon decided to seek a broader audience.

Despite Kipling's recovery of family and discovery of work, the chapter on India in *Something of Myself* is entitled "Seven Years Hard." In part, of course, Kipling wished that title to convey the process of personal toughening through which he acquired a sense of manhood and self-respect. A critical element in this apprenticeship was the Indian environment itself, the ferocity of nature and the proximity of death. "Death was always our near companion," wrote Kipling, while describing how an outbreak of typhoid could decimate a white community of seventy, or kill off a young civilian "at the regulation age of twenty-two."[31] Kipling's second enemy was the heat, especially the killing summer heat of the northern Indian plains in the weeks before the monsoon rains provided some relief. Like many other Anglo-Indians Kipling never adjusted to the premonsoon heat, and if Robinson is to be believed, he suffered more melodramatically than others.[32] Certainly he suffered intensely, as is shown by the most intimate document we possess of Kipling's stay in India, a diary kept sporadically in 1885. In August of that year, after coming down from Simla, he railed at reimmersion into the steamy atmosphere of Lahore after the rains.[33]

To what extent his response to the heat was intensified by his parents' frequent absence in the hills is difficult to estimate. We do know that an incident which Kipling came to regard as a pivotal experience in the realization of his identity as a writer also occurred, as he describes it here, during the hot weather, "when I felt that I had come to the edge of all endurance. As I entered my empty house in the dusk there was no more in me except the horror of a great darkness, that I must have been fighting for some days." In such straits he "picked up a book by Walter Besant which was called *All in a Garden Fair*. It dealt with a young man who desired to write, who came to realize the possibilities of common things seen, and who eventually succeeded in his desire. What its merits may be from today's 'literary' standpoint I do not know. But I do know that the book was my salvation in sore personal need, and with the reading and re-reading it became to me a revelation, a hope and strength."[34]

Such an incident does suggest that the forging of Kipling's identity as a writer was accomplished at great cost, an experience in which his personal demons were conflated with those that swarmed through the stifling summer nights in Lahore. It is, of course, extremely hard to disentangle the developmental crises of adolescence—such as those related to his sense of abandonment as a child—from more deep-seated problems and conflicts that made permanent inroads on his adult behavior and personality.[35] This darker reality is reflected in the family romance itself, in the way childhood fantasy continued to inform Kipling's image of his parents and other adult figures. Even the encomium addressed to the living parents to whom Kipling returned in India, already quoted above, incorporates the ambivalent feeling of an early childhood experience. Although here Kipling affirms his parents as everything he could wish for, he does so in a curiously negative syntax, identifying his mother as not "the sort of woman I don't care for" and his father as not "intolerable." His refusal to allow even "the smallest friction in any detail of our lives" smacks strongly of denial, a way of negating uncomfortable or unacceptable feelings. Kipling's literary work provided one outlet for such unacceptable feelings. He was fortunate also that the warmth and support he received from his parents—his father especially—eased the burden of maintaining them as Olympian, faultless figures. He had emphatically to deny his competitive feelings with his father, even as he carried on the search for strong masculine models with whom to identify.

The intense conflicts Kipling felt over his fledgling independence emerge somewhat more clearly with his mother. Alice Kipling had taken a rather obtrusive part in encouraging Rudyard's literary career. She had arranged, perhaps in collusion with his public school headmaster, to have Kipling's schoolboy verse—poems he had sent out from England for his parents to read—published in India. They appeared in 1881 as *Schoolboy Lyrics*, and Kipling was apparently irritated to discover this surprise when he arrived in Lahore the following year.[36] At least in one instance Alice used her caustic wit to cut her son down to size. During a visit to Simla after an absence of seven months, described in a letter to a friend, Kipling told of his joy when the family dog greeted him "with ecstatic wriggles and jumps and bounds and fawnings such as dogs use to fill in their lack of speech." Though no one in the family had thought she would remember Rudyard, the "dear little beast promptly foreswore her allegiance to both mother and maid who had petted her and fed her as no dog has been fed I am sure, and for the rest of the evening would have nothing of anyone but me whom she nuzzled and whimpered over, thrusting her nose into my hand and demanding imperiously that I should notice her. . . . In a moment of expansiveness I said egotistically:—'I shall think better of myself henceforward.' 'Hear him!' said the Mother. 'Anyone but a man would have said that he would think better of the dog.'"[37]

His mother's remark appears to have prompted Kipling to transfer the issue of possession from the family dog to that of his own place in the family. As he confessed to his friend, "it is owned that I am no longer Ownable and only a visitor in the land. The Mother says that it is so and the Sister too and their eyes see far—'You belong to your self,' says the Mother."[38] With such a formidable mother as Alice Kipling, the issue of possessing or being possessed could not have been far from Rudyard's emotional concerns. Apparently that parental pressure was very strongly felt in his early relations with women. One entry from that 1885 diary, inscribed during his summer residence with his family in Simla, reads: "My own affair entirely. A wet day but deuced satisfactory." From his entry the next day, confessing his suspicion that he had "been a fool," we can be fairly sure that it was a reference to the excitement and disappointment of a brief infatuation.[39] Such "affairs" may have been encumbered by Rudyard's sense of the ubiquitous presence of his parents.

During Kipling's stay in India the shadow of maternal love was never far removed from his romantic involvements. The experienced married woman who makes love to an innocent young man up from the plains is one of the basic themes of Kipling's Simla stories. Rudyard's closest female friend outside of his family was both older and married—an American woman named Mrs. Edmonia Hill, married to a meteorologist in government service. Kipling first met her when he moved over to the *Pioneer* in Allahabad. During the next two years their friendship—though only a friendship—ripened into a daily association and stimulated an interesting correspondence when they were separated by Rudyard's work or his family affairs. To Mrs. Hill we owe one of the most vivid descriptions we possess of Kipling in this period. "Mr. Kipling looks about forty," she wrote in a letter home, "as he is beginning to be bald, but he is in reality just twenty-two. He was animation itself, telling his stories admirably, so that those about him were kept in gales of laughter. He fairly scintillated, but when more sober topics were discussed he was posted along all lines. After dinner, when the men joined the ladies in the drawing room . . . he came to the fireplace where I was standing and began questioning me about my homeland. I am surprised at his knowledge of people and places."[40] Kipling worked hard to impress Mrs. Hill not only with his brilliance, but also with his intimacy with the desirable women of Simla.[41] But there is no evidence that Kipling had a serious or sustained relationship with a young woman during his stay in India. In his letters to England, he comes across clearly as a callow young man.[42]

The wish to appear strong and self-reliant—in romantic matters as in any others—may correspond to an underlying anxiety about inner weakness or dependency. For Kipling, this unreconciled division between strength and weakness was reflected in his public persona. When he felt comfortable, as was almost invariably the case with children, he could be animated, amiable, empathic. When he was not sure of his company, or suspected its hostility, he tended to become either retiring or churlish.[43] As a consequence he sought out social environments, such as the Family Square, in which he was perfectly sure of himself. Kipling responded imaginatively to the distinction between in-groups and out-groups. His involvement in Free Masonry, while in India, was fed at least partially by the peculiar passion of the initiate.[44] Another such in-group for Kipling and other Anglo-Indians, especially unmarried ones, was the club. In his autobiography Kipling tells a story of his humiliation at the Punjab Club in Lahore when his newspaper had taken an unpopular stand on an issue of importance to the British community. He "repaired to the Club which, remember, was the whole of my out-side world." As he entered "the long, shabby dining-room . . . ev-eryone hissed. I was innocent enough to ask: 'What's the joke? Who are you hissing?' 'You,' said the man at my side. 'Your damn rag has ratted over the Bill.' It is not pleasant to sit still when one is twenty while all your universe hisses you."[45] In Kay Robinson's time in Lahore, Kipling apparently avoided dining at the club because of the hostility of one member who disliked him and snubbed him.[46]

Another issue which revolved around the discrepancy between weakness and strength was Kipling's close identification with the military, an identification he sustained throughout his adult life. The public school he attended in England, the United Service College, had been created to guide aspiring officers through the newly established military entrance examination. He had been sent there because of his parents' friendship with the school's headmaster. At U.S.C. he was exposed to the ethos of military service, and more particularly to service in India.[47]

If Kipling had ever aspired to a military career for himself, it had been closed to him because of his poor eyesight.[48] Although he looked older than his years, he was not an imposing figure either temperamentally or physically. He was hardly a courageous person, as suggested in his few tentative forays into the wild mountainous and frontier regions of northern India.[49] In the single most impor-tant sporting skill for Anglo-Indians, horsemanship, Kipling did badly.[50] Yet Kipling was deeply attracted to the military as a caste, and to the values of toughness, audacity, and controlled violence it fostered. His location in Lahore, close to the militarily vital north-west frontier, contributed to the status and the prominence of the military in his daily life and his Indian stories. In *Something of Myself* Kipling proudly describes his comradeship with "the soldiery of those days in visits to Fort Lahore," where his "first and best be-loved Battalion was the 2nd Fifth Fusiliers with whom I dined in awed silence a few weeks after I came out. . . . There were ghostly dinners too with Subalterns in charge of the Infantry Detachment at Fort Lahore, where, all among marble-inlaid, empty apartments of dead Queens, or under the domes of old tombs, meals began with the regulation thirty grains of quinine in the sherry, and ended—as Allah pleased!"[51] "The proudest moment of my young life," Kipling wrote, came on horseback, when he was consulted by Lord Roberts, Commander of the Indian Army. "I rode up Simla Mall beside him on his usual explosive red Arab, while he asked me what the men thought about their accommodation, entertainment, rooms and the like. I told him, and he thanked me as gravely as though I had been a full Colonel."[52]

Kipling admired the leadership qualities of the British officer class and some of his finest literary creations like Bobby Wicks exemplify the values of honesty, loyalty, and self-denial in an almost idolatrous way.[53] Yet the extent to which he identified with authority did not obscure his sympathy for the hard life of the private soldier, although it was a world removed from that of the officer. To the British reading public in the 1890s his re-creation of that world in *Soldiers Three* rivaled in exoticism his stories of native life.[54] "The bare horrors of the private's life" were not far removed in Kipling's mind from his impressions of the native underworld. In his memoir, for example, he criticized the British government's failure to take a sympathetic interest in the private soldier's involvement with native prostitutes. The government denounced prostitution, and therefore "it was counted impious that bazaar prostitutes should be inspected; or that men should be taught elementary precautions in their dealings with them." He deplored the more crowded conditions in which the private soldier lived, leaving him more vulnerable to infectious disease "that could kill all on one side of a barrack-room and spare the other."[55]

Kipling's effort to identify with the British military by becoming its poet helped to close the breach between the passivity of the artist and a more acceptable ideal of manly action. His subject matter— the harshness of India and the hardiness of the men who toiled in it—cemented a precariously divided identity. The splits or divisions in his personality—as an individual, an artist, and an Anglo-Indian—provided a framework within which a particularly compelling image of India could be created. When he left India for London at the age of twenty-four in 1889 to seek a broader audience for his work, that image had already been largely formed. He was only a few months away from being discovered as a writer.

## The Unreality of Empire

To judge by his rapid adoption of a Punjabi or Anglo-Indian political creed, we must take Kipling at his word when he assures us that
his "English years fell away" when he returned to India in 1882. Beyond the obvious pressures on a young man to conform to a rather
narrow social code, a number of other factors affected Kipling's
"conversion." Perhaps the foremost influence was exercised by his
father. Despite Lockwood's artistic interests and his position outside the rigid hierarchies of official Anglo-Indian society, he hewed
to the ascetic and righteous values common to virtually all the British in late-nineteenth-century India.

The elder Kipling's major literary work, *Beast and Man in India*,
published in 1891, is a rambling essay whose ostensible subject is the
native treatment of India's extensive animal life. Along the way it
cites almost every conventional sentiment the Anglo-Indian har-
bored toward his native subjects. Among these are the necessity of
Britain's imperial role in India, the degradation of Hindu religious practices, and the shortcomings of Indian character, rendered
here—thanks to Lockwood's subject—through broad analogies between native Indians and their domestic animals.[56] One of his contributions to the family magazine *Quartette*, produced in Simla in
1885, is even more pointed in its affirmation of a spartan Anglo-
Indian ideology. "Mofussil Jurisdiction" involves the struggle between two British officers in the Punjabi hinterlands for the hand of
a desirable young lady. One, a civil servant, or competition-wallah,[57]
owes his position in India to his intellectual abilities rather than his
character or physique. The other is a well-bred young army officer who is courageous and physically imposing. The competition-
wallah is ridiculed by both the girl and his military adversary. He
makes a fool of himself on a leopard hunt, and tries to take the
credit for killing the beast away from the military man. Needless to
say, he loses the respect and affection of the girl.[58] Through such a
parable of British Indian life Lockwood Kipling affirmed the military model of the Anglo-Indian official that his son also came to
admire.

Even without his father's influence, there were strong pressures
on the young Kipling to conform quickly to a conventional Anglo-

Indian outlook. He returned to India in a period of increasing political tension, and of growing estrangement between the Anglo-Indian and native communities. In the interest of liberal reform Lord Ripon, a representative of the Gladstonian liberalism then in its ascendancy at home, had instituted a number of measures. When he proposed to alter the judicial system to allow Indian judges to try Europeans in the rural areas, however, he provoked a storm of racial resentment from the British community. The *Civil and Military Gazette* was pressured by the Indian government into publishing an editorial supporting Ripon's measure. It was this controversy over the Ilbert Bill that had exposed Kipling to the scathing reception at the Punjab Club, memorialized in *Something of Myself*.[59]

By the fall of 1883 the defense of British supremacy was evident in Kipling's contributions to the newspaper. Five short political pieces can be attributed to him in this period, each of them critical of progressive attitudes. One, an attack on William Morris's socialism, attests to Kipling's conversion from the Pre-Raphaelite "fancies" of his schooldays.[60] With respect to the issues involved in the Ilbert Bill, Kipling's final word came in 1885 in an elaborate parody of Gilbert and Sullivan's comic-opera style entitled "Trial by Judge." His parody ties the relatively narrow question of native judges to the broader issues of self-determination for India. Every native newspaper, he suggests "that serves as a wrap for mussales and ghis" [Indian ingredients] will declare "your honour's just dealing and wisdom and fame." In just a few decades "the thunders of dark justice" would encourage the British to "resign and homeward flee," invoking for India "the New Millennium."[61] In 1885 Kipling published two similar, bitterly satirical pieces. The first of these was a vicious assault on Ripon as the perpetrator of "turmoil and babble and ceaseless strife."[62] In it he drew the same distinction his father had between the effete competition-wallah and the virile military man, saying of Ripon:

> Fittest of rulers was he for a loud-mouthed cackling land
> For ye lived by words where men live by the work
> of their head and their hand.[63]

A second piece called "The Indian Delegates" satirized the claim of a group of educated Indians in London to represent the "real India," the India of native princes, peasant populations, and religious superstition. As long as Hindus of high caste refused to eat with Westerners, and as long as they held their women in bondage to inhumane religious custom, insisted Kipling, there could be no thought of recognizing India's political claims.[64]

When his assignment to the larger *Pioneer* in 1887 made more extensive travel possible, Kipling directed his assault on native political pretensions to their most outspoken center, Bengal. There, where British rule was first established, native political opinion was most advanced. In his sketches of 1887 and 1888, collected under the title *City of Dreadful Night*, Kipling related the ineffectual municipal self-government of Calcutta to the stench created by its inadequate sewage system. "In spite of that stink," he wrote, "they allow, they even encourage, natives to look after the place! The damp, drainage-soaked soil is sick with the teeming life of a hundred years, and the municipal Board list is choked with the names of natives—men of the breed born in and raised off this surfeited muck heap!"[65] He derided the educated Bengali political who sits on the municipal councils as "great on principles and precedents, and the necessity of 'popularizing our system.'" Yet as a rejoinder to the native's pretensions, he observes, "there steals cross the council chambers just one faint whiff. It is as though someone laughed low and bitterly."[66]

The fault, as Kipling sees it here, is in the wild growth of the "exotic plant" of Western education in Bengal. "Now we are choked by the roots of its spreading so thickly in this fat soil of Bengal," wrote Kipling, who argued that the responsibility lay with the misconceived policies that British liberals brought to India. "That torrent of verbiage is ours. We taught him what was consitutional in the days when Calcutta smelt. Calcutta smells still. . . . It is our own fault absolutely."[67] The quite explicitly anal distinction between ordered and anarchic administration, wholesome and unwholesome politics, which Kipling established in these sketches, became the leitmotif of his political commentary for the remainder of his literary career.[68]

Kipling clearly identified with the Anglo-Indian community in its repudiation of native political ambitions, and in its ringing denial that liberal notions of governance could flourish in India's climate. However, it is necessary to distinguish between the *politique* of Kipling's stories and sketches in this period and the full-blown imperialist outlook he espoused later. Even if a British role in India is a governing assumption of these writings, he makes no effort to relate this perception to a global policy of British supremacy in the uncultivated or "uncivilized" areas of the world. He eventually did become a poet of imperialism, most notably in his literary, journalistic, and personal efforts to drum up national enthusiasm for Britain's role in the Boer War at the turn of the century. And he never felt more at one with himself than in those heroic days in South Africa among the British troops.[69]

Kipling's conversion to the imperial cause came not so much from his experience in India as from his disillusionment with English life on his return to Britain in 1889. In a series of verses and sketches sent back to the *Civil and Military Gazette*, he ridiculed the slackness and selfishness he perceived in British social life, as evidenced in the aestheticism of polite London society:

> But I consort with long-haired things
>   In velvet collar-rolls,
> Who talk about the Aims of Art
>   And 'theories' and 'goals,'
> And moo and coo with womenfolk
>   About their blessed souls.
>
> But that they call 'psychology'
>   Is lack of liver-pill,
> And all that blights their tender souls
>   Is eating till they're ill,
> And their chief way of winning goals
>   Consists of sitting still.
>
> It's Oh to meet an Army man,
>   Set up, and trimmed and taut,
> Who does not spout hashed libraries
>   Or think the next man's thought,
> And walks as though he owned himself,
>   And hogs his bristles short.[70]

He was encouraged to view the sacrifices of the British abroad from a new perspective—one not limited to India—when he embarked shortly afterward on two cruises to other areas of British colonization: South Africa, Australia, and New Zealand. The first literary evidence of this global consciousness is demonstrated in an 1891 poem, "The English Flag," written with the help of his mother.[71] Here he contrasts the provincialism of the English public with the sweep and challenge of British possessions overseas, a contrast captured in the poem's opening lines:

Winds of the World, give answer! They are whimpering to and fro—
And what should they know of England who only England know?—[72]

By the mid-1890s his stories "William the Conqueror" and "The Tomb of His Ancestors" were being written, at least partially, to propagandize for the British presence in India.[73] By the Boer War at the end of the decade he had become the poet of the "white man's burden," as reflected in "A Song of the White Men":

> Now, this is the road that White Men tread
>     When they go to clean a land—
> Iron underfoot and levin [lightning] overhead
>     And the deep on either hand.
> We have trod that road—and a wet and windy road—
>     Our chosen star for guide.
> Oh, well for the world when the White Men tread
>     Their highway side by side![74]

Even as partisan of the British imperium overseas, Kipling was never much concerned with its political dimension, and never identified strongly with the architects of its political policies. His heroes were the men and women who did the practical work of empire, the soldiers, administrators, doctors, and engineers. Findlayson, whose creation of a bridge survives the rampaging Ganges in "The Bridge-builders," is presented as having "endured heat and cold, disappointment, discomfort, danger and disease, with responsibility almost too heavy for one pair of shoulders." His bridge, "raw and ugly as original sin, but *pukka*—permanent—" will survive "when all memory of the builder had perished."[75] In eulogizing such work Kipling became a critic of the policies of the central government in Calcutta, and a trenchant commentator on Britain's political objectives. The "Supreme Government" of "On the City Wall" sacrifices its drafts of men for a "pretty idea," but a hopelessly impractical one. The classic statement of this critique comes in "The Head of the District," where a "Black" Bengali is dispatched by the central government in Calcutta to rule over a population of fierce Moslem tribesmen in the foothills of the Himalayas, despite the dire warnings of the British administrator at the scene. As a result the district must pay in anarchy and bloodshed for the blindness of the supposedly enlightened political leadership.[76]

Some of Kipling's skepticism about the upper echelons of the state bureaucracy must be attributed to his presence in the Punjab, where there was a strong tradition of administrative independence at the district level, especially in the frontier areas. At the very least, his experience there reinforced a predisposition to identify with the absolute authority of the isolated and case-hardened administrator.

Kipling drifted throughout his career toward a growing disenchantment with politics itself as an instrument for ordering human relationships. Two of Kipling's futuristic stories, written after the turn of the century, "With the Night Mail" and "As Easy as A.B.C.," document a process by which the political controversies of warring factions have been transformed into technical problems of administration and transportation within a single world order. In "As Easy as A.B.C." the Aerial Board of Control flies about the world rescuing people from "regressive" eruptions of the old politics, in this instance an "outbreak" of democracy in Chicago. Equipped with the latest aerial technology, they whisk the perpetrators away and restore the city to an ordered and antiseptic calm.[77]

The idea of cleansing the world of politics is also apparent in Kipling's correspondence. In the 1890s, after his experience in America, Kipling loved to contrast the anarchy and slovenliness of political democracy with the specialized training, obedience, and discipline of a well-ordered society. In a letter to his literary friend W. E. Henley from Vermont in 1893, Kipling described the fundamental problem of American life in these terms: "the moral dry rot of it all is having no law that need be obeyed."[78] And in correspondence with another friend in 1913 he deplored the tendency of education to incite people to rebellion, when only "sanitation and transportation really matter in a fallen world."[79] Kipling's rejection of politics can be taken more specifically as a rejection of political democracy. But his insistence on distinguishing clearly between administration and politics, and on perceiving one as "wholesome" and the other as "dirty," might suggest emotional conflict and a need for control, as well. In any case, his beliefs should not be identified simply with the political hegemony of imperial power.

Just as the view of Kipling as an ideologue of imperialism must be stringently qualified, so must be the historian Noel Annan's view of him as a coherent social theorist. In a forcefully argued essay Annan has made a brief for Kipling as a literary sociologist. The question that Kipling asked—"what holds society (or an organization) together?"—Annan reminds us, "is exceedingly rarely asked in literature. Equally rarely do creative writers concern themselves with the problem of authority. . . . in his schematic presentation of life we feel that not only is everything to be explained in terms of social processes and relationships, but that when he introduces those alleviations of social processes upon men, such as laughter, mirth, vitality, or love, he is thinking of them equally as social forces existing apart from the individual who experiences them." [80]

In his insistence on focusing on the facts of the social process— "things as they are"—Annan credits Kipling with a decisive break with the abstract or individualistic approach to social issues bred by liberalism and utilitarianism in nineteenth-century Britain. Although he recognizes that Kipling was neither a systematic nor a self-conscious sociologist, he groups him with contemporary continental thinkers, such as Durkheim, Weber, and Pareto, who "rediscovered" society after a century of philosophy and historicism. [81] The group construct through which Kipling operates, Annan says, is the Law, a concept with the same explanatory force and breadth as the anthropologist's notion of culture. This approach "sees human beings moving in a definable network of social relationships which impose upon them a code of behavior appropriate to their environment." [82]

There is no doubt that Kipling is incomprehensible without an appreciation of the broad intent behind his invocation of the Law. Likewise necessary is an understanding of his conviction that ultimate authority and ultimate salvation, insofar as they can be obtained in a "fallen world," rest with the group. The question remains whether Kipling's achievement as an artist and a "sociologist" can be dealt with as such a unified whole, or whether these facets of his work are more profitably treated separately so that the development and complexity of his thought is fully apparent. From a psychological perspective, one might ask whether the Law represents the essence of Kipling's artistic vision, or a defensive retreat from that vision into the relative safety of an established order. Such a question can be answered, in part, by viewing Kipling in a developmental context, for surely the precocious "boy" of twenty-two has to be distinguished from the mature writer in his forties and fifties.

When Kipling became more settled personally, in his family life (he married an American woman in 1892 and they had three children), and in his country estate in Sussex after the turn of the century, his thematic concerns altered accordingly. Such work as *Puck of Pook's Hill*, and many of his stories of the English countryside, are rooted in a curiosity about local history and an almost tactile feeling for the nuance of social structure.[83] In these stories the individual is very much subordinate to the social and historical fabric. Yet even in a fable like "As Easy as A.B.C." the ultimate social ideal is presented as the privacy of the individual and his family, while its nemesis is the invasion of the crowd—the mass man—into private life. The smooth functioning of the administrative order, as guaranteed by the Aerial Board of Control, depends on containing the inevitable eruptions of crowd politics that periodically threaten the individual's privacy.[84] In this context the Law seems better geared to the survival of the beleaguered Hobbesian individual than to the social constructs of Weber or Durkheim.

When applied to Kipling's early Indian stories, Annan's thesis collapses altogether. For these stories focus to a large extent on the individual, the physically and emotionally isolated man, tested beyond endurance by the rigors of his work and the harshness of his environment. One aspect of this experience is conveyed by the narrator of so many of Kipling's Indian stories, especially those from *Plain Tales from the Hills*. Like Kipling, the narrator is a journalist—brash, ironical, and irreverent. And he moves in and out from the margins of these stories, commenting wryly on the action or tentatively involved in it. Whatever Kipling's relation to his own literary creation,[85] he treats the narrator's power to understand and control events in a deeply ironic fashion, as in a story entitled "False Dawn," a tale about a midnight picnic in the Indian hot weather. The party has been organized by a young civilian named Saumarez to create an opportunity to propose to a young woman who is otherwise inseparable from an older sister. The picnic party sets out, only to encounter a violent and blinding dust storm typical of the season. Saumarez is separated from the rest of the party with one of the sisters and proposes to her, only to discover, when the dust has settled, that it was the wrong one. The narrator, who has learned of the error from the desperate Saumarez, sets off after the rejected girl, who has fled in anger and sorrow. He succeeds in retrieving her in a dangerous ride on horseback and, after considerable embarrassment, the error is rectified.

The story itself is absurd, redeemed only by Kipling's power to evoke the chaos and violence of the storm. What is interesting for us, however, is the narrator's movement from the margins to the center of the story. As the tale begins he is very much the outsider, both in his deeper knowledge of the elements of love and of nature, and in the physical arrangement of the party itself: there is one triplet—Saumarez and the two Copleigh sisters; four couples; and the narrator trailing behind alone.[86] In the excitement and confusion of the storm, when the error is discovered, the narrator takes the initiative in involving himself in Saumarez's plight. "It must have been my state of overexcitement that made me so ready to meddle with what did not concern me. Saumarez was moving off to the habit; but I pushed him back and said, 'Stop here and explain, I'll fetch her back!' And I ran out to get at my own horse." And then, though he "hardly knew Miss Copleigh," the drama of the chase takes on emotional overtones. "In cold blood I should never have dreamed of going over such a country at night, but it seemed quite right and natural with the lightning crackling overhead, and a reek like the smell of the Pit in my nostrils."[87] When the storm has subsided and the party has regrouped, the guests now ride by couples, the narrator with the older Copleigh sister. As the narrator confesses in conclusion, "I felt tired and limp, and a good deal ashamed of myself as I went in for a bath and some sleep."[88]

Why the shame on the part of the narrator, otherwise so jaunty and cynical? Clearly enough, it is in part related to his own participation in the story—to the storm of sexual arousal and loss of emotional control which the actual storm unleashes. His desire for involvement, his wish to meddle with the unknown, is itself related to another theme almost universal to these stories—that of knowing. "False Dawn" itself is structured around a central counterpoint: on the one hand, the superior insight of the narrator into the course of events he describes (though the narrator anticipates the storm before setting out, he does not share his knowledge with Saumarez), on the other, the power of nature or of fate to undermine relatively superficial human understanding. As the story begins, the narrator comments, "No man will ever know the exact truth of this story; though women may sometimes whisper it to one another after a dance, when they are putting up their hair for the night and comparing their lists of victims. A man, of course, cannot assist at these functions. So the tale must be told from the outside—in the dark— all wrong."[89] And the storm itself signals the defeat of a reasonable calculability in the world. Only through his involvement in the plot does the narrator assert some control. "All the world was only the two Copleigh girls, Saumarez and I, ringed in with the lightning and the dark; and the guidance of this misguided world seemed to lie in my hands."[90] Yet such knowledge is obtained only at the cost of exposure and shame. The gap between the passivity of the observer and the active world of romantic adventure was too wide to be breached without extreme psychological discomfort.

In general, the problem of knowledge in these stories is informed by the impulse to achieve control, however futile such an ambition may ultimately be. What knowledge means to the cynical narrator— that which keeps the real world and the world of the story at bay— is really the opposite of any form of concrete understanding or involvement. Strickland, the Englishman who has delved too deeply into the magic of native India, best exemplifies the character in these stories who has carried the quest for knowledge too far. He has gained understanding of the immediate environment of native India, but lost perspective on its proper relationship to him as an alien.[91] Ultimate knowledge for these Anglo-Indians, and for the narrator most of all, requires insight into the fabric of illusion and allurement on which their seemingly stable world is actually based. The chronic danger they face is taking things too seriously, believing in the reality of their endeavors and the solidity of their world.

The theme is developed most poignantly in a tale called "Thrown Away" about a "Boy" who "had been brought up under the 'sheltered life' theory; and the theory killed him dead. He stayed with his people all his day, from the hour he was born to the hour he went up to Sandhurst nearly at the top of the list."[92] The Boy, whose experience had been the antithesis of Kipling's, goes out to India, innocently becomes involved in gambling and romance, and takes to heart his losses in both areas. Not even the hot weather sobers the Boy or provides him with any perspective on his problems. The *coup de grâce* comes from the cutting remark of a woman, "a cruel little sentence . . . that made him flush to the roots of his hair."[93] The Boy flees to a deserted house thirty miles away on the pretext of going shooting; but his discerning Major, sensing deeper trouble, pursues him with the narrator in tow. They arrive too late. The Boy has already committed suicide, and all they can do is contrive to make the death look heroic for the sake of the Boy's mother.

Kipling describes the dilemma of "seriousness" at the outset of the story:

Now India is a place beyond all others where one must not take things too seriously—the mid-day sun always excepted. . . . Flirtation does not matter, because every one is being transferred and either you or she leave the Station and never return. Good work does not matter, because a man is judged by his worst output and another man takes all the credit of his best as a rule. Bad work does not matter, because other men do worse and incompetents hang on longer in India than anywhere else. . . . Sickness does not matter, because it's all in a day's work, and if you die, another man takes over your place and your office in the eight hours between death and burial. . . . But this Boy—the tale is as old as the Hills—came out, and took all things seriously.[94]

In preparing the corpse for burial and in camouflaging the nature of the death, the Major confesses that he too was guilty of the "sin" of seriousness when he first came out to India, and that he barely escaped with his own life. In the face of this martyr to seriousness the narrator embarks on a grotesque comic ruse, "the concoction of a big, written lie, bolstered with evidence, to soothe The Boy's people at Home." Through the "hot, still evening" the narrator, with some help from the Major, fabricates a letter eulogizing the Boy's service in India and describing a painless death from some infectious disease. As the night wore on the narrator began to laugh "at the grotesqueness of the affair, and the laughter mixed itself up with the choke—and the Major said that we both wanted drinks. . . . The laughing-fit and the chokes got hold of me again, and I had to stop. The Major was nearly as bad; and we both knew that the worst part of the work was to come."[95]

Such deep brutal laughter rings throughout Kipling's stories on India.[96] At times it seems forced or inappropriate; in other instances it approaches the transcendent stature of tragic insight. In either instance such laughter is a distancing device from the brutal and over-stimulating realities of life as Kipling saw them. Having buried both the "Sheltered Boy" and his story, the narrator suggests rather oddly that he and the Major were left "feeling more like murderers than ever."[97] Indeed, the suggestion intrudes so strangely on the narrative as to raise a question of the author's control of his own creation. As in "False Dawn," the cost of involvement in the story itself is compounded by the uncontrolled feelings of shame and guilt that accompany it. The split Kipling experienced between the passivity of the observer—even if a "chosen" observer—and the need for active intervention rested on such anxieties, as well as on the child's partially repressed desire to know and to control that lived on in the adult.

The phenomenon Kipling is most concerned with in these stories is "breaking strain," the unendurable pressure which is the product of the collision between the isolated individual—the isolated self—and the physical and mental stress of Indian service. The classic statement of this conflict is contained in "At the End of the Passage," the account of four civil servants who are struggling to survive the loneliness of their assignment to remote outposts. Mottram, Lowndes, Spurstow, and Hummil have one consolation, a weekly game of whist to which they travel over long distances. During the hot weather especially, the specter of death hounds these men so closely that "when one of them failed to appear, he would send a telegram to his last address, in order that he might know whether the defaulter were dead or alive."[98] The game itself is desultory and ill-tempered, "the players . . . not conscious of any special regard for each other." Kipling characterizes them as "lonely folk who understood the dread meaning of loneliness. They were all under thirty years of age—which is too soon for any man to possess that knowledge."[99] Their society is necessary, but only as an antidote to the disarming knowledge bred in the bone of the Indian officer. In this story, at least, their special nemesis is the ferocity of the premonsoon heat.

The men flung themselves down, ordering the punkay coolies by all the powers of Hell to pull. Every door and window was shut, for the outside air was that of an oven. The atmosphere within was only 104, as the thermometer bore witness, and heavy with the foul smell of badly-trimmed kerosene lamps, and this stench, combined with that of native tobacco, baked brick, and dried earth, sends the heart of many a strong man down to his boots, for it is the smell of the Great Indian Empire when she turns herself for six months into a house of torment.[100]

In other places Kipling presents the prospects of a rampaging flood, or a devastating outbreak of cholera as the natural enemy, but in each case sudden death shadows the action of the story. In many instances the immediate danger is not physical, but emotional. Sequestered in the gloom of an opium den, as in "The Gate of the Hundred Sorrows," the precise Western sense of time and place is dissolved in the fragmented "Oriental" reality.[101]

"At the End of the Passage" itself proceeds along a path that leads ineluctably from the physical impact of stultifying heat to the emotional collapse of Hummil, the most vulnerable of the four men. When Hummil behaves alarmingly at dinner, Spurstow, the doctor, decides to stay with him and spikes his guns for fear he will commit suicide. Hummil is too agitated to sleep, and not even an injection of morphine provides rest. Instead, he disintegrates before the eyes of the bewildered doctor. "As a sponge rubs a slate clean," some unknown power "had wiped out of Hummil's face all that stamped it for the face of a man. . . . He had slept back into terrified childhood."[102] Despite Spurstow's urging, Hummil refuses to take a medical leave out of concern that a friend, a married man with a wife in delicate health, would have to take his place. When Spurstow returns for the appointed game of whist a week later, he finds Hummil dead. A native servant explains that "he has descended into the Dark Places and there has been caught because he was not able to escape with sufficient speed."[103] A look at the dead man's face and a photograph of the image in the dead man's eyes confirm the diagnosis. "Tisn't in medical science," Spurstow comments laconically.[104]

"At the End of the Passage" differs from similar stories in that there is no relief from the unrelenting reality of the unreality of India. Without Kipling's putting it in so many words, Hummil has taken his desolation and his duty too seriously, and has been driven back into "terrified childhood" in the process. He lacks that tumultuous, cathartic laughter that saves other Kipling characters from a similar fate. After witnessing a similar regression in "The Mark of the Beast," Strickland and the narrator are overwhelmed by a seizure of hysterical laughter. We "had disgraced ourselves as Englishmen forever," the narrator explains.[105] We have already observed this same phenomenon in "Thrown Way," and wherever in these stories an Englishman confronts his ultimate sense of self-coherence or identity he is likely to respond in the same manner. Alan Sandison has suggested that Kipling's India was a *place des signes*, a symbolic screen on which the internal struggles of his protagonist were projected.[106]

In relation to Sandison's suggestion, Kipling's injunction not to take India too seriously can be regarded as the ultimate recognition of its symbolic significance. Re-creating an imaginary dialogue between the outgoing Viceroy, Lord Dufferin, and his replacement Lord Lansdowne, in an article for the *Pioneer* in 1888, Kipling puts the following words into Dufferin's mouth: "You stand on the threshold of new experiences—most of which will distress you and a few amuse. You are the center of a gigantic *Practical Joke*. Strive to enter the spirit of it and jest temperately."[107]

Beyond the reality of the individual trying to retain his balance against formidable odds, everything else ultimately dissolves into a gigantic charade. It is at this point that Kipling invokes the society and the group—or the Law—as an intermediary between the individual and the "dark" world he inhabits. After the violent sacrifice of goat to protect his newborn, illegitimate son in "Without Benefit of Clergy," the protagonist Holden, as we have seen, confesses, "I never felt like this in my life." He proceeds immediately to the club, where a game of pool was under way, and where "the light and company of his fellows" is experienced in marked contrast to his clamorous emotions.[108] Here the club functions as a defense or sanctuary against uncontrollable passion; both "the dread of loss" and "riotous exultation."

In general in these stories, Kipling's identification with the Anglo-Indian community has this same air of imperious necessity. He does not so much associate it with his own values as see in it a place of last resort from the oppressive—often appalling—darkness of native life that threatens the sense of self. If Kipling becomes a "sociologist" in these stories, he does so only to salvage something coherent from his artistic vision and his personal experience. To turn again to the language of politics, Kipling seems less Annan's conservative than a Hobbesian liberal who devises an authoritarian political structure because he perceives life as "nasty, brutish, and short." However often he invokes the society of the Law, his vision remains rooted in the individual psyche.

### Native India "beyond the Pale"

It is a risky undertaking to divine a writer's conscious or unconscious intention through the responses of his readers, even his most perceptive or most lettered readers. Yet when one looks over the initial critical reception of Kipling's stories in England, one finds striking uniformity on this point: it was Kipling's treatment of his native characters, of the feverish exoticism of India, rather than his tales of Anglo-Indian social life, that made the deepest impression on his English audience. As Andrew Lang noted in an 1889 review published in London before Kipling himself returned to England: "His 'black men' . . . are excellent men, full of cunning, revenge, and with a point of honour of their own. We are more in sympathy with their ancient semi-barbarism than with the inexpensive rank and second-hand fashion of Simla."[109] Thomas Humphrey Ward, writing in the *Times Literary Supplement* in March of 1890, credited Kipling's Indian stories with reaching "unknown depths and gulfs of human existence."[110] We have already noted Edmund Gosse's assertion that Kipling's "devils of the East . . . reawaken in us the primitive emotions of curiosity, mystery, and romance in action." Such was the appeal of the early Kipling, before the power of his work was in some measure undermined by political controversies.[111]

Yet Kipling's exoticism must be qualified in two respects. First, in contrast to the romanticism of the French novelist of colonial life, Pierre Loti, to whom he is often compared, Kipling's literary method is that of the journalist, crisp and laconic. His style provides a saving means of distancing himself from his subject matter, rather than becoming immersed in it. "On the City Wall," for example, is a classic instance of a story in which his treatment of the British presence in India provides an ironic counterpoint to his portrayal of the sensuous prostitute. And it is in this virtual opposition between the coldness of his prose and the seductive character of his literary creations that Kipling reveals so much of himself.

With respect to these early stories a second distinction must also be made, between Kipling's exoticism and his reputation as a writer of romance and adventure. In fact, there is little in Kipling's early writing that can genuinely be labeled adventure. "The Man Who Would Be King," written in 1888, might seem a towering exception to this assertion, yet even here the element of adventure is qualified by the heavy symbolic weight of the story as a parable of vaulting imperial ambition. It is striking to note that Kipling—the narrator—drops out of the tale when the adventure itself begins. The narrator's style, perhaps, is too ironic for such an enterprise. Instead, Kipling lets one of the participants, Carnehan, describe the quest for kingship in Kafiristan.[112]

In contrast to "The Man Who Would Be King," the dominant element in Kipling's exoticism is curiosity, and it is in this context that Gosse's characterization of his work as a "peep show" is most apposite. Even in *The Naulahka*, usually dismissed as a lightweight adventure story, the fearless American hero Tarvin is animated more by curiosity than by adventurousness in his quest for a priceless necklace. As Tarvin approaches a particularly frightening abandoned shrine called the Cow's Mouth, Kipling comments that "it was his racial instinct of curiosity rather than any love of adventure that led him to throw himself at the darkness, which parted before and closed behind him."[113] Tarvin, the zealous American, deals with native life more simply and directly than most of Kipling's protagonists. Usually, in stories like "Beyond the Pale," Kipling's approach to native society partakes of a childlike curiosity, a particular blend of excitement and fear that is almost prurient in character. It draws as much from the feelings of the intensely ambivalent child as it does from those of the cynical journalist.

Indeed, it is only in isolating his "insatiable curiosity"—the compulsive character of his interest—that a psychological approach to Kipling's India seems called for. On their surface, at least, Kipling's views of India seem precisely to mirror those of his Anglo-Indian compatriots. Like them, he is agreed on the necessity of British rule in India and on the political incapacity of native subjects. He identifies the "real India" with the toiling agricultural masses, and caricatures the efforts of educated Indians to pattern their thought and behavior on Western models. There is nothing striking or original in a story like "The Enlightenments of Pagett, M.P." to distinguish Kipling as a political or cultural critic from the run-of-the-mill officer or civil servant residing in the Punjab. What differentiated Kipling from his fellow Anglo-Indians, in the final analysis, was what divided his own identity. He was especially sensitive to the struggle between the "black" and "white" elements that split the superficially stable and conventional core of Anglo-Indian social values. His attraction to the passive and the violent elements in his nature led him to project these feelings onto India itself in a way that complemented the magical character of the colonial relationship. He produced as much a symbolic as a real landscape.

The basic component of this projective process was the association of India with some primitive or elemental force. Western logic and pragmatism, to Kipling, seemed flat and superficial when measured against the depths of India, depths that could be calculated in measures of both time and feeling. Pagett, the itinerant M.P., receives his ultimate lesson in India when a "clanking" skeleton from just below the surface of the earth settles at his feet. "Our houses are built on cemeteries," Orde, the knowing civilian, informs him. "There are scores of thousands of graves within ten miles."[114] These skeletons literally obstruct the British effort at material improvement, but more important, they mock in silence the ultimate objectives of British rule. And their mute testimony is supported by the pantheon of Hindu gods to whom the British presence is but a brief and prosaic interlude. "Their Gods! What should their Gods know? They were born yesterday and those that made them are scarcely yet cold," proclaims the Mugger, the crocodile god in "The Bridge-Builders"; "Tomorrow their Gods will die."[115] The elephant god adds: "It is but the shifting of a little dirt. Let the dirt dig in the dirt if it pleases the dirt."[116] In this way Kipling places the considerable achievement of Findlayson into proper perspective.

More often it is the overwhelming force of nature or of mystery that subdues the shallow Western sensibility. The ferocious storm in "False Dawn" plays havoc with the orderly progress of the narrative. In "The Bridge-Builders" the unknown powers of the rampaging river are self-consciously posed against the calculations of the engineer, "comparing, estimating, and recalculating . . . brick by brick, pier by pier." "His side of the sum was beyond question," Kipling comments, "but what man knew Mother Gunga's arithmetic? Even as he was making all sure by the multiplication table, the river might be scooping a pot hole to the very bottom of any of those eight-foot piers that carried his reputation."[117] In "Without Benefit of Clergy," when Holden's tiny son and native mistress are dead, snuffed out in a remorseless outbreak of cholera, the very house in which he had been "master and lord" is virtually destroyed in the ferocious monsoon rains. "He found that the rains had torn down the mud pillars of the gateway, and the heavy wooden gate that had guarded his life hung lazily from one hinge. . . . A gray squirrel was in possession of the verandah, as if the house had been untenanted for thirty years instead of three days."[118]

The physical assault of the elements is more than matched by the power of the native environment to disarm any rational scheme or assumption. The very physiography of native districts in Kipling's stories erodes our concrete sense of time and place. Not only does the opium smoked within "The Gate of the Hundred Sorrows" blot out every concern with mundane reality, but the house itself resists discovery. "You might go through the very gully it stands in and be none the wiser." In such an environment, "where each man's house is as guarded and as unknowable as the grave,"[119] the mystery of native life is yoked to the powers of death and darkness that defy every rational expectation. Traveling as a journalist in the native, still feudalistic states of Rajputana, Kipling is constantly oppressed by the configurations of the native princes' palaces. In the palace in the Dead City of Amber, he finds "crampt and darkened rooms, the narrow, smoothwalled passages with recesses where a man might wait for his enemy unseen, the maze of ascending and descending stairs leading nowither, the ever present screen of marble tracery that may hide or reveal so much." In contrast to the Western sense of concrete reality, he suggests that "it must be impossible for one reared in an Eastern palace to think straightly or speak freely."[120]

Kipling's concern with what is seen or concealed, with dark and cramped recesses, is animated by the awe and terror that mark a child's curiosity. And this childlike feeling of vulnerability is intensified by the sense of being watched in an instance in which his own sight is obscured.

All Palaces in India excepting dead ones, such as that of Amber, are full of eyes. In some, as has been said, the idea of being watched is stronger than in others. In Boondi Palace it was overpowering—being far worse than in the green-shuttered corridors of Jodhpur. There were trap doors on the tops of terraces, and windows veiled in foliage, and bull's eyes set low in unexpected walls, and many other peepholes and places of vantage. In the end, the Englishman looked devoutly at the floor, but when the voice of the woman came up from under his feet, he felt there was nothing left for him but to go. Yet, excepting this voice, there was deep silence everywhere, and nothing could be seen.[121]

The tension of seeing or being seen, heightened in these native palaces with their hidden "evil" eyes, is invested with a primitive power.

The punitive evil eye expresses only one dimension of the elemental in Kipling's India. His view of female sexuality, his aggressive fantasies, and his anxieties concerning his identity are equally involved. What unites all these themes is the fear of regression to an earlier object orientation, a more primitive and more explosive emotional state. This anxiety fueled Kipling's conviction, almost universally shared among Anglo-Indians, that Indian natives, no matter how well educated, were themselves primitive emotionally and must be dealt with as children. Such an assumption was obviously functional within the framework of British rule, for it emphasized the political incapacity of native Indians, their weakness of character, and their dependency upon their British masters.

Like those of other Anglo-Indian writers, one of Kipling's most predictable fictional creations is the Western-educated native whose true character inevitably cracks through a thin veneer of civilization.

For in such characters the two forms of magic—the "primitive" and the "omnipotent"—undergo a tenuous and unsatisfactory fusion. Kipling began portraying this figure quite early in his Indian career, in a sketch for the *Civil and Military Gazette* of January 1885, in which he recounts a meeting with an Anglicized Afghan on a train who "threw back his head and laughed aloud—not with the laughter of civilization, but the laughter that betrayed his origin—mirth, savage and boisterous, that had nothing in common with gold watch-guard, English clothes, patent trunks or first class tickets."[122] More characteristic is the Indian whose civilized pretenses dissolve at the first moment of crisis, like Wali Dad of "On the City Wall," who becomes a violent partisan of his creed when religious strife explodes in Lahore. Thus he is incapacitated for the task of saving an escaped political prisoner, a responsibility then thrust on the shoulders of the English narrator.[123]

Perhaps the most revealing of all such Kipling characters is Michele D'Cruse of "His Chance in Life," a member of India's large half-caste community "which is part English, part Portuguese, and part Native."[124] It represents "the Borderline where the last drop of White blood ends and the full tide of Black sets in," where "the White shows in spurts of fierce childish pride . . . the Black in . . . half-heathenish customs, and strange unaccountable impulses to crime."[125] Michele, placed in a critical situation in his job as a telegraph operator, displays both these responses. He rises to the occasion by organizing resistance to an angry native crowd. But when an Englishman arrives on the scene, "Michele felt himself slipping back more and more into the native; and the tale of the Tibaso Riots ended with the strain on the teller, in an hysterical outburst of tears, bred by sorrow that he had killed a man, shame that he could not feel as uplifted as he had felt through the night, and childish anger that his tongue could not do justice to his great deeds."[126] The degree of white blood a person possesses determines the difference.

The primordial image of the castrating female preoccupied Kipling during his years in India. Throughout much of that period he was at work on a manuscript entitled *Mother Maturin*, which eventually he decided not to publish.[127] Yet the likely nature of his

youthful creation comes through in at least one of his early published works. In "To Be Filed for Reference," the climactic sketch in
*Plain Tales*, *Mother Maturin* is the title of a monumental manuscript
handed on to the narrator by a debauched Englishman on his deathbed. The man, who has "gone native" and married a native woman,
regards the manuscript as the *summa* of his experience of the Indian
underworld, the dark wisdom of the native bazaar.[128] Such a figure
also appears in a satire on the British presence in India entitled "An
Interesting Condition," published in *The Pioneer* in 1888.

> Above all, reposes the East.
> She is old, but she is beautiful.
> A beautiful woman is always old. As old as Beauty.
> She is of moral reputation indifferent. . . .
> With the Tourkh.
> It was an affaire militaire only. . . .
> With the Rajput; with the Hindou.
> It was to pass the time. . . .
> With the Frenchman.
> It was an affair of the heart. . . .
> It is now the Englishman who is kicking her children
> to school. She has a menage of the Britannic ideal—
> solid, sumptuous, and wearying above all. . . .
> The Englishman has taken her by the arm. He
> promenades with her upon Sundays. He laughs.
> He exhibits his teeth. He slaps his leg. He
> also pats her upon the back.
> These things are the marks of the husband
> English. But . . . ask her.
> She has seen many lovers.
> A woman who has seen many lovers will see more.
> This woman will exist for ever, and she will
> always be beautiful.[129]

As with Lalun, the eternal quality of India as female is identified
with her sexual prowess, thus linking the divided images of woman
as mother and as seductress.

   When the element of satire disappears in Kipling's fiction, the image of the seductive female is more directly linked to the dangers of
castration and annihilation. This theme is central to the plot of *The*

# KIPLING

Kipling's mother,
Mrs. J. L. (Alice Macdonald) Kipling
*Collection: Earl Baldwin of Bewdley. Courtesy of*
*Weidenfeld & Nicolson*

John Lockwood Kipling and Rudyard Kipling
*University of Sussex Library, courtesy of The National Trust*
*of Great Britain*

Kipling as a young man
*Courtesy of India Office Library; copyright The British Library*

Page from *The Civil and Military Gazette*, for which Kipling was a correspondent
*Courtesy of India Office Library, copyright The British Library*

Rudyard Kipling, from the etching by William Strang
*Courtesy of The British Museum*

Rudyard Kipling, self-caricature in the manner of
Aubrey Beardsley
*By permission of the Houghton Library, Harvard University, and the
National Trust of Great Britain*

K, k.

Kipling, "The Old and the Young Self"
*By Max Beerbohm, courtesy of Eva G. Reichmann*

Pillars of the Empire, Kipling and Kitchener,
Drawing by F. Carruthers Gould.
From The Struwwelpeter Alphabet, *1908, copyright
The British Library*

Rudyard Kipling as a South African war
correspondent
*By permission of the Houghton Library, Harvard
University.*

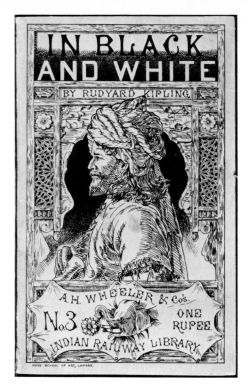

Early Indian editions
*By permission of the Houghton Library, Harvard University.*

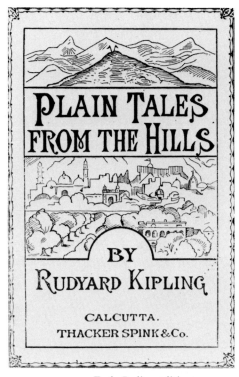

Early Indian editions
*From G. F. Monkshood,* The Less Familiar Kipling and Kiplingana, *1917*

"A Prosperous Year"

"A Lean Year,"
*drawings by Lockwood Kipling, verse by Rudyard Kipling. From Lockwood Kipling,* Beast and Man in India, *189*

Kipling and his characters,
*from the portrait by Cyrus Cuneo. Courtesy of the Illustrated London News Picture Library*

Cary Grant, Victor McLaglen, Douglas Fairbanks Jr. in the movie *Gunga Din*
*Courtesy of National Film Archive/Stills Library, and RKO General Pictures*

The Singer of Empire, *Punch*, 1935
*Copyright Punch/Rothco*

*Naulahka*, where the American hero Tarvin endeavors to extract a priceless necklace—itself a common symbol for the female genital—from an evil native queen, Sitabhai, who manipulates the affairs of a native principality from behind the closed doors of her harem. Sitabhai possesses the sixth sense of the native women in divining Tarvin's thoughts and anticipating his actions. She employs all her wiles in attempting to transform a midnight meeting into a seduction. As she nestles close to him, "his arm slipped unconsciously about her waist." But when he glanced down at her body "he saw the ruby-jewelled jade handle of a little knife at her breast. He disengaged himself from her arms with a quick movement, and rose to his feet. She was very lovely as she stretched her arms appealingly out to him in the half light; but he was there for other things."[130] There is never any grave danger of the strong-willed American yielding to Sitabhai, but only in the face of the threatening knife at her breast does he force himself away from her. Seduction—like the pursuit of the jewels itself—is tainted with the threat of violence and mutilation.

Earlier, in his quest for the jewels, Tarvin descends into the Cow's Mouth, the terrifying but sacred pit in the center of a ruined native city. Goaded by his "instinct of curiosity," Tarvin explores the space in spite of the darkness and "an intolerable smell of musk," until he detects something moving in the slime at the bottom of the pit.

Then he became aware of pale emerald eyes watching him fixedly, and perceived that there was deep breathing in the place other than his own. He flung the match down, the eyes retreated, there was a wild rattle and crash in the darkness, a howl that might have been bestial or human, and Tarvin, panting between the tree roots, swung himself to the left, and fled back over the mud-banks to the ledge, where he stood, his back to the Cow's Mouth and his revolver in his hand. In that moment of waiting for what might emerge from the hole in the side of the tank Tarvin tasted all the agonies of pure physical terror. . . . The Cow's Mouth chuckled and choked out of sight as it had chuckled since the making of the tank, and that was at the making of time.[131]

With its malignant odor and entrapping slime, and the savage teeth of the sacred crocodile waiting at the bottom since "the making of time," the Cow's Mouth might possibly be viewed as a fantasized re-creation of the predatory female genital. Tarvin re-experiences all the archaic terrors of the sexual encounter at their most bestial level. "Never again," Kipling informs us, "for any consideration under the wholesome light of the sun, would he, who feared nothing, set foot in the Cow's mouth." [132]

In "Beyond the Pale," one of the most powerful sketches in *Plain Tales from the Hills*, the entire native quarter of the city is invested with the mystery and danger associated with Kipling's fantasized female. For this reason the native and British communities must be kept rigidly segregated. Kipling explains that "a man should, whatever happens, keep to his own caste, race and breed. . . . Then, whatever trouble falls is in the ordinary course of things—neither sudden, alien, nor unexpected." [133] The man in this case is Trejago, another Englishman who "knew too much" for his own good. He becomes involved in an illicit affair with a fifteen-year-old girl named Bisesa—a widow condemned to spend the rest of her days secluded in her uncle's house—who "prayed the Gods . . . to send her a lover." When Trejago makes his first secret visit to Bisesa's room he dons a native garment called a *boorka* which, Kipling explains, "cloaks a man as well as a woman." Sexual identity is thus confused or threatened in the very act of exploring the narrow alleys of the native quarter in pursuit of his lover.

After a delightful period of such encounters, the affair ends when the jealous Bisesa gets wind of Trejago's meetings with a white woman. "'You are an Englishman,'" she explains, "'I am only a black girl.'—she was fairer than bar-gold at the Mint—'and the widow of a black man.'" [134] But Trejago cannot resist seeking out the grated window of Bisesa in Amir Nath's Gully. "From the black dark, Bisesa held out her arms into the moonlight. Both hands had been cut off at the wrists, and the stumps were nearly healed." [135] If there is any doubt as to the deeper meaning of Bisesa's "stumps"— reminiscent of the child's hand discovered in the garden of Kipling's childhood home in Bombay—it is resolved in the next paragraph when, "as Bisesa bowed her head between her arms and sobbed, someone in the room grunted like a wild beast, and something sharp—knife, sword, or spear—thrust at Trejago in his *boorka*. The stroke missed his body, but cut into one of the muscles of the groin, and he limped slightly from the wound the rest of his days." [136] The crazed Trejago's first act, when he flees the native quarter, is to tear off the *boorka* and throw it away. Thus he reasserts his sexual identity in the face of a sudden and sadistic threat to it. His curiosity about native life is ultimately sexual in character, and the danger such curiosity carries with it is once again that of castration or mutilation. Although here the knife is wielded directly by Bisesa's enraged uncle, the native quarter—"where each man's house is as guarded and unknowable as the grave," and sexual identity itself becomes obscured—is the primary seductress.

Kipling's association of India with the seductive and sometimes castrating female also illuminated the confusion he felt both as a writer and as a member of the Anglo-Indian community. His vigorous identification with the omnipotent image of the British military must be viewed as a defense against the passive component of his characterization of India as female. In fact, he was deeply attracted to both the passive and aggressive aspects of the female, and one might view her as a composite image of these contradictory impulses projected onto native life. Although Kipling—and the Anglo-Indian community in general—strove continually to keep these impulses in check, he ascribed them to distinct segments of the native community in his stories, where he allowed them to war upon one another. This drama of opposing impulses was most commonly represented in the contrast between the peasants and warriors of the Punjab and the natives of Bengal to the south and east—a conventional theme in Anglo-Indian literature.

Yet Kipling not only accentuates these contrasts but distorts them in accordance with his own fantasized fears and desires. His treatment of the northern Indian consistently emphasizes the Oriental qualities he admires: close ties to the land; respect for age and authority; pride and courage. The peasants and landed proprietors, whom Orde parades before the globe-trotting Pagett, all embody these values in one way or another. Kipling takes the opportunity to idealize them, as he does the Jat farmer Jello whose "strongly marked features glowed with russet bronze," and whose "beard and mustache, streaked with gray, swept from bold cliffs of brow and cheek in the large sweeps one sees drawn by Michael Angelo. . . . The drapery of stout blue cotton cloth thrown over his broad shoulders and girt round his narrow loins, hung from his tall form in broadly sculptural folds and he would have made a superb model for an artist in search of a patriarch."[137]

Kipling responds in an even more elemental way to the aggressiveness associated with the farmers and tribesmen of the north. The most telling example of such aggression was the native practice of revenge murder, generally sanctioned in the Punjab, and practiced with special freedom and ferocity by the Pathan tribesmen of the northwest frontier and Afghanistan proper. "Dray Wara Yow Dee" is a monologue which narrates such a quest for revenge, told to an Englishman by a crazed and anguished Afghan horse trader. The story begins with a Biblical quotation—"for jealousy is the rage of man; therefore he will not spare in the day of vengeance"— and the entire tale is suffused with the rhetorical weight and retributive morality of the Old Testament. The horse trader has been humiliated by a man who has committed adultery with his wife. First he punishes the woman: "And she bowed her head, and I smote it off at the neckbone so that it leapt between my feet. Thereafter the rage of our people came upon me, and I hacked off the breasts."[138] Then he sets off in pursuit of her illicit lover. So far, however, his extensive search has been futile and he is spurred on only by the "lust of vengeance." Indeed, his expression of hatred has a sadistic and a sexual component that exceeds mere outrage.

My brother, when the desire of a man is set upon one thing alone, he fears neither God nor Man nor Devil. If my vengeance failed, I would splinter the Gates of Paradise with the butt of my gun, or I would cut my way into Hell with my knife, and I would call upon Those who Govern there for the body of Daoud Shah. What love so deep as hate?

Surely my vengeance is safe! Surely God hath him in the hollow of His hand against my claiming. There shall no harm befall Daoud Shah till I come; for I would fain kill him quick and whole with the life sticking firm in his body. A pomegranate is sweetest when the cloves break away unwilling from the rind. Let it be the daytime, that I may see his face, and delight may be crowned.[139]

And once again the eye—the staring, all-knowing, destructive eye—is an integral part of the horse trader's fantasy of revenge. The intensity of his stare betrays his murderous intention to a woman in the bazaar. Later on, the watchful eye becomes a cosmic symbol of his unrelenting pursuit. "The eye of the Sun, the eye of the Moon and my own unrestful eye—all three are one—all three are one!"[140] In addition, the hill country in which this drama unfolds is idealized, and the Englishman whom he addresses is identified as a kind of blood brother. "The bloom of the peach orchards is upon all the Valley, and *here* is only dust and great stink," the horse trader declares. "It is good in the North now. Come back with me. Let us return to our own people! Come!"[141]

If Kipling, as an Englishman, never fully identified with the "wild men of the north" or their murderous intentions, he did identify with the matrix of values, the clean, manly, vigorous life with which these aggressive fantasies are associated. These values constituted an alternative to the "dust" and "the great stink" which Kipling attributes to the rest of India, and most characteristically to Bengal. In the "Enlightenments of Pagett, M.P.," the Punjabi peasants pour "ironical scorn" on the urban Bengali as a representative of the non-agricultural Indians "whose backs were never bowed in honest work."[142] They castigate Bengali workers as "Black apes" and have only contempt for the Bengali Babu. A similar vein of unmitigated scorn runs throughout Kipling's Indian stories; it seems to rest on two related fantasies. The first of these hinges on the supposed physical frailty and voluptuous involvements of the Hindu. Kipling's most powerful rejoinder to Pagett's naive politics is a "typical" product of the educational system, a callow and bombastic youth whose father is a writer rather than a farmer, and who expounds the cause of political liberty for India. Yet his views, as Kipling presents them, are so shallow that not even the ingenuous Pagett can accept them.

'Sir, I know it all—all! Norman Conquest, Magna Charta, Runnymeade, Reformation, Tudors, Stuarts, Mr. Milton and Mr. Burke, and I have read something of Mr. Herbert Spencer and Gibbon's "Decline and Fall," Reynolds' "Mysteries of the Court," and—'
Pagett felt like one who had pulled the string of a shower-bath unawares, and hastened to stop the torrent with a question as to what particular grievances of the people of India the attention of an elected assembly should be first directed. . . . The student was not, however, prepared with answers to Mr. Pagett's mildest questions on these points, and he returned

to vague generalities, leaving the M.P. so much impressed with the crudity of his views that he was glad on Orde's return to say good-bye to his "very interesting" young friend.[143]

As Pagett discovers, the "subtle Oriental" swallows the "jam" of Western ideas but rejects the pill of moral or religious instruction.[144] Though Mr. Dina Nath talks like "a sort of English schoolboy," he is in fact "married three years" and a physical and moral weakling, "the father of two weaklings." Beneath his bombastic oratory, the Bengali Babu—and all of Western-educated India—is still a victim of his culture's sensuality, his own virility ground down in the stultifying and castrating environment of "mother India." Kipling's hostility to the educated Indian is clearly bound up here with his own divided identity as a writer in a highly masculine culture, the fear of and attraction to his own passive impulses. At a deeper level the Indian claim to independence, like Kipling's own, is viewed within both a political and psychosexual context. There is a clear tie intended here between the verbal torrent which the student Dina Nath unleashes on Pagett and the filth and disease which seem to appear wherever the Babu is present.[145] The further identification of the Indian as basically sensual—as a victim of castration and as essentially passive sexually—echoed the Anglo-Indian cult of manliness, and constituted a vigorous but revealing denial of fantasized fears.

These themes converge in "The Head of the District," Kipling's didactic tale of imperial mismanagement, a tale that can also be read as a parable of conflicting impulse and identity. The story itself is simple. Orde, the hero of "Pagett, M.P." and the Deputy Commissioner of a dangerous frontier district, dies suddenly of fever while serving at his post. The Viceroy, ensconced at a safe distance in Calcutta and hoping to foster the principles of the "New India," installs a Bengali in his place. But the proud and ferocious tribesmen of the hills are aroused by the appointment of a "black" Bengali to rule over them. Before "Mr. Grish Chunder De, M.A.," has even had time to take official charge of the district, the Khusru Kheyl rise in revolt and swarm down from the hills. The Bengali flees at the first scent of trouble, leaving Orde's assistant Tallantire to restore order to the district.

The political lesson of the story is clear enough. India is too divided by region, religion, and race to rule itself. There is in fact no such entity as India, and only a resolute outside force like the British can hold such a fragile construct together. Yet Kipling's characterizations of the Bengalis and the tribesmen make it equally clear that a psychological lesson underlies the political one. His contemptuous portrayal of Grish Chunder De and his venal brother reveal them as the worst type of Babu, "more English than the English, with much curious knowledge of bump-suppers, cricket matches, hunting-runs, and other unholy sports of the alien."[146] He distinguishes the Bengali who "had been born in a hothouse, of stock bred in a hothouse, and fearing physical pain as some men fear sin," from the "lustful" tribal chief Khoda Dad Khan who from "earliest infancy had been accustomed to look on battle, murder, and instant death."[147] In Chunder De's first face-to-face encounter with Khoda Dad Khan, who had revered Orde Sahib, "the eyes behind the gold spectacles sought the floor." The natives of the district ridicule the Bengali as "a black man—unfit to run the tail of a Potter's donkey."[148] At the first sign of resistance to their rule, the brothers begin to cling to their British assistants. As a last resort—the "happy resource of a fertile race!"—Chunder De "falls sick" before he has officially taken charge of the district, leaving Tallantire to clean up the mess the Bengali has created.

Although, in contrast to the effeminacy and cowardice of the Bengalis, the hillsmen are proud, manly, and courageous, no less than the Bengalis themselves they are captives of their own impulsiveness. In the crisis of blood that erupts in the hills there is no restraining their sadistic instincts. Kipling describes their attack on the blind Mullah who is a rival of Khoda Dad Khan for leadership of the Khusru Kheyl.

A grim chuckle followed the suggestion, and the soft *wheep, wheep*, of unscabbarded knives followed the chuckle. It was an excellent notion, and met a long-felt want of the tribe. The Mullah sprang to his feet, glaring with withered eyeballs at the drawn death he could not see, and calling down the curses of God and Mohomed on the tribe. Then began a game of blind man's bluff round and between the fires. . . . They tickled him gently under the armpit with the knife point. He leaped aside screaming, only to feel a cold blade drawn lightly over the back of his neck, or a rifle-muzzle rubbing his beard. . . . Men described to him the glories of the shrine they would build, and the little children, clapping their hands, cried, "Run, Mullah, run! There's a man behind you!" In the end, when the sport wearied, Khoda Dad Khan's brother sent a knife home between his ribs.[149]

Kipling, who had experienced "blindness" himself, savors each excruciating moment of revenge against the blind Mullah, even though he must ultimately condemn the impulse behind the act.[150] The emotional link between sadistic aggression and eyesight is carried even further in the conclusion of the story, when the "remorseful" Khusru Kheyl bring to Tallantire a prize of battle. "Slowly rolled to Tallantire's feet the crop-haired head of a spectacled Bengali gentleman, open-eyes, open-mouthed—the head of Terror incarnate."[151] It is the Babu's brother, and Tallantire has no choice but to punish severely the savage but foolish tribesmen. As Orde comments to Khoda Dad Khan at the beginning of the story, "though ye be strong men, ye are children."[152] As such, the Khusru Kheyl are as much the prisoners of passion as the effeminate, "hothouse" Bengalis.

The reward for the Khusru Kheyl is in Tallantire's promise, "Rest Assured that the Government will send you a man!"[153] The authority of the British, and the respect of their native subjects, depends in the final analysis on their manly self-control, their ability not only to wield arms but to hold them in check. The Bengalis and the hillmen are remote from each other emotionally as well as physically or geographically, and in Kipling's treatment they confront one another like children meeting for the first time. Yet both identify instinctively with the British, who have succeeded by subduing both their subjects and themselves.

### Imperialism and the Day's Work

The historical mythology that evolved out of Britain's presence in the Punjab had its fictional counterpart in Kipling's portrayal of the Anglo-Indian civil servant. Like the mythic John Lawrence, the model of the British administrator Kipling creates in his stories is tailored to the maintenance of a stoical identity and to the dictates of impulse control. Although these impulses are projected onto unruly native subjects in the "Head of the District," they are as often entirely internal, a function of the economy of the individual rather than the confrontation with native society. The phenomenon of "breaking strain," which Kipling examines in stories like "Thrown Away" and "At the End of the Passage," illuminates this essential aspect of the presence of the British administrator in a country where impulsive action is the rule rather than the exception. When Strickland and the narrator give themselves up to hysterical laughter after Fleete's cure in "The Mark of the Beast," the narrator fears that they had "disgraced ourselves as Englishmen forever." [154] And Michele, the half-caste of "His Chance in Life," feels himself "slipping back more and more into the native" in the mere presence of an Englishman, after one heroic effort at self-possession. [155]

Emotional control emerges in these stories as a set of behavioral mandates—an idealized identity structure developed in direct opposition to the unmediated impulse it is designed, in part, to contain. The first of these mandates was itself a mode of denial; the sacrifice of one-self to duty without any hope of reward or recognition. In "A Free Gift," a sketch for the *Pioneer* in 1888, Kipling imagines an exchange between an "underpaid and overworked" Englishman and a self-indulgent Bengali. "'Much better keep on slanging me,'" the Englishman comments. "'I'm paid for it, you know, and I can't hit back. Look here, we'll make a bargain. You call me a thief, a ravisher, an unsympathetic alien, and anything else you like. . . . If you'll only help me to clean up a few sewers now and again.'" [156]

Things are no different on the frontier for Orde and Tallantire. After many years of faithful service, Orde finds himself on his deathbed without enough funds to pay his wife's passage back to England. And Tallantire stays on to hold the district together, despite the fact that he has been wrongfully passed over for promotion to Orde's position. Even though he is left to pacify the Khusru Kheyl, a colleague assures him that he will get no recognition for his efforts: "If you keep things straight, and he [Chunder De] isn't actually beaten with a stick when he's on tour, he'll get all the credit. If anything goes wrong, you'll be told that you didn't support him loyally." [157] Tallantire is willing to sacrifice himself to Orde's memory. But beyond this personal debt, he is hard-pressed to find any redemptive reason for his action. In a country that Kipling has described elsewhere as a "Practical Joke," his selfless behavior possesses at least as much private as "imperial" significance.

In this respect it might be said that Kipling's Indian stories tended to undercut the mythology on which British rule was based, or at least to place it in ironic counterpoint. His celebration of self-control consistently has this reflexive quality, a personal meaning that competes with its value as social product. Ultimately his praise for the practical activity of empire—for its artisans and district administrators—was intended as much to promote the soundness and sanity of the individual as any overriding social or political purpose. In "Without Benefit of Clergy" Holden, who has immersed himself in the world of his native mistress, employs the British society of fact and work as an antidote to his agitated feelings. After the birth of his illegitimate child, as we have seen, he seeks out his club where "the talk beat up around the ever-fresh subject of each man's work, and steadied Holden till it was time to go to his dark empty bungalow."[158] And when the child dies suddenly and he is overcome by grief, "one mercy only was granted to Holden. He rode to his office in broad daylight and found waiting for him an unusually heavy mail that demanded concentrated attention and hard work."[159]

Beyond its defensive function in an alien environment, the devotion to work was positively valued and formed an essential component of Kipling's identity. He had a genuine infatuation with "things as they are," with work that took concrete or material shape. On his travels for the *Pioneer* in 1887, after a meeting with a group of English canal officers and engineers, he remarked that "after long residence in places where folk discuss intangible things . . . in an abstract and bloodless sort of way, it was a revelation to listen to men who talk of Things and People—crops and ploughs and water—supplies, and the best means of using all three for the benefit of a district."[160] And on this same trip he praises a group of Europeans managing the woolen mills at Dhariwal for "compassing their heads and hands real, concrete and undeniable Things. As distinguished from the speech which dies and the paperwork which perishes."[161] According to Kipling, these men have recognized that "too much progress is bad."[162] They are too absorbed in spinning cotton to conjure with abstractions. Indeed, Kipling maintained a life-long interest in the skilled workman and the operation of mechanical devices, and testified to it early in his career by detailed sketches of mechanical operations like the Giridih coal fields.[163]

Kipling's interest in Findlayson the bridgebuilder is not only in his technical achievement, but also in his struggle against the natural elements, and ultimately against the "gods" who have been unleashed by them. It is "the still small voice of fact" which he contrasts to the blackness and inscrutability of India, as well as to the posturing and idealism of well-meaning but deluded Europeans. In "The Judgment of Dungara" this contrast is realized in the distinction between a naive missionary couple, trying to convert their native charges to Christianity, and the hard-headed assistant collector who understands the limitations of what can be accomplished in his district. In contrast to the high-blown sentiments of the Krenks, who are "playing against the Devil for the living soul," Gallio believes "one creed as good as another."[164] Having said this, "Gallio departed to risk his life in mending the rotten bamboo bridges of his people, in killing a too persistent tiger here or there, in sleeping out in the reeking jungle, or in tracking the Suria Kol raiders who had taken a few head from their brethren of the Boria clan. He was a knock-kneed, shambling young man, naturally devoid of creed or reverence."[165] When the Krenks' fatuous efforts to convert the natives are undermined by intrigue—supposedly the judgment of Dungara, the local deity—they mourn their failure, while Gallio bursts into irreverent laughter. The missionaries are another of the type who take India too seriously.[166] After the Krenks' departure the jungle quickly overruns their school and their chapel, but Gallio's practical work in the district goes on.

This is the lesson that Leo the Lion and the other characters in "Children of the Zodiac"—the parable which Kipling wrote in London after leaving India—must master. Although they are offspring of the gods, the children gradually learn of their mortality after their descent to earth. And through that knowledge they accept the necessity of dedicating their lives to honest toil. After learning of his ultimate fate from Cancer the Crab, Leo wanders aimlessly until he encounters another of the children, the Bull, plowing a field. "You cannot pull a plough," said the Bull, with a little touch of contempt. "I can, and that prevents me from thinking of the Scorpion."[167] Leo accepts the Bull's invitation to sing, and thus discovers his own vocation, trampling over the world singing that the "children of men must not be afraid."[168] The work of Leo and the Girl is so engrossing that "in their wanderings they came across the Bull, or the Ram, or the Twins, but all were too busy to do more than nod to each other across the crowd, and go on with their work."[169] Of course, only some people understand the real nature of Leo's song. After hearing it, Kipling tells us, some young men "grew impossibly conceited" and others "strove to be God and failed." But those who genuinely knew Leo's meaning "accomplished four times more work than they would have done under any other delusion."[170] The genuine workers of the world—the true workers of empire—remain an elite, and they do so by rejecting cosmic ambitions and focusing narrowly on the immediate.

Ironically, the other side of the need to fix rigid limits—and a reflection of the fantasy that informs it—is the desire for omnipotent authority. Such an ambition functions as a motive force behind the apparent modesty and matter-of-factness of "the day's work." Only within a carefully delineated sphere of action and jurisdiction could unlimited power be established and maintained. As noted, Kipling attributed this sort of mythic stature to the administrator and engineer who labored on specific projects in the remote areas of India, beyond the reach of bureaucratic influence. The one concern that inspires the rather cynical young Gallio is "a longing for absolute power which his undesirable district gratified."[171] Like the "omnipotent Assistant Collector," Kipling's other administrative heroes struggle against intruders from outside their jurisdictions as well as the anarchic elements within them. After the blunders of the central government have worked their havoc, Tallantire is able to subdue the Khusru Kheyl quickly and efficiently only by exceeding all his authority, and thus escaping the shackles of bureaucratic inertia. Hitchcock, Findlayson's assistant in "The Bridge-Builders," is forced to travel to London at his own expense to correct the bureaucratic bungling of the "Government of India" that has upset all their minute calculations.

Only absolute power, based on genuine knowledge of concrete conditions, will achieve orderly and efficient governance. Orde, whose authority is bred in the bone, is Kipling's paragon, as reflected in this contrast with the superficial, globe-trotting Pagett: "Orde in a shooting-coat, riding breeches, brown cowhide boots with spurs, and a battered flax helmet . . . had ridden some miles in the early morning to inspect a doubtful river-dam. The men's faces differed as much as their attire. Orde's, worn and wrinkled about the eyes and grizzled at the temples, was the harder and more square of the two."[172] Orde's physical toughness reflects a mental and emotional strength: he lives without illusion, knows his work and his territory intimately, and can stare his subjects in the eye. He is the living embodiment of untrammeled authority and of dedication to "things as they are."

Kipling's composite picture of the ideal "head of the district" represented a matrix of influences that cannot be easily disentangled. He was as much the captive of an ongoing myth of imperial order as he was the creator of one. His experience in India left him receptive both to the blandishments of British authority, and to the "dark" reminders of the shaky foundations on which it rested. Critics have noted how quickly the teenage Kipling adapted to the basic ideological posture of his fellow Anglo-Indians. Throughout his life, in fact, Kipling sought out and identified with powerful, authoritative individuals, the most notable being Cecil Rhodes. His friendship with Rhodes cemented his involvement in the Boer War at the end of the nineteenth century.[173] Kipling's identification with authority, his insistence on the concrete actuality of imperial rule—its omnipresence—seems to reflect a personal need for strong external authority as much as a political imperative.[174] As he comments in *Plain Tales*: "Never forget that unless the outward and visible signs of Our Authority are always before a native he is as incapable as a child of understanding what authority means, or where is the danger of disobeying it."[175] Authority, for the adult Kipling, needed to be buttressed by external force, a watchful eye that bears likeness to a primitive and predatory psychic "object." Nor is it insignificant that this statement on "the outward and visible signs of Our Authority" is drawn from "His Chance in Life," Kipling's story of the half-caste Michele D'Cruze, an especially dangerous "object" for Kipling, in view of his conflicting attractions to the black and white worlds.

In considering the objection that Kipling's Indian stories lack moral or emotional depth, Alan Sandison has suggested that such dissatisfaction among critics stems not from a lack of conflict or struggle within the stories, but from Kipling's almost reflexive adherence to the ultimate necessity of British rule, an adherence that seems to close off rather than to resolve the conflict within the stories themselves.[176] In these instances Kipling identified with the external embodiment of white authority so rigidly in order to ward off or segregate those "black" impulses he struggled to master. Kipling presented his own personal conflict as a universal political conflict, a struggle in which the regressive pull of instinctual behavior would bring down fragile civilizations unless external authority were strictly maintained. India, of course, worked as an object lesson to reinforce this conviction. But he could apply such a stern doctrine to Western politics as well, as in the political sketches he produced on returning to England from India. In "A Little Civilization" he depicted "an apostle of light . . . but one week divorced from his drawing room" under attack from the masses. He described "his mouth full of unprintable language,—bashing in a grand piano with a blood-stained gun butt. It had cost him thirty years to attain Insight, Repression, and Calm. Seven days turned him into a Turco. . . . For this is the nature of civilization."[177]

Both Kipling's preoccupation with emotional and social anarchy and the strategies he put forward for redressing it suggest, as noted throughout, deeply rooted concerns with control, his effort to reduce politics to administration, and administration, in turn, to sanitation. Perhaps the classic statement of this intent is contained in a sketch he published in the *Civil and Military Gazette* in 1888 entitled "New Brooms." In its conclusion a despairing district officer has this dialogue with the Government of India about Ram Buksh, the archetype of the educated Indian.

"But he's educated," said the Government of India.

"I'll concede everything," said the Englishman. "He's a statesman, author, poet, politician, artist, and all else that you wish him to be, but he isn't a Sanitary Engineer. And while you're training him he is dying. Goodness knows my share in the Government is very limited nowadays, but I'm willing to do all the work while he gets all the credit if you'll only let me have some authority over him in his mud-pie making."

"But the Liberty of the Subject is sacred," said the Government of India.

"*I* haven't any," said the Englishman. "He can trail through my compounds; start shrines in the public roads; poison my family; have me in the courts for nothing; ruin my character; spend my money, and call me an assassin when all is done. *I* don't object. Let me look after his sanitation."

"But the days of a paternal Government are over; we must depend on the people. Think of what they would say at Home," said the Government of India. "We have issued a Resolution—indeed we have!"

"What are you going to do?"

"Constitute more boards," said the Government of India. "Boards of Control and Supervision—Fund Boards—all sorts of Boards. Nothing like system."

The Englishman looked at the Resolution and sniffed. "It doesn't touch the weak point of the country."

"What *will* touch the weak point of the country, then?" said the Government of India.

"I used to," said the Englishman. "I was the District Officer, and I twisted their tails. You have taken away my power, and now—"

\* \* \*

"Never mind me," said the Englishman. "I'm an effete relic of the past. But Ram Buksh will die, as he used to do." [178]

As the former district officer asserts, he used to touch the weak point of the country when he "twisted their tails." And in his appeal of the Government of India he pleads to "let me have some authority over him in his mud-pie making." Even the exercise of imperial authority is imagined here as control over a modeling or shaping process associated with children's play.

Like the image of "mud-pie making," this ambition may have been encouraged by the "colored" or "black" pigment of the native Indian. Writing some years after his Indian experience to an American friend, R. A. Duckworth Ford, stationed in the Philippines, Kipling alluded to the emotional satisfaction of drilling native troops: "It's curious the fascination that white men feel drilling queer material into shape." [179] In a letter to Ford a year later bewailing the spread of democracy in the world, Kipling linked the love of drill to the possession of real power. "Power with responsibility is all that any man wants, and works and will cheerfully die for; and the more 'democratic' a land is the more urgently does one wish to flee from it and go out and drill Tugalongs or whatever you call your rapporees."[180] Kipling's image of the colonial administrator—of the men, as he once wrote to W. E. Henley, "who have built bridges and slain niggers and administered countries"[181]—is born out of this wish to flee reality in pursuit of a lost world, a child's world, of magical power and omnipotent control.

In the final analysis the phrase "drilling queer material into shape" can stand as an epitome of the imperial experience in Kipling's India. It expresses both his personal struggle with the power of "blackness" and the need to domesticate that power to the narrow discipline of work. To some extent, Kipling tries to redeem this rigid and oppressive ethic with laughter, healing laughter, the laughter of self-irony and hard-won insight. The "Children of the Zodiac" learn to laugh and, through that laughter, to achieve humanity. Laughter prevents his Anglo-Indians from taking their lot "too seriously." And ultimately, as in *Kim*, Kipling fixes on the notion of "the Great Game" to suggest the murky and remorseless process of imperial politics. In the last analysis the British presence in India has no clear-cut purpose, beyond the clichés such as "White Man's Burden" that Kipling throws off in his later, more political, period. His vision of India remains primarily just that—an intensely personal image that, despite the conventional views on which he draws, cannot be reconciled simply to any political or social reality.

## Conclusion

# Lord Curzon and the Eclipse of the Punjab Style

*Now it is not good for the Christian's health to hustle the Aryan Brown,*
*For the Christian riles, and the Aryan smiles, and he weareth the Christian*
*    down;*
*And the end of the fight is a tombstone white with the name of the late*
*    deceased,*
*And the epitaph drear: 'A Fool lies here who tried to hustle the East.'*
                                                              —*Rudyard Kipling*

Ｉn contrast to his lackluster predecessors, George Nathaniel Curzon made so striking an impression as Viceroy that even during his term in office he was finding his place in the pantheon of heroes of British India and the Punjab. One of his admirers, H. Caldwell Lipsett, wrote in 1903:

Two of the titulary deities of the Punjab down to the present day are "Jan Laren" [John Lawrence] and Nikalsayn [John Nicholson], strong men both, of an iron hand and indomitable resolution. It is safe to prophesy that in the coming years the name of "Curzon Lat Sahib" will be added to theirs as one of the great Englishmen who have impressed the imagination of India. He has shown himself a ruler of high ideals and strenuous performance. Lord Curzon is not a popular Viceroy and it would be affectation to pretend that he is. It is not the strong man's part to court popularity, but to rule the Empire committed to his charge wisely and well.[1]

Despite Curzon's acknowledged position among the giants of the Punjab, he never actually saw service in the province. Indeed, one of his most controversial and successful acts as Viceroy was to divide the Punjab, creating an independent administrative unit along the northwest frontier. Yet as much as any Englishman in India, Curzon embraced the legacy of Lawrence and Nicholson. He shared their "iron hand and indomitable resolution," always prepared, as Lipsett reminds us, to sacrifice his popularity to the demands of his conscience. He worked tirelessly on behalf of his paternalistic vision of British India, and in his devotion to the virile traditions of the frontier was the very embodiment of the Punjab Style. Indeed, under Curzon's rigorous leadership the administrative and political ideals initially associated with the Punjab at mid-century might be said to have reached their apogee in India.

At the same time, however, Curzon's period witnessed a turning point in the fortunes of the Indian nationalist movement. As a consequence of his policies, Indian nationalists achieved far greater organizational strength than they had previously attained. After Curzon's departure from India in 1905 a radical or extremist wing emerged within the Congress Party that was much more militant in its demands for representative institutions and eventual self-rule. In the same period the British government introduced its first significant reform measures, in an effort to appease at least moderate nationalist sentiment. In retrospect, Curzon's tenure in office signaled both a high point of the Punjab Style in India, and its apparent bankruptcy as a sustained source of imperial values.

## Education in Imperialism

Although both George Nathaniel Curzon and Rudyard Kipling became identified with British imperialism, their involvement with empire followed along almost opposite lines. And despite their shared reputation for brilliance and their conservative political views, the two men, though acquaintances, were never personally close. Kipling first met Curzon at Oxford in 1897 at a dinner party that included Henry James. Curzon later invited Kipling to be his guest at Simla in 1899, an invitation which Kipling refused, expressing the sentiment that "viceroys were not much in his line."[2]

Kipling shunned personal publicity and maintained a dim view of politics. Curzon remained an unremittingly public man, in spite of a rather mercurial political career in which he fell in and out of favor. Kipling came to his imperialist ideology through a tortuous process that was as much personal and aesthetic as it was political.

Curzon, by contrast, was attracted to imperialism at an early age, and it provided the leitmotif of his public career. On the eve of his departure for India in 1898, he told of his first infatuation with the British Empire in his student days at Eton. It occurred after an address by Sir James Fitzjames Stephen, "but just returned from India," who declared to the assembled boys "that there was in the Asian continent an empire more populous, more amazing, and more beneficent than that of Rome; that the rulers of that great dominion were drawn from the men of our own people; that some of them might perhaps in the future be taken from the ranks of the boys who were listening to his words." Since that day, Curzon stated, "the fascination, and, if I may say so, the sacredness of India have grown upon me, until I have come to think that it is the highest honor that can be placed upon any subject of the Queen that in any capacity, high or low, he should devote such energies as he may possess to its service."[3]

Curzon's recollection is interesting in a number of respects, not least in that it was Stephen, that adamantine authoritarian, who first planted the seed of British India in Curzon's imagination. The passage is also expressive of Curzon's secure place within the British political establishment. A few years after Curzon had left Eton and gone on to Balliol College, Kipling—whose parents could afford neither Eton nor Oxford—was expressing his envy of his first cousin Stanley Baldwin, who was in the sixth form at Harrow, Eton's rival as a bastion of upper-middle-class and aristocratic elitism.[4] It is no small irony that the same Stanley Baldwin was later to best Curzon for the leadership of the Conservative Party and the prime-ministership in 1923. More to the point, for all his ultimate identification with England and empire, Kipling was very much an outsider in social and political terms. He was literally "born" to India, as reflected in his emotional and artistic attachment to it. Curzon was no less complex a person, and in his own way deeply involved with the Oriental attributes of Indian life, but his interest in India was first of all expressive of his social position and his political ambition.

Curzon's public image was that of a strong-willed, sometimes arrogant individual. As the eldest son of the Rev. Alfred Nathaniel Holden Curzon, the fourth Baron Scaresdale, he was proud of his aristocratic connections,[5] and from his arrival at Balliol he cultivated both Tory politics and a taste for refined living,[6]—qualities well captured in an admiring letter from an American who was a contemporary of Curzon's at Oxford:

As an undergraduate at Oxford I attended the Union debates and noted the best speakers. As an unprejudiced observer I was interested more in studying the types of men than in weighing their political arguments. You were the only man I found who perfectly filled my ideal of what a young representative of the Conservative, and especially the aristocratic, party should be. It was the intense aristocratic turn of your disposition which forcibly struck me.[7]

Curzon's biographer, Lord Rolandshay, described him at Oxford as "A striking figure, tall, straight and rigid, bearing himself with a loftiness uncommon among men of his age, he made an immediate impression upon all with whom he came into contact."[8] An older friend, Richard Farrer, wrote to him on his twenty-first birthday: "There is no fellow among my friends and acquaintances who starts on his majority with greater gifts, or who shows more likelihood of turning them to good account. Only beware of the besetting danger of any young man possessed of talent, position and good looks—I mean that of trying to do too many things at once."[9] The epithet "a most superior person"—a line from a doggerel verse written by a friend of Curzon's—branded him in his early twenties and the description stuck, much to the delight of detractors later on in his political career.[10] Beyond his aristocratic hauteur and political ambitions, Curzon possessed genuine intellectual ability. He had swept the field of academic prizes at Eton, and at a time when personal distinction at such a school provided credentials for the highest political circles, friends were already referring to "the brief interval which must intervene between Eton and the Cabinet."[11] Curzon's performance at Oxford did nothing to detract from his reputation. Although he allowed his studies to take second place to his social and political activities, he accomplished the unprecedented feat of winning two major history prizes in his final year, and received a coveted nomination as a Fellow to All Souls College.[12]

During the period from his graduation in 1882 to his appointment as Viceroy to India in 1898, Curzon served in Parliament and rose within the ranks of the Conservative Party as a spokesman for its foreign policy. After an eloquent maiden speech in the House of Commons in 1886, he was regarded as one of the House's most accomplished and most florid orators. He served initially as a private secretary to Lord Salisbury and then, under a Tory cabinet organized by Salisbury in the 1890s, as Under Secretary of State for Foreign Affairs and as a member of the Privy Council.

More influential, perhaps, than Curzon's parliamentary experience for his views on foreign policy were his extensive travels in Asia. During these years he undertook two trips around the world, and through his journalistic accounts, published in *The Times* (of London), and books he established himself as a noted authority on Asian culture and politics. He first visited India in 1887, returning to Central Asia the following year to gather materials for a book on Russian expansion in that area and its implications for the British Empire. A trip to Persia next produced the book for which he is best known, *Persia and the Persian Question*, an exhaustive two-volume treatment of Persian culture, society, and politics. He made two further Asian expeditions in the early 1890s, one to the Far East and the other to the Himalayan region, before the pressures of political office and marriage began to impinge on his freedom to travel. By virtue of his Asian experience, and the grave problems on the northwest frontier created by the forward policy, Curzon was regarded as a natural choice to succeed Lord Elgin as Viceroy when he was appointed in 1898. He was the first Viceroy since Lawrence to be equipped for his position with a specialized knowledge of Indian society and Asian politics.

Curzon's outlook was compounded of an unusual blend of aristocratic pride, romanticism, and moral rectitude. As might be expected, James Stephen's early influence left Curzon with an understanding of Britain's world role in which omnipotent control was wedded to the ideal of political and social order. Writing to his father of his impressions of Singapore, Curzon wrote that "the strength and omnipotence of England everywhere in the East is amazing. No other country or people is to be compared with her; we control everything, and are liked as well as respected and feared."[13] He linked such control to the enlightened leadership of the British "proconsul." "I record it to our credit and praise that—so far as my experience goes—our home Government is served by as able and enlightened a body of men as ever carried or sustained a conquering flag in foreign lands," he declared with youthful enthusiasm. "The industry, the capacity and the service of these men are beyond praise."[14]

Curzon's conception of the British Empire was a romantic one. Like Disraeli, he prided himself on the expansion and splendor of British sovereignty overseas. Among the Viceroys of British India he was the greatest advocate of Oriental pomp and circumstance, as expressed in the elaborately staged Coronation Durbar of 1903 in honor of King Edward VII.

It was a scene that made one catch one's breath in wonder; for those who saw it nothing will ever dim the memory of the solemn irresistible march of the elephants, the swaying howdahs of burnished gold and silver, the proud Maharajahs seated on high, the clanging bells and the strains of martial music, the silent, motionless enveloping troops, the uncountable crowds in radiant vestments, and the majestic setting, the mighty cathedral mosque and the vast red fort, and the umbrageous park between. The Durbar can be repeated again, but not that unforgettable spectacle.[15]

Like Kipling, Curzon was fascinated by the mysteries of Eastern life that frustrated rational comprehension. In enlarging on the contrasts between East and West in his work on Persia, Curzon asked, "Do we ever escape from the fascination of a turban, or the mystery of the shrouded apparitions that pass for women in the dusty alleys? . . . How mute and overpowering the silence that prevails over the lone expanse, so different from the innumerable rural sounds that strike the ear at home."[16] Even more impressive were the contradictions that marked "the elements and conditions" of Oriental life. After citing the extremes of nature where "the transition is as awful as from life to death," he pointed to the extremes of Persian personality.

The finest domestic virtues co-exist with barbarity and supreme indifference to suffering. Elegance of deportment is compatible with a coarseness amounting to bestiality. The same individual is at different moments haughty and cringing. A creditable acquaintance with the standards of civilization does not prevent gross fanaticism and superstition. Accomplished manners and a more than Parisian polish cover a superb faculty for lying and almost scientific imposture. The most scandalous corruption is combined with a scrupulous regard for specific precepts of the moral law.[17]

The magic of Persia—and of all of Asia, for that matter—was imagined by Curzon in terms of abrupt and violent contrast. And reciprocally, Curzon described as a form of magic "the wand of a European magician"—the imperialist impulse of the British and other European nations.[18]

## Curzon as Viceroy

Arriving as Viceroy of India in 1898, Curzon responded to the magical character of native life—to its "sluggish pools of superstition" and its allegedly mercurial population—with an imperious magic of his own. In his exacting devotion to work, in his paternalistic vision of Britain's role in India, and in his romantic attachment to the frontier, he confronted the magic he perceived in native life with the magic we have associated with the Punjab Style.

Although lacking the evangelical conviction of some of his predecessors in India, Curzon was attracted to the rhetorical and moral force of the Old Testament, and to the fervor of the New Testament, as the taproot of his imperial idealism. In his last speech before leaving India in 1905, he proclaimed that "the Almighty has placed your hand on the greatest of His ploughs, in whose furrows the nations of the world are germinating and taking shape, to drive the blade a little forward in your time, and to feel that somewhere among these millions you have left a little justice or happiness or prosperity, a sense of manliness or moral dignity, a spring of patriotism, a dawn of intellectual enlightenment, or a stirring of duty, where it did not before exist—that is enough, that is the Englishman's justification in India."[19] Curzon saw himself and the Raj as the incarnation of righteousness and moral order in India. Echoing James Stephen, he ascribed Britain's success in India above all to her adherence to the law, an irreproachable sense of justice that enabled a "handful" of Englishmen to subdue a civilization with traditions that predated those of their own society.[20]

As Viceroy, Curzon administered the law with an impartiality toward all the races in India—both native and European—that reawakened some of the animosity within the Anglo-Indian community that had been kindled twenty years earlier by the Ilbert con-

troversy. But unlike Ripon then, Curzon was firm enough and convinced enough of the fragility of Britain's position in India to resist
pressure from fellow Anglo-Indians.[21] "I know," Curzon stated,
"that as long as Europeans, and particularly a haughty race like the
English, rule Asiatic people like the Indians, incidents of *hubris* and
violence will occur, and that the white men will tend to side with
the white skin against the dark. But I also know, and have acted
throughout on the belief, that it is the duty of statesmanship to arrest these dangerous symptoms and to prevent them from attaining
dimensions that might even threaten the existence of our rule in the
future."[22]

Although wedded to administrative impartiality, and astute enough
to recognize the potential pitfalls of racial arrogance, he nonetheless
espoused the moral superiority of the English to his native audi-
ences. Speaking to the students at Calcutta University, he attributed
the Englishman's imperial success to "universal belief in his integrity, his sincerity, and his purpose. People know that his heart is in
his task, and that, when the pinch comes, he will stick to his post."
Then he went on "without a trace of national vanity" to say, "Go
you and do likewise"[23]—the phrase Jesus addressed to his disciples.
In keeping with the great Punjabis of the mid-nineteenth century,
he seemed to thrive on work. All his biographers agree that, like
John Lawrence, he drove himself and his subordinates relentlessly.
He relished the effective exercise of power and struck against the
bureaucratization of Indian government at "both ends," praising the
energetic "man on the spot" in the best Punjab tradition, while trying to tighten the slack reins of viceregal authority at the expense of
the bureaucratic departments and the provincial governments.[24]
Like many driven men, he found it difficult to delegate authority
effectively.

Unfortunately for Curzon and India, the "magic" of character
and of work was dynamically related to the growing sense of isolation that dogged the Anglo-Indian community in the closing years
of the nineteenth century. The widely shared sense of self-sacrifice
to an unappreciative native population found no more articulate
spokesman than Lord Curzon. Under the burden of viceregal work
he depicted himself as a horse who "staggers and drops between the
shafts" until "another animal is brought to take its place."[25] To him,

as to Kipling, the isolated and unappreciated civil servant was the backbone of empire.

I think you only see the Civil Service at its very best when it is working under the strain of some great affliction or disaster in India, such, for instance, as plague or famine. Plague was continuous through my time; famine marked a considerable portion of it. It is at those moments that you realize, more fully than at any other, the real devotion of the Service, not only to the cause of duty, but to the interests of the people of India themselves. Our Civil Servants on those occasions will work themselves to the bone in the discharge of their duty. Very often the eye of no official lights upon their labours; sometimes, perhaps too often, no order shines upon their breasts. And yet they go on working up to the end even, sometimes, at the sacrifice of their lives.[26]

And yet the pain of official neglect was nothing against the sting experienced from the native Indians' lack of appreciation of the sacrifices made in their behalf. Reflecting many years later on his opposition to racial injustice in India, he commented: "I spent many anxious hours in dealing with cases of racial injustice. But it counted as dust in the balance when I was unable to make political concessions for which I held—and possibly I was not wrong—that the country was not yet ripe."[27]

In expressing himself in these terms, Curzon suggested the fateful conflict between a wish to be admired by native Indians and a chronic inability—one almost universally shared within the Anglo-Indian community—to view them, perhaps even potentially, as equals capable of political autonomy. As Viceroy, Curzon voiced the conventional sentiments out of which the "illusion of permanence" had been fabricated. He reaffirmed the fundamental principle of a British *corps d'élite* to administer India, arguing that "partly by education, partly by heredity, partly by upbringing, the knowledge of principles of Government, the habits of mind, and the vigour of character," only the British were capable of effective rule in India.[28] The corollary to this conviction was a disparaging notion of Indian political capacity, expressed in private if not in public. In a letter to Arthur Balfour during his term in office, Curzon maintained, in response to a proposal to include a native on his Executive Council, "that in the whole continent there is not one Indian fit for the post."[29]

Curzon was also enamored of the contrast between the "real" Indian and his unnatural counterpart, the deracinated Western-educated native. He deplored the influence of Thomas Macaulay on Indian education in the nineteenth century;[30] and, along with other Anglo-Indian officials, actively disliked the class of dissident lawyers and congressmen which, he felt, Macaulay's reforms had fostered. He advised young Indian students to avoid politics and devote themselves instead to the struggle against backwardness and ignorance. In this spirit he dedicated his own administration to improving the lot of "the real people of India, the patient, humble, silent millions, the 80 percent who subsist by agriculture, who know very little of policies, but who profit or suffer by their results. . . . he cannot read at all; he has no politics. But he is the bone and sinew of the country, by the sweat of his brow the soil is tilled."[31]

For Curzon the plight of the humble millions constituted a mandate for viewing domestic politics purely in administrative terms; he regarded administrative efficiency as "a synonym for the contentment of the governed."[32] If detractors have exaggerated in suggesting that in his zeal for administrative reform Curzon lost sight of the more general objectives of government,[33] such criticism points to the degree to which administrative reform, like the partition of Bengal, was posed as an alternative to political change. In contrast to preceding administrations, Curzon did provide dynamic leadership and achieved an enviable, if sometimes controversial, record of reform. In their broad intent Curzon's policies were very much the incarnation of the Punjab Style, even when applied at the upper echelons of the government. By improving the character and quality of British administration, Curzon hoped to stave off the demand for political reform, and to strengthen traditionally conservative elements in Indian society at the expense of progressive and politically dissident ones.

In this regard Curzon's first preoccupation as Viceroy was with the bureaucratic procedures of the central administration. Early in his Viceroyalty Curzon described the bureaucratic system as a "gigantic quagmire or bog, into which every question that comes along either sinks or is sucked down."[34] He attempted to accelerate decision-making and reduce paper work to reasonable proportions, while enhancing his own position at the head of the bureaucracy.

He was responsible for a major overhaul of the Indian railway system in the interest of efficiency and profitability, and for a concentrated effort to improve and protect traditional Indian agriculture. True to his declared resolve to govern for the benefit of the peasantry, he sponsored extensive irrigation projects and the development of improved agricultural husbandry. Of more immediate concern, he introduced the Punjab Land Alienation Act of 1900, and supported legislation to establish rural co-operative credit societies as an alternative source of agricultural financing.[35]

Perhaps Curzon's concern with the reform of Indian education best reflected the priorities inherent in the Punjab Style. After a few years as Viceroy, he was convinced that Western education had been artificially grafted onto India, producing a graduate inclined "to a tone of mind and to a type of character that is ill-regulated, averse from discipline, discontented, and in some cases actually disloyal."[36] The reforms he initiated, though too broad in scope and too complex to be discussed here, were designed in large part to arrest the influence of political Westernization as against pragmatic modernization. One facet of this program was a much greater stress on education in the vernacular at the primary level. For higher education Curzon tried to fashion a policy that would provide for greater governmental control of university policy, and encourage the study of science and technology. These areas had been neglected—as they had been in Britain itself—because of the classical and humanistic focus of nineteenth-century British education.[37] These reforms aroused the ire of Indian critics who saw them—not inaccurately—as an effort to undermine the potential of the universities as a political training ground. In general, it might be said, Curzon's efforts to divorce the issue of administrative functioning from the political working of government simply accelerated the opposition of Indian nationalists to his policies.

Perhaps the purest expression of Curzon's imaginative involvement with the Punjab Style was his infatuation with the northwest frontier. He felt the magic of the frontier as keenly as any of the Punjabis at mid-century—a fact reflected in his explorations in the Himalayas in the 1890s, and in the degree to which he was drawn to the problem of the Russian "menace" during the decade or so before he became Viceroy. In office he continued to respond to the starkness and the grandeur of the mountains, and to the elemental qualities of the natives who inhabited them. And like the earlier Punjabis he employed Biblical figures to articulate his feelings. "I am never so happy as when on the Frontier," he confided to his friend St. John Brodrick in 1900. "I know these men and how to handle them. They are brave as lions, wild as cats, docile as children. You have to be very frank, very conciliatory, very firm, very generous, very fearless. It is with a sense of pride that one receives the honest homage of these magnificent Samsons, bearded, instinct with loyalty, often stained with crime."[38] Like his predecessors, Curzon reacted both to the contradictory qualities he perceived in the Pathan, and to a strain of independent spirit with which he strongly identified. "Those wild clansmen have an individuality . . . a manliness in their patriotism and a love of independence in their blood that is akin to our own."[39]

Curzon was equally attracted to the British officers who endured the hazards of frontier service, and whose independence and resourcefulness were akin to those of the Pathans. And like Henry Lawrence, he was enamored of the energy and youthfulness frontier service demanded. He expressed his admiration for "the young officer who exceeds his instructions or who takes the bit between his teeth. . . . We employ, and we rightly employ, the greybeards in our councils and in positions of supreme control; but on the outskirts of civilization we require the energy, the vitality, and physical strength of youth."[40] He saw the northwest frontier much as he saw the American frontier earlier in the nineteenth century. It provided for Britain the physical and moral terrain necessary for an expansive and "imperialistic" race. Just as American character had blossomed only through the frontier experience, Curzon saw "a corresponding discipline for the men of our stock . . . on the outskirts of Empire, where the machine is relatively impotent and the individual is strong . . . an ennobling and invigorating stimulus for our youth, saving them alike from the corroding ease and the morbid excitements of Western civilization."[41]

It is one of the ironies of Curzon's tenure in India that, despite his involvement with the mythology and politics of the Punjab, he was responsible for its dismemberment. In 1901 Curzon received support from the Cabinet in London to set up a new northwest frontier province that would be directly responsible to the Viceroy. Curzon's principal motives were to achieve more direct control over frontier policy in the event of a major outbreak of violence, and to create a provincial administration specifically with frontier policy in mind. Despite strenuous resistance from career officers in the Punjab, and fear in London that Curzon would use the new province as a base for a dangerously aggressive frontier campaign, his policy was soon recognized as a success.

Curzon retreated from the forward positions established along the frontier in the 1890s after the tensions produced by these outposts ignited a series of costly conflicts with the native tribes. He held on only to a few strategic positions, and tried to enlist support among co-operative tribes as an alternative to British military presence. His policy might be seen as a compromise between the "masterly inactivity" of the Lawrences and the forward policy of Lansdowne and Elgin. The consequence was a remarkable period of peace along the frontier, which left Curzon a freer hand in imperial diplomacy. The only troubling aspect of his foreign policy was the abrasive manner in which he had overridden the objections of the Punjab's Lieutenant-Governor, Macworth Young, and other officers in the province, for it foreshadowed the highhandedness that was his undoing in his last two years as Viceroy.[42]

Curzon resigned his office in the summer of 1905, early in his second term as Viceroy, after a protracted struggle with Lord Kitchener, Commander-in-Chief of the Indian army, and with the home government. By the end of his tenure Curzon felt exhausted and isolated, his authority undermined by the India Council in London and by the persistent attacks of native critics.[43] Was his resignation to be attributed to the eclipse of the Punjab Style, the dissipation of the "illusion of permanence" in the face of the political demands of a determined Indian nationalist movement? This, surely, is part of the story, but the historical record is much more complex. It is true that the Morley-Minto reforms—named for the Secretary of State and the new Viceroy respectively—which followed Curzon's departure constituted the first serious attempt to come to terms with native political aspirations. No doubt it would have been a hazardous undertaking to establish another purely paternalistic government in India after Curzon's downfall. Nonetheless, neither Curzon's unmitigated paternalism nor Indian political critics brought him down. His resignation was forced by an accumulating pattern of strained relations with responsible ministers in Whitehall, and by the charismatic appeal of Lord Kitchener as Commander-in-Chief. Part of this predicament was brought on by Curzon himself, as supercilious and highhanded in his dealings with his political peers as he was with native Indians. And he proudly resisted any limit on his autocratic authority originating in London. When disputes arose over his handling of the Punjab, the Coronation Durbar of 1903, or the administration of the Bengal, he could become unyielding and irascible.[44]

Curzon's dispute with Kitchener is another matter. Here he faced an opponent as stubborn and supercilious as himself, and he is entitled to much sympathy for the treatment he endured at Kitchener's hands. Although, not surprisingly, their disagreement rapidly degenerated into personal vituperation, it revolved around a grave matter of policy: whether the civil or the military government would have ultimate control over the Indian army. After a Machiavellian series of intrigues and maneuvers by both parties, Kitchener and the army won out, not so much on the merits of the case as by virtue of the overwhelming popularity of Kitchener in Britain. It boiled down to a choice between the two men, and Curzon was regarded by the government in London as the more expendable. Feeling betrayed and abandoned, he saw no alternative but to resign his post.[45]

It would be mistaken, nonetheless, to underestimate the alienation of middle-class Indians—especially Bengalis—in the later stages of Curzon's term in office. The issue around which native dissent crystallized was the administrative division of Bengal, an action which placed both the strengths and limitations of the Punjab Style in sharp perspective. More than anything else, the controversy that raged in Bengal in 1904 illustrated the sharp division between Curzon's administrative orientation and the political aspirations of native Bengalis. Curzon was probably correct in his view that Bengal, as the largest administrative unit under British control, was too unwieldy to be ruled effectively. And, most likely, his political animus against Bengali nationalists took second place to his concern with the efficient and effective administration of the area. Yet from the first the plan was received by the province's intellectuals as an attack upon the growing solidarity of Bengali nationalism. And in campaigning for his reform in Bengal in 1904, he confronted the universal hostility of the native press, and mass demonstrations against partition.[46]

Public resistance, however, only deepened Curzon's determination to carry through with his program. He responded by dismissing the extent of opposition to partition, or by branding that opposition as unreasonable or seditious. Even a sympathetic biographer like Lawrence Zetland (Lord Ronaldshay) cites his "almost contemptuous indifference toward the agitation which his proposals had aroused."[47] Writing to St. John Brodrick in 1904, Curzon belittled the Bengali opposition in these terms:

> You can scarcely have any idea of the utter want of proportion, moderation or sanity that characterises native agitation in this country. Starting with some preposterous fiction or exaggeration, the Bengali, after repeating it a few times, ends by firmly believing its truth. He lashes himself into a fury over the most insignificant issues, and he revels in his own stage thunder in the happy conviction that owing to the circumstances of the case it can provoke no reply.[48]

After partition had been forced through, the scars of the struggle were apparent in Curzon's speech at Calcutta University in 1905, when he told the students, "I hope I am making no false or arrogant claim when I say that the highest ideal of truth is to a large extent a Western conception."[49]

The wounds on either side of the dispute over Bengal never healed fully. Curzon's arrogance and shortsightedness further isolated him both from native Indians and his supporters in London. The episode helped immeasurably to strengthen the nationalist movement in Bengal and elsewhere in India. Within Bengal itself the *swadeshi* or "own country" struggle against administrative partition marked a high point of agitational politics. Moreover, it accelerated the further growth of a nationalist press in that region. Outside of Bengal, *swadeshi* elicited the support of radicals like the west Indian leader Bal Gangadhar Tilak and promoted the growth of nationalism on an all-India basis. In the wake of the agitation the Indian National Congress came to resemble an organized party rather than a collection of loosely tied groups. An extremist wing emerged within the Congress under Tilak's direction that pressed the party to formulate a more radical program. At the same time terrorist movements were organized in Bengal, western India, and the Punjab.

The British responded to these developments by chastising extremists and terrorists while trying to mollify more moderate opinion. Tilak was jailed on a charge of seditious behavior in 1909. But in that same year the Morley-Minto reforms were instituted to appease nationalist sentiment. Although the Indian Councils Act, as it was formally known, fell far short of creating representative institutions, it provided for the expansion of the Imperial Legislative Councils and for the indirect election of twenty-seven of its sixty members. Moreover, the powers of the Council were expanded in a way that foreshadowed full parliamentary government. In 1911, when the capital was moved from Calcutta to Delhi, the partition of Bengal was revoked, much to the satisfaction of Bengali public opinion. Thanks to these conciliatory policies the full force of Indian nationalism was not felt until a few years later under the impact of World War I. But for many Indians the struggle with Curzon had laid open to question the very legitimacy of the British Raj.[50]

### Kipling and Curzon

The controversy over the division of Bengal revealed not only the limitations of Curzon's ideological outlook, but also some of his personal limitations. This is no place for a full-scale psychological treatment of Curzon, except to note in passing how some of his early experiences and his personality traits paralleled those of Kipling and harmonized with the behavioral mandates of the Punjab Style.

Both Kipling and Curzon were apparently harshly treated in childhood by a parental substitute. In comparison to Kipling's mistreatment by Aunty Rosa, Curzon's was administered in a more conventionally Victorian manner by a governess who assumed the primary responsibility for his upbringing from distant and seemingly indifferent parents. As he described her in diaries written many years later, "this remarkable woman controlled the first five of our family for over ten years and left on all of us a mark which has never been effaced. She taught us good habits, economy, neatness, method, and a dislike of anything vulgar or fast. But in her savage moments she was a brutal and vindictive tyrant and I have often thought since that she must have been insane."[51]

This Miss Paraman so terrorized Curzon and his siblings that they never had the courage to tell their father or mother, a secret suffering like that which Kipling also preferred to endure. And many of the public humiliations reported by Kipling—such as being paraded through the streets with the sign "liar" on his back—were similar to those to which Curzon was exposed. Curzon described one such incident: "She shut us up in darkness, practiced upon us every kind of petty persecution, wounded our pride in dressing us (me in particular) in red shining calico petticoats (I was obliged to make my own) with an immense conical cap on our heads round which, as well as on our breasts and back, were sewn strips of paper bearing in enormous characters written by ourselves the words Liar Sneak Coward Lubber and the like."[52]

Curzon emerged into adulthood as a deeply divided personality. Not unlike Kipling, Curzon could be warm and personable in surroundings where he felt comfortable. He was admired by his friends for his wit and charm, and in the aristocratic circles in which he passed his social life he had a reputation as a practiced romancer.[53] Like Kipling, he married an American woman and idealized her in the best Victorian tradition. He became quite dependent on her emotionally and was prostrated by her death in 1906, an event whose tragedy surpassed his defeat in India the year before.

This image of the warm private man must be balanced by that of the "most superior person." Curzon's biographers agree that he quickly became aloof and superior when uneasy in a public situation. He had great difficulty in sharing responsibility, and carried out all his activities—both public and private—with an obsessive attention to details that he rationalized as the mark of all great men.[54] He threw himself into his work compulsively, to the point of physical and mental exhaustion. Such self-mastery and personal power were purchased at the price of a sharp sense of isolation and—to use Kipling's term—"breaking strain." As with Kitchener, Curzon seemed always to personalize public disputes. He was extremely sensitive to criticism throughout his career, to the point of paranoia in his later cabinet post as Foreign Minister under Lloyd

George.[55] And ironically, in the light of his criticism of the Indian officials' lack of staunch character, he could be emotionally unstable in a crisis, breaking easily into tears as he did in one of his confrontations with Kitchener.[56] Beside the stalwart image of Curzon as the incarnation of the Law must be placed that of a hypersensitive and isolated figure driven almost to breakdown by imperial office.

The contradictions apparent in Lord Curzon's personality—and in that of Kipling as well—encompassed the contrasting elements that characterized the Punjab Style. The conflict between the paternalism of the Punjab heroes, with its strong affective content, and their rigid adherence to the Law as a sanctuary against personal and public anarchy, divided Anglo-Indian culture in the latter half of the nineteenth century as decisively as it did the personalities of Kipling and Curzon. And it found expression in the institutional and social life of British India in the late nineteenth century, as well as in its mythology. Only in the Punjab did these contradictory responses achieve a brilliant if unstable fusion. There, for a time, a special set of historical circumstances allowed a direct and zealous style of imperial administration—one sanctioned by the language and moral urgency of evangelical conviction—to contain the dissident elements out of which Britain's imperial rule was constituted. Such a fortuitous amalgam may, by its very nature, have been only temporary; but it remained, at the very least, an important emotional and ideological bulwark for the Anglo-Indian community into the twentieth century.

If Kipling and Curzon may be cited as two prototypical exponents of the Punjab Style, they can also be placed in emotional or cultural opposition to each other. Within the spectrum of figures we have considered, Kipling came closest to genuine identification with native India, the "dark" dimension of the Anglo-Indian imagination that was drawn to fantasized images of native life. The conflict between his empathy with native India and his self-conscious adherence to the Law of Anglo-Indian society was, we have suggested, largely responsible for the underlying appeal of his work. Curzon, by contrast, was the very incarnation of the official values of British India, as well as the sense of moral superiority and of arrogance that were components of these values. Their positions on opposite ends of such a spectrum can be regarded as a measure of their respective stature. Kipling came closest to representing the imperial imagination in its full breadth and complexity. Curzon embodied as much as anyone the exacting sense of justice that has since become the legacy of the British experience in imperial administration.

At the same time it must be acknowledged that the limitations of men like Kipling and Curzon—expressed in feelings of isolation or fantasies of omnipotent power—must also be seen as part of the fabric of the British imperial experience in India. In the long run the Punjab Style was too unstable, too magical in its aspirations for omnipotent control, to respond flexibly to the pressures exerted by native Indians for recognition as independent and autonomous people in their own right. The need to contain the regressive impulses that found symbolic expression in native culture made it impossible for the British to recognize their own "object hunger" and their desire for absolute control at both the emotional and political levels. Under the threat of loss—expressed in native demands to participate in the political and administrative institutions introduced into Indian culture by the British themselves—these magical aspirations crystallized around a mythology of imperial rule that had become increasingly grandiose and increasingly empty by Curzon's time in India. It may be merely trite to say that the very greatness of the British Raj contained the seeds of its ultimate dissolution; but it is nonetheless clear that such a style of imperial rule successfully masked the emotional foundations of British government in India, and helped to render political transformation all the more traumatic when it finally came.

# NOTE ON SOURCES

The research materials for this book included both published and unpublished primary sources. For published materials on nineteenth-century British India and on Anglo-Indian fiction, I used the collections at Widener Library, Harvard University, and the British Library in London. Unpublished papers on major figures in British India, such as John Lawrence and Henry Lawrence, were examined at the India Office Library, London. Volumes of the first newspaper in India for which Kipling wrote, the *Civil and Military Gazette*, were studied at the newspaper division of the India Office Library. I examined a variety of unpublished materials on Rudyard Kipling, including the Kipling Collection at the Houghton Library, Harvard University; the Carpenter Collection at the Library of Congress; the Berg Collection at the New York Public Library, and letters from Kipling to W. E. Henley at the Morgan Library in New York.

# CHAPTER NOTES

## *Preface*

1. Edmund Gosse, "Rudyard Kipling," quoted from *Kipling: The Critical Heritage*, ed. Roger Lancelyn Green (London: Routledge & Kegan Paul, 1971), pp. 106–07. Gosse attributed the same impact to the French writer on exotic subjects, Pierre Loti.

2. Rudyard Kipling, "The Man Who Would Be King," *The Phantom Rickshaw: The Burwash Edition of the Complete Works and Verse of Rudyard Kipling* (New York: AMS Press, 1970), 3:195. All subsequent references to Kipling's works will be taken from this edition, unless otherwise indicated.

3. "Without Benefit of Clergy," *Life's Handicap*, Works 4:159–61.

4. *Ibid.*, p. 161.

5. Alan Sandison, "A Matter of Vision: Rudyard Kipling and Rider Haggard," in *The Age of Kipling*, ed. John Gross (New York: Simon and Schuster, 1972), p. 128.

6. The most prominent recent work that has criticized psychohistory through the weakness of psychoanalytic theory is David F. Stannard's *Shrinking History: On Freud and the Failure of Psychohistory* (New York: Oxford University Press, 1980). Stannard examines not only what he sees as the logical flaws and the theoretical weakness of psychoanalysis, but also what he argues is its failure to justify itself as a model of therapy. In explicating and criticizing the theory, Stannard focuses almost exclusively on Freudian constructs and pays no systematic attention to more recent developments in psychoanalytic ego psychology. In a recent review the historian Dominick Cavallo provides a critique of Stannard's argument; see *Social Science History* 5 (Fall 1981), 492–95.

7. A highly polemical critique of scientific approaches to history, including both psychohistory and quantitative history, is contained in Jacques Barzun's *Clio and the Doctors: Psychohistory, Quanto-History, and History* (Chicago: Chicago University Press, 1974).

8. A continual theme in Erikson's writing, this is perhaps most explicitly emphasized in his treatment of the concept of identity. See *Identity, Youth and Crisis* (New York: Norton, 1968).

9. In *Psychoanalytic Theory, Therapy, and the Self* (New York: Basic Books, 1971), Harry Guntrip provides a short account of the development of an object relations approach among British psychoanalysts, including discussions of Melanie Klein, Ronald Fairbairn, and Donald Winnicott. Otto Kernberg, in *Borderline Conditions and Pathological Narcissism* (New York: Jason Aronson, 1975), describes borderline personality organization as characterized by chronic anxiety, multiple neurotic symptoms, and severe character pathology. See Ch. 1, "The Syndrome," pp. 3–47.

10. Otto Kernberg discusses this process in depth in *Object Relations Theory*

*and Clinical Psychoanalysis* (New York: Jason Aronson, 1976). See especially pp. 19–107.

11. In *Psychoanalytic Sociology* (Baltimore: Johns Hopkins University Press, 1973), Gerald Platt and Fred Weinstein describe the development of psychoanalytic theory toward a concern with shared social and cultural values. They establish what is essentially an object relations approach to the mechanisms by which such shared assumptions influence motivation and behavior at an individual level.

12. Erikson has employed the term "originology" to describe the effort to trace motivations in history to their sources in individual pathology. See *Young Man Luther* (New York: Norton, 1962), especially p. 18. For a thoughtful treatment of the problem of reductionism, along with other methodological issues facing psychohistorians, see Robert J. Brugger, "The House of Many Gables," in *Ourselves/Our Past: Psychological Approaches to American History*, ed. Robert J. Brugger (Baltimore: Johns Hopkins University Press, 1981), pp. 1–34.

13. D. C. Hamer makes this point in a recent essay on the nineteenth-century British politician William Gladstone. See "Gladstone: The Making of a Political Myth," *Victorian Studies* 22 (Autumn 1978), 29.

14. In "Leader and Led, Individual and Group," *The Psychohistory Review* 9 (Spring 1981), 214–37, Bruce Mazlish argues that the meaning that an individual or a leader has for a group should be a major focal point of psychohistorical investigations.

15. Gerald Platt, "Thoughts on a Theory of Collective Action: Language, Affect and Ideology in Revolution," in *New Directions in Psychohistory*, ed. Mel Albin (Lexington, Mass.: D. C. Heath, 1980), p. 83.

16. *Ibid.*, p. 83.

17. Jacob Arlow, "Ego Psychology and the Study of Mythology," *Journal of the American Psychoanalytic Association* 9 (July 1961), 375.

18. This view is presented by Max H. Stern in "Ego Psychology, Myth and Rite: Remarks about the Relationship of the Individual and the Group," *The Psychoanalytic Study of Society*, Vol. 3, ed. Warner Meunsterberger (New York: International Universities Press, 1964), p. 90.

19. See Dennis Kinkaid, *British Social Life in India 1608–1937* (London: G. Routledge, 1938), and Francis Hutchins, *The Illusion of Permanence* (Princeton: Princeton University Press, 1967), especially Ch. 5, "British Indian Society: A Middle Class Aristocracy," pp. 101–18.

20. Octave Mannoni, *Prospero and Caliban: The Psychology of Colonialism* (New York: Praeger, 1964), p. 82. See Mannoni's chapter "The Cult of the Dead and the Family," pp. 49–59, for a description of ancestral worship among the Malagasies.

21. *Ibid.*, p. 64.

22. See Mannoni's chapter "Crusoe and Prospero," pp. 97–109, in *Prospero*.

23. See Erikson's *Identity, Youth and Crisis* for an example of such an approach.

24. In their essay on the integration of psychoanalysis and sociology, *Psychoanalytic Sociology*, p. 89, Weinstein and Platt describe the relationship between society and the individual as that between two "somewhat related action systems." They argue that there is a partially unconscious commitment in both the individual and social "systems" to the same set of generalized symbolic codes. At the same time they maintain that within this generalized symbolic relationship there are significant individual variations that account for "unique, discrete personalities." In general the essay is the most authoritative discussion of the social implications of psychoanalytic theory.

## Introduction

1. Leonard Woolf, *Growing: An Autobiography of the Years 1904 to 1911* (London: Hogarth, 1961), p. 46.
2. "Anglo-Indian" is a term used conventionally to designate the British community in India during the nineteenth century. In the twentieth century "Anglo-Indian" has come to be used to identify Indians of mixed European and Indian descent.
3. Woolf, *Growing*, p. 46.
4. Alice Fleming, "Some Childhood Memories of Rudyard Kipling," *Chambers Journal* (March, 1939), p. 171. Kipling's autobiographical story "Baa, Baa Black Sheep," *Wee Willie Winkie, Works* 3 : 285–315, deals in an especially vivid way with the treatment he experienced during this period. A similar account of his childhood experience is in his memoir *Something of Myself, Works* 24 : 355–68. Charles Carrington, Kipling's biographer, reconsidered the nature of Kipling's stay in England in "'Baa, Baa Black Sheep'—Fact or Fiction," *Kipling Journal* 182 (1972), 7–14. There have been many psychoanalytically oriented discussions of the impact of separation and loss in early childhood. Among these see John Bowlby, "Grief and Mourning in Early Childhood," *Psychoanalytic Study of the Child* 15 (1962), 9–52; and Gregory Rochlin, *Griefs and Discontents* (Boston: Little Brown, 1965), especially "The Dread of Abandonment" and "The Loss Complex," pp. 1–62.
5. Hutchins, *Illusion*, pp. x–xii.
6. Thomas Metcalf discusses the link between radicalism and evangelicalism in *The Aftermath of Revolt, India, 1857–1870* (Princeton: Princeton University Press, 1964). He distinguishes between those reformers who regarded religious conversion as the instrument of liberation from traditional values, and those who felt that conversion to Christianity would follow naturally from a Western education in rational thinking and morality. See "Introduction: The Era of Reform," pp. 3–45.
7. This thesis is presented by Stokes in *The English Utilitarians in India* (Oxford: Oxford University Press, 1959), especially Section IV, "The Utilitarian Legacy," pp. 234–322. In this section Stokes discusses the views of both Jeremy Bentham and James Mill that "conflicting egoisms of men could be harmo-

nized only artificially by the legislator." He also points out that both men were influenced by the optimism of the eighteenth century Enlightenment to believe that ultimately human character would be transformed by education and good government, and legal restraints would become superfluous. See pp. 293–95.

8. *Ibid.*, p. 345.

### The Mutiny and After

9. Philip Mason, *A Matter of Honour: An Account of the Indian Army, Its Officers and Men* (London: Cape, 1974), pp. 263–68, presents a detailed account of the greased cartridges controversy.

10. In an article entitled "The Martial Races of India" in *The Modern Review* 49 (Calcutta, 1931), 219, the Indian scholar Nirad Chaudhuri quoted from the standing regulations of the 11th Sikh Regiment: "Men will observe the customs of their faith. A Sikh found smoking tobacco, or with his beard, moustache, or the hair of his head cut, or who dyes or pulls out the hair of his beard or face—and a Musalman found drinking alcoholic liquor . . . will render themselves liable to punishment for disobedience of regimental standing orders."

11. Quoted from Hira Lal Singh, *Problems and Policies of the British in India, 1885–1898* (New York: Asia Publishing House, 1963), p. 9.

12. Philip Mason [Philip Woodruff]. *The Men Who Ruled India*, Vol. 2, *The Guardians* (London: Cape, 1953).

13. Rudyard Kipling, "The Judgment of Dungara," *In Black and White, Works* 2 : 227–29.

14. See Kincaid, *British Social Life in India*, pp. 83–137, for a graphic account of the extravagant and dissolute life style of the Nabobs in Calcutta.

15. The term "civilian" was commonly used by Anglo-Indians to designate a member of the Civil Service, especially the elite section of the Civil Service, the Covenanted Civil Service, staffed almost exclusively by the British. Along with the military, the Civil Service constituted one of the two official hierarchies in British India. One measure of their significance in Anglo-Indian social life is the title of Kipling's newspaper in Lahore, *The Civil and Military Gazette*.

16. The traditional view of the moral views and practices of the Victorian middle classes has been challenged in recent writings on Victorian society and culture. Attention has been turned to the so-called "underside" of Victorian life in studies of the rampant prostitution and pornography that also characterized Victorian society. In "Victorian Counterculture," in *Victorian Studies* 18 (March 1975), 257–76, Morse Peckham has suggested that two cultures coexisted in Victorian Europe, a public culture of sexual constraint and a private culture of sexual license. Among the major works to be consulted in this area are Steven Marcus, *The Other Victorians* (New York: Basic Books, 1966) and Judith Walkowitz, *Prostitution in Victorian Society* (Cambridge, Eng.: Cam-

bridge University Press, 1980). This scholarship complements the present study insofar as this work undertakes to explore the underside of the British imagination in India, as reflected in patterns of attraction and aversion to the sensual dimension of Indian life.

17. Michael Banton and Jonathan Harwood, *The Race Concept* (London: David and Charles, 1975). See Ch. 3, "Race and Culture," pp. 61–90.

18. Christine Bolt, *Victorian Attitudes to Race* (London: Routledge and Kegan Paul, 1971), discusses the concept of polygenesis, or multiple creation, in her treatment of the scientific approach to racism. See Ch. 1, "The Scientific View," pp. 1–28.

19. *Ibid.*, p. 188.

20. *Ibid.*, p. 169.

21. George O. Trevelyan, *Competition Wallah* (London: Macmillan, 1866), p. 216.

22. George O. Trevelyan, *Cawnpore* (London: Macmillan, 1910), p. 36, quoted from Hutchins, *Illusion*, p. 110.

23. Letter from Lord Northbrook to Lord Ripon, 24 Oct. 1883, Ripon Papers, British Library, quoted from S. Gopal, *The Viceroyalty of Lord Ripon, 1880–1884* (London: Oxford University Press, 1953), p. 116.

24. Quoted from Mason, *Guardians*, p. 172.

25. The civilian Henry Beveridge, in *The District of Bakarganj: Its History and Statistics* (London, 1876), pp. 211–12, wrote: "It seems to me . . . the most important thing about an individual man is the character of his parents, and about a people the race to which it belongs. Certainly, I do not think, in looking at the Bakarganj people, that the most important thing about the majority of them is whether they are Hindus or Mahomedans." Quoted from Lord Beveridge, *India Called Them* (London, 1947), cited in Hutchins, *Illusion*, p. 61.

26. Quoted from Mason, *A Matter of Honour*, pp. 368–69.

### The "Real India": The Rugged Frontier

27. Bengali resentment on this point is captured in Walter Lawrence's *The India We Served* (Boston: Houghton Mifflin, 1929), pp. 263–65.

28. S. S. Thorburn, *Mussalmans and Money-Lenders* (London, 1886), p. 54.

29. Kipling's short story "The Head of the District," *Life's Handicap, Works* 4, is constructed around this dichotomy.

30. Alan J. Greenberger, *The British Image of India: A Study in the Literature of Imperialism, 1880–1960* (Oxford: Oxford University Press, 1967), pp. 156–58.

31. See Flora Annie Steel, *On the Face of the Waters* (New York: Macmillan, 1897); Maud Diver, *The Hero of Herat* (New York: G. P. Putnam's, 1913). Maud Diver (1867–1945) was born in India in an army family, and later lived in India as the wife of an army officer. She began to write her novels after settling in England in 1896. Flora Annie Steel (1847–1929) lived in India from 1867 to 1889 as the wife of a civil servant posted in the Punjab. The popularity of these and other female Anglo-Indian novelists reflects the prominence of women in Victorian Britain as authors of romance and light fiction. See Benita Parry,

*Delusions and Discoveries: Studies on India in the British Imagination, 1880–1930* (London: Allen Lane, 1972), Chs. 2 and 3, pp. 70–130, for a treatment of these female writers.

32. Malcolm Darling, *Apprentice to Power: India 1904–1908* (London: Hogarth, 1966), p. 104.

33. Maud Diver, *The Great Amulet* (New York: John Lane, 1908), p. 104.

34. Gosse, "Rudyard Kipling," p. 117.

35. *Ibid.*, pp. 107–08.

## One: Post-Mutiny India and the Development of the Punjab Style

1. Alice Perrin, *The Waters of Destruction* (London: Chatto & Windus, 1909), p. 115. Perrin was the daughter of an Indian army officer and lived for some years in India when her husband, Charles Perrin, was with the Indian Public Works.

2. *Ibid.*, p. 115.

### Authoritarian Rule in Post-Mutiny India

3. Metcalf, *Aftermath of Revolt*, pp. 16–17.

4. Stokes, *English Utilitarians*, p. 118.

5. See John William Kaye, *A History of the Sepoy War in India, 1857–1858* (London: W. H. Allen, 1864), pp. 338–39. Kaye's history was regarded as the authoritative account of the Mutiny in the nineteenth century, but his account of the Bengal army before the Mutiny is replete with Victorian prejudices regarding Indian character and religious practices. For a more balanced treatment which presents the economic, religious, and disciplinary issues that account for the worsening relations between officers and men, see Mason, *A Matter of Honour*, pp. 247–62.

6. Metcalf, *Aftermath of Revolt*, p. 326.

7. *Ibid.* See especially ch. 4, "Restoration of the Aristocracy," pp. 132–73.

8. David Lelyveld, *Aligarh's First Generation: Muslim Solidarity in British India* (Princeton: Princeton University Press, 1978). See pp. 213–48 for an account of Morison's activities at the Mohammedan Anglo-Oriental College at Aligarh.

9. Theodore Morison, *Imperial Rule in India* (London: Archibald Constable, 1899), pp. 44–45.

10. Lovat Fraser, a biographer of Curzon's and an observer at the Durbar, described the scene in *India under Curzon and After* (London: Heinemann, 1911), pp. 232–33: "For sheer spectacular magnificence no sight I have ever seen can be compared with the elephant procession at the State Entry. Pictures convey no adequate conception of that marvelous moment when the Viceroy, on a gigantic elephant, with all the greatest princes of India in his train . . . entered Delhi slowly, impressively, the central figure in a vision so resplendent that at first the awestruck crowds forgot to cheer."

11. Salisbury to Disraeli, 7 June 1876, Salisbury Papers, Christ Church Library, Oxford, quoted from Seal, *Emergence of Indian Nationalism*, p. 193.

12. S. Gopal, *British Policy in India* (Cambridge, Eng.: Cambridge University Press, 1965), pp. 115–16.

13. Stephen to Lytton, 2 May 1876, quoted from J. Roach, "Liberalism and the Victorian Intelligentsia," *Cambridge Historical Journal*, Vol. 13, p. 64.

14. Metcalf, *Aftermath of Revolt*, p. 318.

15. James Fitzjames Stephen, "Foundations of the Government of India," *The Nineteenth Century* (October, 1883), quoted from Singh, *Problems and Policies*, p. 9.

16. Letter from Mayo to the Duke of Argyll, 1 Sept. 1871, Mayo Papers, Cambridge University Library, quoted from S. Gopal, *British Policy in India*, p. 121.

17. See Seal, *Emergence*, pp. 159ff, for a description of the Indian Civil Service's resistance to Lord Ripon's reform program in the 1880s.

18. *Ibid.*, p. 136.

19. William Wilson Hunter, *The Earl of Mayo* (Oxford: Oxford University Press, 1891), p. 199. The British maintained a penal colony on the Andaman Islands and Mayo had been concerned about the state of discipline there. The Pathan who assassinated Mayo had been sentenced to life imprisonment for murdering a blood-feud enemy at Peshawur in the frontier area of the Punjab.

20. Letter from Mayo to General Strachey, 9 Feb. 1872, Mayo Papers, Cambridge University Library, quoted from Gopal, *British Policy*, p. 121.

21. Letter from Curzon to the Secretary of State, 3 May 1899, cited in John Zetland (Lord of Ronaldshay), *Life of Lord Curzon*, Vol. 2 (London: Ernest Benn, 1928), 64.

22. This refers specifically to the administrative system of the Lawrence brothers in the Punjab.

### Beginnings of Indian Dissent

23. *Civil and Military Gazette* 15 (September 1888), 3.

24. O'Moore Creagh, *Autobiography* (London: Hutchinson, 1924), p. 130.

25. *Ibid.*, pp. 244–45.

26. An excellent discussion of the regional interests involved in the support of the Congress movement in these years is contained in Seal, *Emergence*.

27. Singh, *Problems and Policies*, p. 245.

28. *Ibid.*, p. 256.

29. Quoted from *Ibid.*, p. 13.

30. For a general discussion of the obstacles encountered by native Indians wishing to enter the Civil Service, see *ibid.*, especially Ch. 1, "Problems of Indianization in the Civil Services," pp. 13–74.

31. John Strachey, *India* (London: Kegan, Paul, Trench, 1888), p. 358.

32. *Ibid.*, p. 36.

33. Seal, *Emergence*, p. 141.

34. *Ibid.*, p. 183.

35. Christine Dobbin, "The Ilbert Bill: A Study of Anglo-Indian Opinion in India, 1883," *Historical Studies Australia and New Zealand* 12 (October 1965), 87–102.

36. The *Englishman*, 22 Aug. 1883, quoted from Dobbin, "The Ilbert Bill," p. 98.
37. The *Bombay Gazette*, 16 March 1883, quoted from Dobbin, "The Ilbert Bill," p. 95.
38. The *Englishman*, 15 Oct. 1883, quoted from Dobbin, "The Ilbert Bill," p. 95.
39. Gopal, *The Viceroyalty of Lord Ripon*, p. 145.
40. *Civil and Military Gazette*, 1 Dec. 1883. This and subsequent references to the *Civil and Military Gazette* were obtained from the Newspaper Collection, India Office Library, London.
41. *Ibid.*, 13 Sept. 1883.
42. Gopal, *Viceroyalty of Lord Ripon*, p. 152.

### The Punjab Style

43. For a discussion of this aggressive frontier policy see C. Collin Davies, *The Problem of the North-West Frontier* (Cambridge, Eng.: Cambridge University Press, 1932), especially Ch. 5, "The Forward Policy in the 'Nineties," pp. 71–98.
44. *Works* 16:391.
45. *Departmental Ditties, Works* 25:88.
46. Olaf Caroe, *The Pathans: 550 B.C.–A.D. 1957* (New York: St. Martin's, 1958), p. xiii. "Pathan" is the name by which the tribesmen of the northwest frontier were generally known.
47. Richard Temple, who served under John Lawrence in the Punjab, made this observation in his biography, *Lord Lawrence* (London: Macmillan, 1893), p. 153.
48. One such exception was the work of John Nicholson in subjugating the tribesmen of the frontier district of Bannu in the early 1850s. See L. J. Trotter, *The Life of John Nicholson* (London: J. Murray, 1898), pp. 144–70.
49. Quoted from Sir Herbert Edwardes and Herman Merivale, *Life of Sir Henry Lawrence* (London: Smith, Elder, 1872), 2:219.
50. Robert Needham Cust, *Pictures of Indian Life; Sketched with the Pen from 1852–1881* (London: Trubner, 1881), p. 101.
51. Many entries in a journal Honoria Lawrence kept in India in the late 1830s and early 1840s reflect Christian earnestness and a concern with the problems of rearing her children in a non-Christian land. See Honoria Lawrence Journal, Henry Lawrence Collection, India Office Library, London, England.
52. *Memorials of the Life and Letters of Sir Herbert B. Edwardes*, Vol. 1, edited by his wife (London: Kegan, Paul, Trench, 1886), 356.
53. *Ibid.*, pp. 86, 304.
54. For example, Malcolm Darling's encounter with Baluch tribesmen in the first decade of the twentieth century reminded him of the Book of Genesis. See Darling, *Apprentice to Power*, p. 50. Davies, *North-West Frontier*, discusses the Hebraic descent theory; see pp. 42ff.
55. In his satirical account of Anglo-Indian society, *The Chronicles of Dustypore: A Tale of Modern Anglo-Indian Society* (London, 1875), 1:22, Henry S. Cunningham commented that at a boarding school for British girls the religious edu-

cation focused on the chronicles of Israel rather than specifically Christian texts, hymns, or the Sermon on the Mount.

56. Cust, *Pictures of Indian Life*, p. 267.

57. Quoted from R. Bosworth Smith, *Life of Lord Lawrence*, 2 vols. (New York: C. Scribner's, 1885), 2:81–82.

58. *Ibid.*, 1:320.

59. A.L.S. From Temple to John Lawrence, 14 April 1865, Richard Temple Collection, India Office Library. While Chief Commissioner of the Central Provinces in 1865 Temple wrote to Lawrence, then Viceroy, denying any special favoritism to "Punjabi" civil servants in his appointments in the Central Provinces. The letter suggests such accusations were widespread during Lawrence's viceroyalty.

60. "William the Conqueror, Part I," *The Day's Work, Works* 6:168.

61. Darling, *Apprentice*, p. 51.

62. *Ibid.*, pp. 108–09.

63. H. W. H. Coxe (An Old Punjabee), *The Punjab and the Northwest Frontier* (London, 1878), pp. 164–65.

64. P. H. M. van den Dungen's *The Punjab Tradition* (London: Allen and Unwin, 1972), presents an authoritative account of the agricultural problems created by British policies in the Punjab. Also see Thomas R. Metcalf, "The British and the Moneylender in Nineteenth Century India," *Journal of Modern History* 34 (1962), 390–97.

65. Van den Dungen, *Punjab Tradition*, pp. 174–75.

66. See S. S. Thorburn, *The Punjab in Peace and War* (London, 1904), pp. 229–42.

67. Thorburn, *Musselmans and Moneylenders* (London, 1886), pp. 37–38.

68. *Ibid.*, p. 23.

69. In the *Punjab Tradition*, p. 213, van den Dungen reports that the then Lieutenant-Governor of the Punjab, Dennis Fitzpatrick, received constant complaints from landowners against moneylenders during a tour of the Jhelom district, of which Thorburn was then the commissioner. Although Fitzpatrick felt that Thorburn might have been exaggerating the scope of the problem, he found enough evidence of alienation of land to justify a formal inquiry.

70. Darling, *Apprentice*, p. 181.

### "East" and "West" in Opposition

71. Maud Diver, *The Englishwoman in India* (London: W. Blackwood, 1909), pp. 55–56.

72. *Ibid.*, p. 11.

73. See Hutchins, *Illusion of Permanence*, Ch. 5, "A Middle-Class Aristocracy," pp. 101–18.

74. John Beames, *Memoirs of a Bengal Civilian* (London: Chatto and Windus, 1961), p. 132, quoted from *ibid.*, p. 108.

75. Quoted from Hilton Brown, *The Sahibs* (London: Hodge, 1948), p. 27.

76. Darling, *Apprentice*, p. 38.

77. G. R. Elsmie, *Thirty-five Years in the Punjab, 1858–1893* (Edinburgh: D. Douglas, 1907), p. 291.

78. Alice Perrin, *The Anglo-Indians* (London, 1912), p. 28.

79. Darling, *Apprentice*, p. 53.

80. In *Cults, Customs and Superstitions of India* (London: T. Fisher Unwin, 1908), p. 324. J. C. Oman, who worked in the Punjab as a professor of natural sciences at Government College, Lahore, makes this generalization on the strength of his experience with the Indian natives.

81. Flora Annie Steel, *Voices in the Night* (London: Macmillan, 1900), p. 79.

82. Henry Lawrence, *Essays, Military and Political* (London: W. H. Allen, 1859), p. 264.

83. *Civil and Military Gazette* 23 Feb. 1886.

84. In *Voices in the Night* Steel writes that Davenant "despite five years of England and his wife's incessant instructions, had never been able to grasp that exclusive use of certain rooms. . . ." See p. 79.

85. Maud Diver, *The Hero of Herat*, pp. 23–24.

86. I. A. R. Wylie, *The Native Born* (Indianapolis: Bobbs-Merrill, 1910), pp. 410ff.

87. Diver, *The Englishwoman in India*, pp. 67–68.

88. *Civil and Military Gazette* 3 Sept. 1887.

89. Quoted from J. C. Elliott, *The Frontier 1839–1947* (London: Cassel, 1968), p. 7.

90. In making this point in *A Matter of Honour* Philip Mason distinguishes between the myth of the "noble savage" inherited from 18th century literature and the revised version of the myth which had currency in the post-Mutiny army. While the earlier version of the myth stressed the chivalry, generosity and trustworthiness of the idealized native, Mason suggests that the issue of obedience—personified in the simple and unquestioning native servant—was also an important aspect of the "noble savage" ideal in the British lore of the post-Mutiny period. See p. 315.

91. *Memorials of Sir Herbert Edwardes*, p. 360.

92. Caroe, *The Pathans*, pp. 332, 345.

93. G. W. Steevens, *In India* (London: William Blackwood & Sons, 1899), pp. 212–14.

94. See Oman, *Cults*, pp. 303–04, for a description of this sense of immersion in a native quarter of an Indian city.

95. In the preface to *Cults*, p. viii, which describes some of these rituals, Oman chastises a puritanical critic of his research into these activities: ". . . . no account of Indian life and religion can be anything but misleading unless it affords some glimpses at least of the objectionable forms in which, *under present circumstances*, Hinduism, even at the present time, finds practical, if covert, expression; and therefore I have. . . . ventured reluctantly to lift, just a very little, the veil which shrouds these dark places of Hinduism from public knowledge. . . ." For a discussion of one such ritual see pp. 67–83.

96. The British attitude toward Kali worship will be discussed in the next chapter.

97. George MacMunn, *The Underworld of India* (London: Jarrolds, 1933), p. 201. Writing in the 1860s John Kaye, the historian of the Afghan wars and the

Mutiny, wrote of the homosexuality of the Sikh ruler Ranjit Singh that "it was a melancholy thing to see the open exhibition . . . of all those low vices which were destroying the life, and damning the reputation of one who, but for these degrading sensualities . . . was one of the most remarkable men of modern times." Quoted in Arthur Swinson, *North-West Frontier, People and Events, 1839–1947* (London: Hutchinson, 1967), p. 28.

98. MacMunn, *The Underworld of India*, p. 201.

99. O'Moore Creagh, *Indian Studies* (London: Hutchinson, n.d.), pp. 32–45.

100. In *The Anglo-Indians*, pp. 122–23, Perrin presents such a portrait of uncontrolled passion and aggression "behind the veil."

101. Diver, *Englishwoman*, p. 76.

102. *Ibid.*, p. 74.

103. In *The Waters of Destruction*, pp. 174–75, Perrin contrasts the "suffocating" seductiveness of an Englishman's native wife with bright and cheerful scenery that reminds him of England.

104. Flora Annie Steel, *Hosts of the Lord* (London: Macmillan, 1900), pp. 129–41.

105. Steel, "On the Second Story," *Indian Scene* (London: Edward Arnold, 1933), pp. 294–95.

106. Diver, *Englishwoman*, pp. 168–69.

107. *The Naulahka* was written in collaboration with Kipling's friend Wolcott Balestier. For an account of their friendship and literary collaboration, see Charles Carrington, *Rudyard Kipling, His Life and Work* (London: Penguin, 1970), pp. 220–30.

108. Kipling, "The Enlightenment of Pagett, M.P.," *Many Inventions, Works* 5.

109. Walter Lawrence, *The India We Served*, p. 117.

## Two: Magic and Magical Thinking in British India

1. Lawrence, *The India We Served*, pp. 42–43.

### "Magic" and Control

2. Geza Roheim, *Magic and Schizophrenia* (Bloomington: Indiana University Press, 1962), p. 11.

3. Sigmund Freud, *Totem and Taboo* (New York: Norton, 1950). See especially Ch. 2, "Taboo and Emotional Ambivalence," pp. 18–74.

4. Roheim, *Magic*, p. 6.

5. Sandor Ferenczi, "Stages in the Development of the Sense of Reality," in *Contributions to Psychoanalysis* (Boston: R. G. Badger, 1916), pp. 181–203, describes this process in terms of different types of magical thinking.

6. John P. Jones, *India: Its Life and Thought* (New York: Macmillan, 1908), contains a characteristic statement of such convictions. See especially Ch. 7, "Popular Hinduism," pp. 190–219.

7. John Strachey, *India*, p. 24.

8. See Oman, *Cults*, for an account of some of these activities.

9. Diver's *Englishwoman in India* is replete with references to the danger presented from contact with native servants.

10. "Little Henry and His Bearer," in *The Guardianship of God* (London: Macmillan, 1903), pp. 167–91.

11. "At the End of the Passage," *Life's Handicap*, *Works* 4:318.

12. Kisch rose to the post of Commissioner of the Dacca Division in Bengal during his tenure in the Indian Civil Service.

13. *A Young Victorian in India: Letters of H. M. Kisch*, ed. Ethel Waley Cohen (London: Cape, 1957), pp. 118, 126–27, 142–43.

14. George O. Trevelyan, *Competition Wallah*, p. 347.

15. As its title suggests, Mason's novel is constructed around "the broken road" as a symbol of the obstacles the British face in India. See A. E. W. Mason, *The Broken Road* (New York: Scribner's, 1907).

16. The indifference to sanitary facilities provided the central theme in Rudyard Kipling's derogatory essays on native life in Calcutta. See *City of Dreadful Night* (New York, 1899). These essays are discussed in Ch. 4.

17. Anne C. Wilson, *After Five Years in India: Life and Work in a Punjab District* (London, 1895), p. 281.

18. Lawrence, *India We Served*, p. 42.

19. Alice Perrin, *The Waters of Destruction* (London: Chatto and Windus, 1909), p. 62.

20. *Ibid.*

21. Kipling's "The Phantom Rickshaw," in which a civil servant is haunted and eventually destroyed by the ghost of a former lover, illustrates this phenomenon.

22. Arthur Nethercot, *The First Five Lives of Annie Besant* (Chicago: University of Chicago Press, 1960), presents an account of the movement. Among the influential Anglo-Indian converts to theosophy were the editor of the newspaper *The Pioneer* in Simla, A. P. Sinnett, and the founder of the Indian National Congress, A. O. Hume.

23. Thorburn, *The Punjab in Peace and War*, p. 166.

24. George Campbell, *Memoirs of My Indian Career*, Vol. 1 (London, 1893), 56.

25. *Ibid.*, p. 56.

26. Cust, *Pictures of Indian Life*, p. 101.

27. Darling, *Apprentice to Power*, pp. 108–09.

28. Oman describes this phenomenon in *Cults*, pp. 286–90. In his article on "Stages of Development," 193, Sandor Ferenczi points out an animistic period in early childhood in which every external object seems endowed with life.

29. Lawrence, *India We Served*, p. 145.

30. In Valentine Chirol's *Indian Unrest* (London, 1910), pp. 100–03, the seditious tendencies he observes in contemporary India are associated with "buried" elements in Hinduism related to the worship of the Mother Goddess. More recent commentators on Hindu mythology have focused on the distinction between Hindu and Western attitudes. For example, Philip Spratt, *Hindu Culture and Personality: A Psychoanalytic Study* (Bombay: Manaktalas, 1966), pp. 5–26, suggests that Hindus are distinguished from Westerners by a narcissistic personality primarily oriented toward maternal symbols and maternal

images. Wendy Doniger O'Flaherty, in *Asceticism and Eroticism in the Mythology of the Siva* (London: Oxford University Press, 1973), pp. 317–18, also attempts to distinguish Hindu and Western perspectives in a structuralist approach to the mythology of the Hindu god Siva: "Hindu mythology does not seek any true synthesis of opposites, Hinduism is content to keep each as it is; in chemical terms one might say that the conflicting elements are resolved into a suspension rather than a solution. The aesthetic satisfaction of the myth lies here, where the god seems to savour fully and perfectly both of the extremes."

31. Oman, *Cults*, p. 28.
32. Flora Annie Steel, *Miss Stuart's Legacy* (London: Macmillan, 1893), p. 105.
33. Cust, *Pictures of Indian Life*, p. 111.
34. See Herbert Edwardes, *A Year on the Punjab Frontier in 1848–1849* (London, 1851).
35. Maud Diver, *Candles in the Wind* (New York: John Lane, 1909), p. 235.
36. Flora Annie Steel (?), *The Garden of Fidelity* (London: Macmillan 1929), p. 92.
37. Diver, *Candles in the Wind*, p. 235.
38. In *Psychoanalytic Sociology*, p. 39, Platt and Weinstein argue: "The analysis of different levels of anxiety and of increased control over anxiety, which are experienced at different libidinal stages and stages of object relations, would lead logically—if projected onto social problems—to an historical investigation of the changing character of social relationships and especially of relationships to authority."
39. At this point the infant has neither the capacity to tolerate frustration, nor the ability to distinguish itself as an entity from the mother. Its tendency is to identify completely with her through primitive ego mechanisms such as introjection and projection. Through these mechanisms self images assume the traits of the primary object images, and vice versa. Furthermore, the primary object is divided into positive and negative components. They correspond to the infant's deeply divided feelings of sensual fulfillment and intolerable deprivation in the nurturing process. Edith Jacobson, *The Self and the Object World* (New York: International Universities Press, 1964), p. 44, describes this phenomenon in the pre-Oedipal child in these terms: "These cathectic processes are reflected in introjective and projective mechanisms based on the child's unconscious fantasies of incorporation and ejection of the love object. At this stage the child displays submissive, clinging, following attitudes or behavior alternating with temporary grandiose ideas showing his 'magic' participation in the parents' omnipotence. There are erratic vacillations between attitudes of passive, helpless dependency on the omnipotent mother and active, aggressive strivings for self expansion and a powerful control over the love objects."
40. *Ibid.*, p. 43. According to Jacobson: "Such magic, illusory fantasies indicate how much the child wants to maintain the mother as a part of himself and to adhere to the primitive aim of merging with her without distinction and consideration of the external and his own, inner reality."

41. Otto Kernberg discusses the role of splitting in early object relationships in "Structural Derivation of Object Relations," *International Journal of Psychoanalysis* 44 (1966), 236–52.

42. On this one occasion the usual restrictions of caste, sex, status, and age that pertain to Hindu religious observations are disregarded.

43. Steel, *Miss Stuart's Legacy*, pp. 236–37.

44. Kipling, "On the City Wall," *In Black and White, Works* 2 : 323.

45. Perrin, *Waters of Destruction*, pp. 161–62.

46. Jacobson, *The Self and the Object World*, pp. 63–67. Jacobson points out that the achievement of a new orientation toward the love object frees the ego for a more realistic relationship to a wider environment, encouraging greater self-identity and self-discipline. The infant's desire to be part of its love objects is compromised by the rather different wish to attain a realistic likeness of them.

47. *Ibid.*, pp. 51–52. Jacobson relates the threat of regression or relapse to the degree of "true" as opposed to "narcissistic" object relations achieved by the child: "Of course, the child will be protected from relapses into the world of magic fantasies of fusions and early infantile types of identifications to the extent to which he succeeds in building up true object relations which no longer display the narcissistic qualities described above. This again presupposes the constitution of well-defined self representations separated by distinct, firm boundaries from the likewise realistic representations of his love objects."

48. *Ibid.*, p. 101. Another approach to this problem involves the issue of power over objects and the heightened ambivalence characteristic of the obsessional neurotic. Karl Abraham, *On Character and Libido Development* (New York: Norton, 1966), was the first to point out the connection between the achievement of the anal retentive stage in psychosexual development and an essentially ambivalent and retentive attitude toward the love object. In underscoring that point in "Characteristic Superego Identification of Obsessional Neurosis," *Psychoanalytic Quarterly* 28 (1959), 23, Philip Weissman writes: "In the anal-retentive stage phase objects are ambivalently fused in what becomes an increasingly retentive tendency in contrast to the preceding destructive phase. These are newly fused good and bad objects being introjected and becoming newer identifications of the developing archaic superego. These new identifications gradually modify the (archaic) superego so that destruction is not, as formerly, its main instinctual drive. In this way the developing ego finds a way—by gradual compromise—to retain the love object." The distinction between an ambivalent and preambivalent attitude toward the love object may be said to correspond to the distinction between an essentially anal versus an essentially oral orientation. In many respects the values associated with Anglo-Indian society may be described as anal in character, while those associated with native culture may be described as oral. Michael Paul Rogin, *Fathers and Children: Andrew Jackson and the Subjugation of the American Indian* (New York: Knopf, 1975), makes such an analysis of the conflict between

American society and the American Indian. See especially the introduction, "Liberal Society and the Indian Question," pp. 3–15.

49. George Steevens, *In India*, pp. 90–91, observed in his travels that both the Babu and the sweeper were equally antagonistic to Western sanitary techniques.

50. *Civil and Military Gazette*, 3 March 1886.

51. Steel, *Voices in the Night*, p. 77.

52. *Memorials of Sir Herbert Edwardes*, 1:390, states such an attitude. Edwardes argues forcefully that native character can never equal British character in a crisis situation.

53. Cust, *Pictures of Indian Life*, p. 249.

54. See *The Punjab in Peace and War*, p. 262. Although Thorburn was referring metaphorically to British success controlling the flood-prone rivers of the Punjab, it was no less a reference to the British capacity to contain the violence and anarchy present before their assumption of power.

55. Mason, *Broken Road*, p. 343.

56. Oman, *Cults*, p. 29.

57. Diver, *Candles in the Wind* (New York, 1909), p. 45.

58. *Ibid.*, p. 356.

59. Steel, *Voices in the Night*, p. 124.

60. *Ibid.*, pp. 116–27.

61. Chirol, *Indian Unrest*, pp. 102–03.

62. Steel, "On the Second Story," pp. 278–79.

63. *Ibid.*, p. 324.

64. I. A. R. Wylie, *The Daughter of Brahma* (Indianapolis: Bobbs-Merrill, 1912), pp. 305–06.

65. Kaye, *Sepoy War*, 2:312.

66. T. R. Holmes, *A History of the Indian Mutiny* (London: Macmillan, 1904), p. 219.

67. Ascott Hope, *The Story of the Indian Mutiny* (London, 1896), p. 49.

68. G. B. Malleson, *The Indian Mutiny of 1857* (London, 1891), p. 81.

69. Weissman, "Characteristic Superego Identification," pp. 23–24, considers obsessional conflicts and identifications: "Such identifications are superimposed upon the primitive preambivalent, nonfused object relationships which contain the capacity to threaten with fears of annihilation of object, or self, or both. The fear of unmodified annihilation or destruction underlies the threat of loss of the love object in the obsessional neurotic. The obsessional neurotic achieves identification with ambivalent objects. In melancholia, omnipotent introjected, preambivalent, nonfused good and bad object attached identifications predominate in a less well differentiated ego in which also self-representation and object representation tend to be fused. To this more primitive psychopathology, the obsessional neurotic sometimes regresses." In another article, "Ego and Superego in Obsessional Character," *Psychoanalytic Quarterly* 23 (1954), 529–43, Weissman describes the same process as the regression from mature to archaic superego identifications. These archaic iden-

tifications with omnipotent paternal introjects, according to Weissman, are magical in character and threaten both destruction and loss of the love object. See pp. 535–38.

## The Retreat to the Law

70. Darling, *Apprentice to Power*, p. 127.
71. Kipling, "Without Benefit of Clergy," *Life's Handicap, Works* 4 : 148.
72. *Ibid.*
73. Edmund Candler, *Abdication* (New York: E. P. Dutton, 1922), p. 13.
74. See Stokes, *The English Utilitarians and India*, Part IV, "The Utilitarian Legacy," pp. 234–322.
75. Quoted from *ibid.*, pp. 301–2.
76. Strachey, *India*, pp. 367–68.
77. Algernon Durand, *The Making of a Frontier* (London: John Murray, 1899), p. 44. Durand subsequently served as military advisor to the Viceroy from 1894 to 1899.
78. Strachey, *India*, p. 365.
79. Lawrence, *India We Served*, p. 177.
80. Morison, *Imperial Rule in India*, p. 146.

## The Fear of Loss

81. C. T. Buckland, *Sketches of Social Life in India* (London, 1884), p. 143.
82. S. S. Thorburn, *David Leslie, A Story of the Afghan Frontier* (London, 1879), p. 146.
83. Steel, "Little Henry," p. 173.
84. Coxe, *Punjab*, p. 154.
85. Platt and Weinstein, *Psychoanalytic Sociology*, "On Social Stability and Social Change," pp. 91–122, describe the social impact of the threat or reality of object loss.
86. James Fitzjames Stephen, Letter to *The Times* (London), 3 Jan. 1883, quoted from Seal, *Emergence*, 165.
87. Jules Nydes, "The Paranoid-Masochistic Character," *Psychoanalytic Review*, 50 (1963), 216.
88. Isidor Bernstein, "The Role of Narcissism in Moral Masochism," *Psychoanalytic Quarterly* 26 (1957), 375, points out the function of splitting in masochism: "It may be noted that the dynamic formulations for masochism are, to some extent, the same as those for depression: introjection of the object and a regressive splitting of the object and self-representations into the idealized good parent-child with all the love and aggression embodied in the superego and the bad parent-child with all of the hatred and devaluation directed toward it as the object embodied in the ego."
89. Diver, *Candles in the Wind*, pp. 207–08.
90. Maud Diver, *Honoria Lawrence: A Fragment of Indian History* (Boston: Houghton Mifflin, 1936), p. 389.
91. Steevens, *In India*, pp. 353–54.
92. Michael O'Dwyer, *India as I Knew It* (London: Constable, 1925), p. 129,

points out the protests against the Colony Bill of 1907 in Lahore, Lyallput, and Rawal Pindi as an example of such agitation.

93. George MacMunn, "The Bomb Parasts," *The Underworld of India*, pp. 254–55.
94. *Ibid.*, p. 259.
95. "At the End of the Passage" *Works*, 4, is a classic instance of a story which revolves around the dual themes of madness and suicide.
96. Lockwood Kipling, *Beast and Man in India* (London, 1891), p. 291.

## Three: British Heroism in India: History as Mythology

1. Richard Temple, *Lord Lawrence* (London: Macmillan, 1893), p. 136.

### The Mythological Present

2. In *The Hero with a Thousand Faces* (Princeton: Princeton University Press, 1974), pp. 10–20, Joseph Campbell states: "The Hero, therefore, is the man or woman who has been able to battle past his personal and local historical limitations to the generally valid, normally human forms. Such a one's visions, ideas and inspirations come pristine from the primary springs of human life and thought. Hence they are eloquent, not of the present, disintegrating society and psyche, but of the unquenched source through which society is reborn."
3. Lawrence, *The India We Served*, p. 18.
4. *Ibid.*
5. *Kim, Works* 16:375, 248.
6. For example, in I. A. R. Wylie's *The Native Born* (Indianapolis: Bobbs-Merrill, 1910), one of the exemplary British officers is named Nicholson, while in Diver's *Candles in the Wind* the British protagonist is named Laurence. Diver's hero expresses humility concerning his name: "I'm Laurence with a 'u'; and I'm afraid there's precious little of the man of mark about me." (p. 71).
7. *Candles in the Wind*, pp. 32–33.
8. Maud Diver, *The Great Amulet* (New York: John Lane, 1908), p. 211.
9. *Ibid.*
10. Diver, *The Hero of Herat*, p. xi. An artillery officer, Eldred Pottinger, infiltrated Afghanistan on an intelligence mission disguised first as a horse trader and then as a holy man. He arrived at Herat in 1837, and under the protection of its Afghan rulers led the city's resistance to a siege by Persian forces. An account of his life and exploits in Afghanistan is contained in John William Kaye's *Lives of Indian Officers*, Vol. 2 (London, 1867), 145–208.
11. R. Bosworth Smith, *Life of Lord Lawrence*, Vol. 1 (New York, 1885), 59.
12. *Ibid.*, pp. 100–01.

### The Lawrence Brothers: Poetry versus Prose

13. Diver, *Honoria Lawrence*, p. 376.
14. J. L. Morison, *Lawrence of Lucknow, 1806–1857* (London: G. Bell, 1934), p. 179.
15. Smith, *Life* 1:2.
16. Kaye, *Sepoy War* 2:9.

17. Quoted in Edwardes and Merivale, *Henry Lawrence*, 2:200.
18. Morison, *Lawrence*, p. 151.
19. Edwards and Merivale, *Henry Lawrence* 2:154.
20. Smith, *Life* 1:351.
21. Kaye, *Lives*, 2:472.
22. Edwardes and Merivale, *Henry Lawrence* 2:115.
23. *Ibid.*
24. Smith, *Life* 1:33.
25. *Ibid.*, p. 158.
26. Charles Aitchison, *Lord Lawrence* (Oxford, 1892), p. 192. Aitchison, who had served under Lawrence in the Punjab, was Lieutenant-Governor there in the early 1880s.
27. *Ibid.*, p. 197.
28. Smith, *Life* 2:330. Smith also quotes George Campbell's description of the rather harsh, obsessive side of Lawrence's personality. "Sir John was a very strict disciplinarian. As he did not spare himself, so he did not spare others. He had a very active horror of idleness. . . . No doubt he carried this to such a point that he was considered, in some degree, to be a hard man." See 1:456.
29. Smith, *ibid.*, pp. 43–44, presents this anecdote of Lawrence's fearlessness: "On one occasion, during the second Sikh war, when insurrection was rife all around, he was sleeping in a lonely station, after a hard day's work, the sleep of the just and fearless. At dead of night there was an alarm, and one of his assistants came in, pale with terror, and exclaimed in an excited tone, 'Do you know we are in a cul-de-sac?' 'Hang the cul-de-sac,' replied the awakened and intrepid sleeper, and turned over in his bed and had the rest of his sleep out."
30. Temple, *Lord Lawrence*, pp. 109–10.
31. *Ibid.*, p. 68.
32. Smith, *Life* 1:358.
33. This is the judgment made by Henry Lawrence's close friend Herbert Edwardes in Edwardes and Merivale, *Henry Lawrence* 2:113: "It was a hard destiny, doubtless; and so it was deemed by many an honourable friend and staunch partisan of his own, and to a considerable extent, by the public voice of India. But yet fairness compels even a biographer to admit, that those who sympathize with him and admire him most had scarcely a right to deem him, in the main, treated with injustice."

### John Nicholson: The Avenging Angel

34. Kaye, *Lives* 2:427.
35. *Ibid.*, pp. 466ff.
36. Quoted from Smith, *Life* 2:193.
37. Quoted from L. J. Trotter, *The Life of John Nicholson* (London, 1898), p. 205.
38. In his *Lives of Indian Officers*, p. 448, Kaye quoted Herbert Edwardes's account of a "Nikkul Seyn" sect: "A brotherhood of Fakeers in Hazareh abandoned all forms of Asiatic monarchism and commenced the worship of 'NikkulSeyn;' which they still continue. Repeatedly they have met John Nicholson since,

and fallen at his feet as their Gooroo (religious or spiritual guide). He has flogged them soundly on every occasion, and sometimes imprisoned them; but the sect of the 'Nikkul Seynees' remains as devoted as ever. . . . On the last whipping, John Nicholson released them, on the condition that they would transfer their adoration to John Becher;—but arrived at their monastery in Hazareh, they once more resumed the worship of the relentless 'Nikkul Seyn.'"

39. Trotter, *Nicholson*, p. 187.

40. R. G. Wilberforce, *An Unrecorded Chapter of the Indian Mutiny* (London, 1894), p. 25.

41. Smith, *Life* 2:194.

42. Trotter, *Nicholson*, p. 128.

43. *Ibid.*

44. *Ibid.*, p. 180.

45. Caroe, *Pathans*, p. 351.

46. Trotter, *Nicholson*, p. 255.

47. Nicholson's biographer Trotter, *Nicholson*, p. 253, employed the description "heroic disregard of orders"; Bosworth Smith, *Life* 2:83, characterized Nicholson's behavior as "contempt of all authority and rule."

48. Smith, *Life* 2:111–12.

49. Quoted from Trotter, *Nicholson*, p. 253.

50. *Ibid.*, p. 46.

51. *Ibid.*, p. 80.

52. A. L. S. from Nicholson to Herbert Edwardes, 28 May 1857, London, India Office Library, Herbert Edwardes Collection. In that same letter Nicholson also appealed to Edwardes, who was stationed at the Punjab frontier town of Peshawur, to "select a fitting victim among the town's influential native residents." The more moderate Edwardes responded that he was against employing what he termed vindictive Indian methods that resulted in a loss of caste for the British. See A. L. S. from Edwardes to Nicholson, 6 June 1857, India Office Library, Herbert Edwardes Collection.

53. Flora Annie Steel, *On the Face of the Waters: A Tale of the Indian Mutiny* (New York, 1895), pp. 390–91.

54. Smith, *Life* 2:61–62.

55. *Ibid.*, p. 143.

56. Trotter, *Nicholson*, pp. 291–93, described the condition of Nicholson's command: "Our men, in fact, had little strength or spirit left for another call upon their courage and endurance. They were utterly spent and worn out. . . . They had 'stormed the gates of Hell,' had done their duty like good soldiers, and felt that, for the present, they could do nothing more."

57. From the point of view of Heinz Kohut's self psychology the group, especially under the pressure of a threat to its identity, can be seen as cohering around a shared conception of the grandiose self. For an extensive treatment of the concept of the grandiose self in the context of the psychoanalytic treat-

ment of narcissistic personality disorders, see Heinz Kohut, *The Analysis of the Self* (New York: International Universities Press, 1971). In reference to Hitler and the Nazi movement, Kohut provides some suggestion of the possible application of his self psychology to groups. See *the Restoration of the Self* (New York: International Universities Press, 1977), p. 129; and "Narcissism and Narcissistic Rage," *Psychoanalytic Studies of the Child* 27 (New York: Quadrangle, 1973), 382. For a somewhat more complete discussion of the potential application to groups of Kohut's approach, see Ernest S. Wolf, "Psychoanalytic Self-Object Psychology and Psychohistory," in *New Directions in Psychohistory*, pp. 37–48.

### The Conquest of Character

58. Kaye, *Sepoy War* 2:59–60.
59. Hope, *The Story of the Indian Mutiny*, pp. 49–50.
60. Malleson, *Indian Mutiny*, p. 81.
61. Holmes, *History of the Indian Mutiny*, p. 221.
62. *Ibid.*, pp. 221–22.
63. Kaye, *Sepoy War* 2:208.
64. See Holmes, *History of the Indian Mutiny*, pp. 96–104.
65. Kaye, *Sepoy War* 2:208.
66. Smith, *Life* 2:227.
67. *Ibid.*, pp. 150–51.
68. *Ibid.*, p. 227.
69. Holmes, *History of the Indian Mutiny*, p. 221.
70. Kaye, *Sepoy War* 2:403.
71. Smith, *Life* 2:197.
72. In comparing the two brothers Smith, *Life* 1:160–61, suggests that Henry Lawrence's rise was accelerated by patronage from above, while John Lawrence had to rise slowly and independently through the ranks.
73. Temple, *Lord Lawrence*, p. 3.
74. *Ibid.*, p. 5.
75. Aitchison, *Lord Lawrence*, p. 190.
76. Alfred H. Miles and Arthur John Pattle, *Fifty-Two Stories of the Indian Mutiny and the Men Who Served India* (London, 1895), p. 139.
77. Stokes, *The English Utilitarians in India*, pp. 308–10.

### Four: Kipling's India: In Black and White

1. Kipling, "On the City Wall," *In Black and White, Works* 2:305–06.
2. *Ibid.*, pp. 307–08.
3. *Ibid.*, pp. 303, 310.
4. *Ibid.*, p. 305.
5. *Ibid.*, p. 310.
6. *Ibid.*, p. 319.
7. *Ibid.*, p. 329.
8. Kipling, *Plain Tales from the Hills, Works* 1:213.

9. Kipling, *Kim, Works* 16:370–74.

10. A. L. S. from Kipling to Charles Eliot Norton, Rotingdean, England, 15 Jan. 1900. Kipling Collection, Houghton Library, Harvard University, Cambridge, Mass.

### The Family Square

11. *Something of Myself*, pp. 382–83.

12. J. I. M. Stewart, *Rudyard Kipling* (New York: Dodd Mead, 1966), p. 40.

13. *Something of Myself*, p. 383.

14. In *Something of Myself*, p. 417, Kipling stated: "I think I can with truth say that those two made for me the only public for whom then I had any regard whatever till their deaths, in my forty-fifth year."

15. *Ibid.*, p. 394.

16. Carrington, *Rudyard Kipling*, pp. 100–01, describes how the Kiplings became friendly with the Viceroy Lord Dufferin and his family during their first season at Simla in 1885. When the Viceroy's son became romantically attached to Trix, however, the social gap was too great for the viceregal family and they sent their son away.

17. A. W. Baldwin, *The Macdonald Sisters* (London: Davies, 1960), p. 132, says that Lockwood expressed such sentiments in a letter to a family friend, Miss E. R. Plowden, late in life.

18. Frederic William Macdonald, *As a Tale That Is Told* (London: Cassell, 1919), p. 334.

19. E. Kay Robinson, "Kipling in India," *McClure's Magazine* 7 (July 1896), 99.

20. *Something of Myself*, p. 382.

21. Jonathan Gathorne-Hardy's *The Rise and Fall of the British Nanny* (London: Hoddes and Stoughton, 1972) presents this as a central argument in his book on child-rearing in the Victorian period.

22. *Something of Myself*, p. 356.

23. In "Tod's Amendment," for example, the young son of a government official is able to suggest an important amendment to a bill on land tenure because of his familiarity with native concerns. See *Plain Tales from the Hills, Works* 1:239–48.

24. *Something of Myself*, p. 355.

25. *Ibid.*, p. 356.

26. *Ibid.*, p. 392.

27. Robinson, "Kipling in India," p. 104. Mrs. Edmonia Hill, an American friend of Kipling's during his stay in India, also reports his "affection for the 'wild men of the north.'" See "The Young Kipling," *Atlantic Monthly* 157 (April 1936), 409.

28. *Something of Myself*, p. 383.

29. *Ibid.*, pp. 385–86.

30. Carrington, *Rudyard Kipling*, p. 114.

31. *Something of Myself*, p. 383.

32. Robinson, "Kipling in India," p. 104. According to Carrington, Kipling was

advised by his doctor in 1888 not to spend another hot season on the Indian plains. See Carrington, *Rudyard Kipling*, p. 156.

33. See Kipling's August entries from Lahore in his 1885 diary, Kipling Collection, Houghton Library.

34. *Something of Myself*, p. 400.

35. See Erik Erikson's essay, "Identity Confusion in Life History and Case History," *Identity, Youth and Crisis* (New York: Norton, 1968), pp. 142–207.

36. Carrington, *Rudyard Kipling*, p. 85, reports Trix's story that Rudyard sulked for three days when he discovered that his mother had published *Schoolboy Lyrics* without his knowledge.

37. Letter to Mrs. Edmonia Hill from Simla, 22 June 1888. Quoted in Carrington, *Rudyard Kipling*, pp. 153–54.

38. *Ibid.*, p. 154.

39. Taken from the August 4 and 5 entries in Kipling's 1885 diary.

40. Hill, "The Young Kipling," p. 406. The Hill article is based on letters sent home from Allahabad at that time.

41. *Ibid.*, pp. 407–08.

42. See Kipling's letters to his cousins in England quoted in Carrington, *Rudyard Kipling*, pp. 102–09.

43. In an unpublished manuscript which focuses on Kipling's stay in America, "Kipling in America." Washington, D.C., Library of Congress, Carpenter Collection, W. M. Carpenter draws from a Miss Cabot, a house guest of the Kiplings, who complains of Kipling's unpredictable behavior when opposed or confronted. In one instance Kipling bolted from the dinner table when he was upset by one of his guest's comments.

44. M. Karim, "Rudyard Kipling and Lodge Hope and Perseverance," *Kipling Journal* 189 (1974), 4–12, discusses Kipling's activities as a Mason in India. Kipling first joined Lodge Hope and Preservation in Lahore in 1885, when he was still some months below age, because the lodge needed a secretary. He became a lifelong Mason, and masonic themes and symbols appear in his work throughout his career.

45. *Something of Myself*, p. 390.

46. Robinson, "Kipling in India," pp. 1–4.

47. One of the Stalky stories, based on his experiences at school, illustrates this exposure. See "A Little Prep," *Stalky and Co., Works* 14:225–50.

48. Hill "The Young Kipling," p. 408, reports that Kipling was disappointed that his eyesight prevented him from following an army career.

49. In a letter to an old school companion (quoted in Carrington, *Rudyard Kipling*, p. 111), Kipling recalls an experience of his near the Khyber Pass in a humorous vein: "*Nota Bene.* Never close with an Afghan. Plug at him from a distance. There's no glory if he sticks you and precious little if you pot him. I had an experience at Jumrood which brought this home to me. I stood afar off and heaved rocks at my adversary like David did and providentially smote him on the mouth insomuch that he lost interest in me and departed. He had a knife and seemed to object to my going on foot towards the Khaiber. Nar-

row-minded sort of cuss who couldn't appreciate the responsibilities of journalism. That's been all the active service I've seen, and I didn't like it."

50. See Kipling's entries for May 8 and 9 in his 1885 diary. Robinson, "Kipling in India," p. 107, also makes this point. There is a further account of Kipling's difficulty in handling a horse and buggy quoted from the memoirs of Miss Cabot in Carpenter's manuscript on "Kipling in America."

51. *Something of Myself*, p. 393.

52. *Ibid.*, p. 394.

53. See "Only a Subaltern" in *Under the Deodars, Works* 3:95–113.

54. See early reviews of Kipling's stories published in England, reprinted in Green, *Kipling: The Critical Heritage*, pp. 34–159.

55. *Something of Myself*, pp. 393–94.

## The Unreality of Empire

56. *Beast and Man in India*, p. 152, compares the peasant cultivator to his ox with regard to indifference, equanimity, and passivity.

57. This term arose from the competitive examination for prospective officers of the Indian Civil Service established around mid-century to replace the patronage system introduced by the East India Company.

58. Lockwood Kipling, "Mofussil Jurisdiction," *Quartette. The Christmas Annual of the Civil and Military Gazette,* by Four Anglo-Indian Writers (Lahore, 1885), pp. 107–24.

59. As Kipling pointed out in *Something of Myself*, p. 390, the *Civil and Military Gazette* offered some support to Ripon because it held a government printing contract.

60. See Kipling, "William Morris's Poem 'The Day is Coming,'" *Civil and Military Gazette*, 7 Nov. 1883.

61. Kipling, "Trial by Judge," *Civil and Military Gazette*, 16 Sept. 1885.

62. Kipling, "A Lost Leader," *Civil and Military Gazette*, 31 Aug. 1885.

63. *Ibid.*

64. Kipling, "The Indian Delegates," *Civil and Military Gazette*, 21 Nov. 1885.

65. Kipling, "A Real Live City," *City of Dreadful Night* (New York, 1899), pp. 25–36.

66. "The Council of the Gods," *ibid.*, p. 28.

67. *Ibid.*, p. 30.

68. In a letter to his friend Rider Haggard in 1925, quoted from Morton Cohen, ed., *Rudyard Kipling to Rider Haggard: The Record of a Friendship* (London: Hutchinson, 1965), p. 156, Kipling comments: "Nice to notice how the *real* [his italics] progress of civilization translates itself into improved sanitary plumbing."

69. Julian Ralph, *War's Brighter Side* (New York: D. Appleton, 1901), describes how Kipling spent long periods of time among the troops in South Africa and helped to edit a newspaper that was published for them.

70. Kipling, "In Partibus," *Uncollected Prose, Works* 23: 177–78. On the same theme, see a sketch entitled "The Three Young Men," *ibid.*, pp. 227–31.

71. Carrington, *Rudyard Kipling*, pp. 226–27.
72. Kipling, "The English Flag," *Barrack Room Ballads, Works* 25:289.
73. In "The Tomb of His Ancestors," *The Day's Work, Works* 6:93–133, the protagonist John Chinn is part of a family which has served with distinction in India throughout the nineteenth century, and becomes legendary among a native tribe in the central part of the country.
74. Kipling, "A Song of the White Men," *Early Verse, Works* 28:209.
75. Kipling, "The Bridge-Builders," *The Day's Work, Works* 6:3, 5.
76. Kipling, "The Head of the District," *Life's Handicap, Works* 4:109–37. This is also a familiar theme of *Plain Tales from the Hills*, as in "Tod's Amendment."
77. Kipling, "As Easy as A.B.C.," *A Diversity of Creatures, Works* 9:1–36.
78. A. L. S. from Kipling to W. E. Henley, Battleboro, Vermont, 8 January 1893, Morgan Library, New York.
79. A. L. S. from Kipling to W. Cameron Forbes, Bateman's, England, 21 Aug. 1913. Kipling Collection, Houghton Library.
80. Noel Annan, "Kipling's Place in the History of Ideas," in *Kipling's Mind and Art*, ed. Andrew Rutherford (Stanford: Stanford University Press, 1966), p. 122.
81. *Ibid.*, pp. 99–101.
82. *Ibid.*, p. 102.
83. A classic example of such a story is "A Habitation Enforced," which appeared in a collection entitled *Actions and Reactions* (1909). See *Actions and Reactions, Works* 8:309–49.
84. Kipling, "As Easy as A.B.C.," *Works* 9:1–36.
85. Is such a character meant to be Kipling? This is a question which has engaged not only readers of these stories, but also, in other contexts pertinent to this one, critics of fiction in general. The possible relationships between an "implied author" and a dramatized narrator are virtually unlimited, a function both of technical and normative problems. See Wayne C. Booth's *The Rhetoric of Fiction* (Chicago: University of Chicago Press, 1961) for a discussion of these issues. Much of the meaning of these stories is expressed through the ironic distance between the author and his dramatized counterpart. The stories are animated by so many of the concerns of a precocious adolescent that they invite a reading that tentatively identifies Kipling with the dramatized narrator.
86. Kipling, "False Dawn," *Plain Tales from the Hills, Works* 1:60.
87. *Ibid.*, p. 64.
88. *Ibid.*, p. 66.
89. *Ibid.*, p. 57.
90. *Ibid.*, p. 65.
91. "Miss Youghal's Sais," *Plain Tales, Works* 1:31–37, illustrates this.
92. "Thrown Away," *Plain Tales, Works* 1:20.
93. *Ibid.*, p. 23.
94. *Ibid.*, pp. 20–21.

95. *Ibid.*, pp. 25–26.
96. Also observe Strickland's laughter in "The Mark of the Beast," *Life's Handicap, Works* 4:225–40, after helping to save a friend from being transformed into a wolf. See pp. 239–40.
97. "Thrown Away," p. 28.
98. "At the End of the Passage," *Works* 4:172.
99. *Ibid.*, pp. 172–73.
100. *Ibid.*, p. 183.
101. "The Gate of the Hundred Sorrows," *Works* 1:329–39.
102. "At the End of the Passage," p. 187.
103. *Ibid.*, p. 192.
104. *Ibid.*, p. 194.
105. "The Mark of the Beast," *Works* 4:240.
106. Sandison, *The Wheel of Empire* (New York: St. Martin's, 1967), p. 108.
107. "A Free Hand," *The Pioneer* 10 (November 1888). This and subsequent references to Kipling's contributions to *The Pioneer* are taken from a collection of these contributions privately printed in 1922. The collection is contained in the Kipling Collection, Houghton Library.
108. "Without Benefit of Clergy," *Life's Handicap, Works* 4:147–48.

### Native India "beyond the Pale"

109. Andrew Lang, review of *In Black and White* and *Under the Deodars* in *Saturday Review*, 8 Oct. 1889, reprinted in Green, *Kipling: The Critical Heritage*, pp. 44–46.
110. Thomas Humphrey Ward in *Times Literary Supplement*, 25 March 1890, reprinted *ibid.*, p. 51.
111. Robert Buchanan, "The Voice of the Hooligan," *Comtemporary Review* 76 (December 1899), 774–89, was the first major attack on Kipling's politics.
112. "The Man Who Would Be King," *The Phantom Rickshaw, Works* 3:189–241. See especially p. 211.
113. *The Naulahka, Works* 15:306.
114. "The Enlightenments of Pagett, M.P.," *Works* 5:129.
115. "The Bridge-Builders," *Works* 6:27.
116. *Ibid.*, p. 28.
117. *Ibid.*, pp. 18–19.
118. "Without Benefit of Clergy," *Works* 4:167.
119. "Gate of the Hundred Sorrows," *Works* 1:331.
120. Kipling, "Letters of Marque," *From Sea to Sea*, Vol. 1, *Works* 17:18.
121. *Ibid.*, pp. 149–50.
122. "A Civilized Indian," *Civil and Military Gazette*, 12 Nov. 1885.
123. "On the City Wall," *Works* 2:325.
124. "His Chance in Life," *Plain Tale from the Hills, Works* 1:96.
125. *Ibid.*, p. 95.
126. *Ibid.*, p. 100.
127. In a letter to his cousin, Miss Edith MacDonald, from Simla, 30 July 1885,

Kipling described the project and some of his family's mixed reactions to it. Cited in Carrington, *Rudyard Kipling*, p. 103. According to Carrington, p. 424, Kipling used the manuscript in 1899 to provide ideas for *Kim*, and then probably destroyed it.

128. "To Be Filed for Reference," *Plain Tales from the Hills, Works* 1:383–94.

129. Kipling, "An Interesting Condition," *The Pioneer*, 20 Dec. 1888.

130. *The Naulahka, Works* 15:450–52.

131. *Ibid.*, pp. 286–87.

132. *Ibid.*, p. 389.

133. "Beyond the Pale," *Plain Tales from the Hills, Works* 1:213.

134. *Ibid.*, p. 218.

135. *Ibid.*, pp. 218–19.

136. *Ibid.*, p. 219.

137. "The Enlightenments of Pagett, M.P.," *Works* 5:111–12.

138. "Dray Wara Yow Dee," *In Black and White, Works* 2:216.

139. *Ibid.*, p. 220.

140. *Ibid.*

141. *Ibid.*, p. 214.

142. "Enlightenments of Pagett, M.P.," *Works* 5:105.

143. *Ibid.*, p. 116.

144. *Ibid.*, p. 118.

145. A good example of this imagined connection is contained in a sketch entitled "Venus Annodomini," *Plain Tales from the Hills, Works* 1:307, which concerns an administrator of a "particularly unpleasant part of Bengal . . . full of Babus who edited newspapers" and "a good deal of cholera and dysentery abroad for nine months of the year."

146. "The Head of the District," *Works* 4:125.

147. *Ibid.*, p. 122.

148. *Ibid.*

149. *Ibid.*, pp. 132–33.

150. In *Something of Myself, Works:* 24, p. 366, Kipling described himself as becoming "half-blind" as a child before he was fitted with spectacles. His autobiographical novel, *The Light That Failed, Works:*15, is about a young artist who loses his eyesight.

151. "The Head of the District," p. 136.

152. *Ibid.*, p. 114.

153. *Ibid.*, p. 137.

### Imperialism and the Day's Work

154. "The Mark of the Beast," *Works* 4:220.

155. "His Chance in Life," *Works* 1:100.

156. "A Free Gift," *The Pioneer*, 9 March 1888.

157. "The Head of the District," *Works* 4:119.

158. "Without Benefit of Clergy," *Works* 4:149.

159. *Ibid.*, p. 156.

160. "A District at Play," *The City of Dreadful Night and Other Sketches* (Leipzig: B. Tauchnitz, 1900), p. 250.
161. *Ibid.*, p. 257.
162. *Ibid.*
163. In terms of Kipling's interest in craftsmanship, it might be argued that some of the influence of the Pre-Raphaelites such as William Morris was sustained in his journalism and literary work. Kipling's increasing interest in mechanical devices became a point of criticism among some of his fellow writers. In a letter to Mrs. Grace Norton in 1897, quoted in Carrington, *Rudyard Kipling*, p. 408, Henry James criticized Kipling's increasing preoccupation with engines: "he has come down steadily from the simple in subject to the more simple—from the Anglo-Indians to the natives, from the native to the Tommies, from the Tommies to the quadrupeds, from the quadrupeds to the fish, and from the fish to the engines and screws."
164. Kipling, "The Judgment of Dungara," *Works* 2:227, 228.
165. *Ibid.*, p. 229.
166. Kipling generally had a negative view of missionaries as a young man. As he stated in a letter written in 1895 to the Rev. J. Gillespie, quoted from Carrington, *Kipling*, p. 426: It is my fortune to have been born and to a large extent brought up among those whom white men call 'heathen'; and while I recognize the paramount duty of every white man to follow the teachings of his creed and conscience as 'a debtor to the whole law', it seems to me cruel that white men, whose governments are armed with the most murderous weapons known to science, should amaze and confound their fellow creatures with a doctrine of salvation imperfectly understood by themselves and a code of ethics foreign to the climate and instincts of those races whose most cherished customs they outrage and whose gods they insult."
167. "The Children of the Zodiac," *Many Inventions, Works* 5:428–29.
168. *Ibid.*, p. 431.
169. *Ibid.*, pp. 431–32.
170. *Ibid.*, p. 434.
171. "The Judgment of Dungara," *Works* 2:229.
172. "Enlightenments of Pagett, M.P.," *Works* 5:97.
173. See Carrington, *Rudyard Kipling*, especially pp. 328–35, for a treatment of his relationship with Rhodes and his general involvement in South Africa.
174. The intensely felt need continuing into adult life of the support and guidance of some external authority figure has been referred to as "object hunger" in the psychoanalytic literature. Heinz Kohut, *The Analysis of the Self* (New York: International Universities Press, 1974), pp. 44–49, dicusses the vulnerability of the newly internalized superego to severe disappointment and, subsequently, "object hunger." This discussion is particularly relevant to Kipling because of his separation from his parents at age five.
175. "His Chance in Life," *Works*: 98.
176. Sandison, *Wheel of Empire*, p. 101.

177. "A Little Civilization," *St. James Gazette*, 11 March 1890.

178. "New Brooms," *Uncollected Prose, Works* 23, 86–87.

179. A.L.S. from Kipling to R. A. Duckworth Ford, from Bateman's, England, 16 Sept. 1907, Kipling Collection, Houghton Library.

180. A.L.S. from Kipling to Ford, from Capetown, South Africa, 10 Feb. 1908, Kipling Collection, Houghton Library.

181. A.L.S. from Kipling to W. E. Henley, Brattleboro, Vermont, 8 January 1893, Morgan Library, New York.

### Conclusion: Lord Curzon and the Eclipse of the Punjab Style

1. H. Caldwell Lipsett, *Lord Curzon in India, 1898–1903* (London: R. A. Everett, 1903), p. 109.

### Education in Imperialism

2. See Carrington, *Rudyard Kipling*, pp. 309, 423.

3. George Curzon, "Speech at a Dinner Given by Old Etonians," London, 28 Oct. 1898, in *Lord Curzon in India, 1898–1905*, ed. Sir Thomas Raleigh (London: Macmillan, 1906), pp. 3–4.

4. Carrington, *Rudyard Kipling*, p. 94. In a letter to his cousin, Miss Edith Macdonald, from Lahore in November 1884, Kipling commented: "I'd give something to be in the Sixth at Harrow as he is, with a University Education to follow."

5. Curzon was reared in the family's ancestral home Kedleston Hall, built on a site in Derbyshire inhabited by Curzons for eight centuries. See Lawrence Zetland (Earl of Ronaldshay), *The Life of Lord Curzon* (London: Ernest Benn, 1927), 1:17.

6. *Ibid.*, Vol. 1, Ch. 2, "Life at Balliol," pp. 37–50. Curzon's taste for refinement was, of course, one respect in which he was out of keeping with the Punjab Style.

7. *Ibid.*, pp. 42–43. The letter, from a Mr. L. R. Johnson of Bollinger County, Missouri, was written a few years after Curzon had left Oxford, and included a request for a photograph.

8. *Ibid.*, Vol: 1, p. 40.

9. Quoted from Kenneth Rose, *Superior Person: A Portrait of Curzon and His Circle in Late Victorian England* (London: Weidenfeld and Nicolson, 1960), 53.

10. Leonard Mosley, *The Glorious Fault: The Life of Lord Curzon* (New York: Harcourt, Brace, 1960), pp. 31–32.

11. Zetland, *Curzon*, 1:37.

12. *Ibid.*, pp. 51–55. Much to the surprise of his peers and professors, and to Curzon's own chagrin, he received only a second-class degree from Oxford. All Curzon's biographers attribute this failure to his neglect of formal studies and a late start in preparing for his final examinations.

13. Quoted from David Dilks, *Curzon in India*, Vol. 1 (London: Hart-Davis, 1969), 27.

14. Quoted from Rose, *Superior Person*, pp. 197–98.

15. Fraser, *India under Curzon*, p. 233.

16. George Curzon, *Persia and the Persian Question*, Vol. 1 (London, 1892), 13.

17. *Ibid.*, pp. 14–15.

18. *Persia*, 2:602.

### Curzon as Viceroy

19. George Curzon, "Speech at Dinner Given by Byculla Club," Bombay, 16 Nov. 1905, in *Lord Curzon in India*, ed. Raleigh, p. 589.

20. *Ibid.*, "Speech on Presentation of Freedom of City of London," 20 July 1904, p. 35.

21. Dilks, *Curzon in India*, 1:211–13. Dilks points out that Curzon insisted on the thorough investigation and punishment of British soldiers accused and found guilty of abusing Indian natives. Such insistence on the letter of the law aroused the enmity of much of the British military stationed in India.

22. *Ibid.*, pp. 211–12.

23. Curzon, "Speech at Convocation of Calcutta University," 15 Feb. 1902, in *Lord Curzon in India*, ed. Raleigh, p. 483.

24. Zetland, *Curzon*, 2:51–66, deals with the administrative reforms initiated by Curzon shortly after his arrival in India.

25. Curzon, "Seventh Budget Speech (Legislative Council at Calcutta)," 29 March 1905, in *Lord Curzon in India*, ed. Raleigh, p. 152.

26. Curzon, "The Indian Civil Service," *Subjects of the day; being a selection of speeches and writing by Earl Curzon of Kedleston*, ed. Desmond M. Chapman-Huston (London: Allen and Unwin, 1915), p. 57.

27. George Curzon, *British Government in India*, Vol. 2 (London: Cassell, 1925), 136.

28. Curzon, "Sixth Budget Speech (Legislative Council at Calcutta)," 30 March 1904, in *Lord Curzon in India*, ed. Raleigh, p. 143.

29. Quoted from Dilks, *Curzon in India*, 1:95.

30. *Ibid.*, p. 244.

31. Curzon, "Speech at Byculla Club," p. 584.

32. Quoted from Singh, *British in India, 1885–1898*, p. 9.

33. S. Gopal, *British Policy in India*, p. 222, argues: "Within India, efficient administration, on which a premium had been laid ever since the Crown assumed responsibility, now became an end in itself. Curzon was determined to administer well, and, sparing neither himself nor his subordinates, succeeded in doing so; but so much effort was spent in perfecting the methods of administration that its objectives were lost from view."

34. Letter from Curzon to the Secretary of State, 3 May, 1899, quoted from Zetland, *Curzon*, Vol. 2, 64.

35. For a discussion of Curzon's reform programs, see Ibid., Vol. 2, Ch. 22, "A Great Reformer," 290–304.

36. Michael Edwardes, *High Noon of Empire: India Under Curzon* (London: Eyre & Spottiswoode, 1946), p. 146.

37. Zetland, *Curzon*, 2:184–94, presents a detailed treatment of Curzon's educational reforms.

38. Quoted from Dilks, *Curzon in India*, 1:227.

39. Curzon, "Speech at Dinner Given by Royal Societies' Club," London, 7 Nov. 1898, in *Lord Curzon in India*, ed. Raleigh, pp. 9–10.

40. *Ibid.*, p. 11.

41. George Curzon, *Frontiers* (Oxford: Oxford University Press, 1907), pp. 55–57.

42. Zetland, *Curzon*, Vol. 2, Ch. 8, "A North West Frontier Province," 122–40, recounts the establishment of the new province.

43. The India Council was the agency of the India Office in London directly responsible for finances and administration in India. It was staffed largely by retired members of the Indian Civil Service.

44. Dilks, *Curzon in India*, 1:249–53, deals with an example of such behavior, Curzon's dispute with the British Cabinet over the Coronation Durbar of 1903.

45. Dilks, Vol. 2, focuses on the dispute with Kitchener and Curzon's eventual resignation. See especially pp. 177–242.

46. *Ibid.*, pp. 200, 202, 204.

47. Zetland, *Curzon*, 2:326.

48. Dilks, *Curzon in India*, 2:203–04.

49. Quoted from Zetland, *Curzon*, 2:363. The statement was made at a Convocation of Calcutta University in 1905.

50. See Leonard A. Gordon's treatment of the *swadeshi* movement in *Bengal: The Nationalist Movement, 1876–1940* (New York: Columbia University Press, 1974), pp. 77–100.

### Kipling and Curzon

51. Quoted from Mosley, *Glorious Fault*, p. 11. Curzon was the second child and eldest son among eleven children born between 1857 and 1873.

52. *Ibid.*, p. 12.

53. See Rose, *Superior Person*, for the best account of Curzon's social life in the 1890s, especially in the period before his marriage in 1895.

54. *Ibid.*, p. 27.

55. Mosley, *Glorious Fault*, p. 242.

56. *Ibid.*, pp. 139–40.

# INDEX